JULES RIMET STILL GLEAMING?

England at the World Cup

Ken Jones

First published in Great Britain in 2003 by
Virgin Books
Thames Wharf Studios
Rainville Road
London W6 9HA

A catalogue record for the book is available
from the British Library.

ISBN 1 85227 087 X

Typeset by TW Typesetting, Plymouth, Devon
Printed and bound in Great Britain by
Mackays of Chatham PLC

CONTENTS

1. 1934 TO 1950

England's 3–2 defeat of Italy at Highbury on 14 November 1934 brought the football correspondent of *The Times* to this conclusion: 'The true verdict of the match, in spite of appearances, is that England is still supreme in a game essentially her own.' Four months earlier, Italy had beaten Czechoslovakia in Rome to win the second World Cup, a tournament whose very name was sneered at in Britain. As in 1930, when England stood loftily aside from the inaugural World Cup in Uruguay, they and the other home countries had again refused to take part. Having withdrawn from FIFA in 1928 over the question of 'broken time' payments at the Olympics in Amsterdam, they were not even eligible. In any case, as the acknowledged masters of world football England took the view that nothing could be gained from expanding international activity beyond annual tussles for a mythical British 'Triple Crown' and close-season tours. They could arrogantly sit back and wait for the World Cup to take its course, then challenge the winners to a contest on English soil, defeat this upstart of a nation and promptly assume the mantle of world champions.

This was the reason for Italy's visit to London in 1934. At England's invitation, the two countries met for the unofficial championship of the world in an encounter so violent that the Football Association seriously considered abandoning matches against foreign teams. One of seven players selected from Arsenal, the England left-back and captain Eddie Hapgood had his nose broken by an elbow in the face. The centre-forward Ted Drake, also of Arsenal, left the field with blood pouring from a leg wound and was later seized around the neck after a typically robust challenge on the Italian goalkeeper. The Arsenal wing-half Wilf Copping, whose rugged features bore the blue scars of hard toil underground in the Yorkshire coalfield, remarked, 'It was dirty trick after dirty trick until me and Jack Barker [the Leeds and England centre-half] showed them what tackling was all about.'

And Copping, with Barker's eager assistance, had literally put the boot in. Fifteen years later, I came under Copping's harsh supervision as a teenage professional with Southend United. He needed very little encouragement to recall that his violent assaults had caused three of the Italians to leave the field for running repairs. 'Got three of the bastards off in ten minutes,' he would growl. Even if prematurely aged by the effects of a fall from scaffolding during war service, as a physical training instructor Copping was the archetypal British football hard case: standing about 5ft 9in and sturdily built, the vast expanse of his forehead sat above a brutalised nose and a bristling square jaw. Utterly contemptuous of cowardice, Copping's hardness was legendary. He taught tackling from the top down, 'forehead in first', and stressed the importance of numerical superiority. In the days before substitutes, 'It's easier to play against ten men than eleven, even easier against nine' was one of his favourite expressions. No wonder the Italians flinched from him.

Copping was never sent off or cautioned once throughout his career with Leeds and Arsenal, and he went on to make a total of 20 appearances in England's colours, but it was the Battle of Highbury that defined his reputation as much as it reinforced the myopia of English football. Blind to the misdeeds of Copping, Barker and the tough Manchester City outside-left Eric Barker, considering them to be hard but fair in the best English tradition, officials of the Football Association seethed over Italy's behaviour, more convinced than ever that the World Cup was a bad idea, one they could happily ignore.

By the time England and Italy next met, drawing 2–2 in Milan in May 1939, the seven founding members of FIFA had been joined by 44 others but there had been no change in the attitude of the British associations. In the words of FIFA secretary Dr Ivo Shricker, they remained in 'splendid isolation'. Importantly, FIFA did not put any obstacles in the way of those member nations who wanted to play against the British, though strictly speaking this was not in order. Between the Battle of Highbury and the outbreak of World War Two, England won eleven of sixteen matches against foreign opposition while engaging in tougher struggles at home against the Scots and the Welsh. For example, in October 1938, four months after Italy retained the World Cup with a 4–2 victory over Hungary in Paris, a Wales team that included six players born in Merthyr Tydfil, where unemployment topped 80 per cent, defeated England by the same score in Cardiff.

Britain may not officially have been part of the world game, but it held an unofficial world record: the £14,000 fee paid by Arsenal to

Wolverhampton Wanderers in 1938 for one of the Merthyr men, Bryn Jones. Held under working conditions that imposed a wage ceiling of £10 per week and an equally iniquitous retain and transfer system that would remain unchallenged for a further 23 years, Jones had no say in his future. Regarded by administrators as a cornerstone of the English game, the system survived not on merit but because it had never been challenged in the civil court. Footballers of the time were glad enough merely to be paid for enjoying their sport. If it occurred to them that it was absurd to perform before paying crowds of 80,000 or more for what amounted to a pittance, few baulked at the prospect. It was infinitely better than working at a coalface or joining the dole queue.

Happy in Wolverhampton, where he was hugely popular – when news of Arsenal's offer broke supporters threatened to tear down the goalposts at Molineux – Jones was sold against his wishes. The transfer was so sensational that it drove talk of war from the front pages of national newspapers and caused questions to be asked in Parliament, but it was worth very little to Jones himself. When he dared to ask for more than the standard £10 signing-on fee, Arsenal's autocratic manager George Allison turned purple with rage. Calling on his assistant to bear witness, Allison turned on the shy young Welshman whom he was about to make the world's most expensive footballer. 'Repeat in front of this man what you said to me and I'll make sure that you never kick another ball,' he snapped. 'You are joining a great club. You will get the very best treatment but not a penny more than the rules allow.' Jones signed for the maximum wage of £10, falling to £8 during the close season, and bonuses of £2 for a win and £1 for a draw. From Wolves he received six months' accrued share of benefit, amounting to £75. In an impassioned speech to the Trades Union Congress fifteen years later, Jimmy Guthrie, chairman of the Players Union, stated that his members were still being held to slave contracts and sold off like cattle. It was not far from the truth.

Change was always slow to come. Much of the credit for Italy's back-to-back successes in the World Cup had been given to their manager Vittorio Pozzo, an egotist and an autocrat who used bombast to gain the trust of his players. England, however, saw no gain in the recruitment of a coach, even on a temporary basis. Indeed, coaching itself was still viewed with suspicion in the English game. Often appointed in vague circumstances, club managers were aloof, office-bound figures who seldom visited the training ground. Instruction was left to trainers, who concentrated on tenets passed down from generation to generation. Conditioning was basic, involving laps, sprints and body exercises; some trainers actually held the view that keeping players away from the ball increased their hunger for it on matchdays. Detailed team talks were rare, the team formation standard.

In 1939, the Everton wing-half Joe Mercer was one of England's rising stars. Many years later, when manager of Manchester City, he recalled, 'Most of what I learnt came from older players. Around them, you were expected to keep your eyes and ears open and your mouth shut. There was a strict hierarchy. Reserves weren't welcome in the first-team dressing room. Some of the older guys wouldn't give you the time of day, wouldn't pass on anything because they were frightened of losing their place in the team. Mostly, you learnt as you went along. Shortly after breaking into the Everton team, I made the mistake of throwing the ball infield instead of up the touchline. My ears rang for the next fifteen minutes.' Mercer's first cap came against Ireland in November 1938, the match in which Willie Hall of Tottenham Hotspur scored five times, all the goals made by the mesmeric dribbling of Stanley Matthews. 'Apart from being told to go out and play my own game, whatever that meant, I didn't get one word of advice,' Mercer stated. 'Looking back, I think the majority of players preferred it that way. They conformed to a basic team structure but the rest was pure instinct.'

The late Walter Winterbottom, who in 1946 became the first official England team manager and director of coaching, turned out for Manchester United in the late 1930s while studying physical education at Carnegie College in Leeds. He also remembered the lack of imagination at most clubs. 'The older players decided the tactics. Full-backs pivoted around the centre-half so there were plenty of opportunities to find wingers with long crossfield passes. Nobody had worked out even simple things like drawing players out of position. In the main, managers made very little contribution, just signed the cheques.'

When winning the League Championship in 1936 and the FA Cup a year later, Sunderland were managed by Johnny Cochrane, a diminutive Scot who was seldom seen without his bowler hat. A number of missed penalty kicks spurred Cochrane into action.

Entering Sunderland's dressing room shortly before a game, Cochrane placed his bowler on the floor and called for attention. 'There's nothing to taking a penalty,' he declared. He then swung a foot and sent his bowler into the ceiling, muttering, 'Sod it, missed it.' The great Sunderland and England inside-forward Raich Carter shook his head. A man of massive ego, Carter would carry his scorn for instruction into management. 'They can either play or they can't,' he would say when in charge at Middlesbrough 25 years later. 'Team talks won't make any difference.'

Carter was out of favour when the FA touring party to play Italy, Yugoslavia and Romania left London on 7 May 1939 to connect with the Orient Express in Calais. Three weeks earlier, watched by an official British record attendance of 147,000, England had beaten Scotland 2–1 at Hampden Park, their first victory in Glasgow for twelve years and a win that prevented Wales from becoming outright winners of the British Championship for the fourth time since 1932. This convincing success, one in which Matthews and Mercer were outstanding, persuaded even the most caustic critics that a fine England team, perhaps the best ever, was taking shape.

Matthews, at 24, was already established as one of the game's great players, becoming internationally famous long before an explosion in the communications industry raised football to a global passion. And no one held Matthews in greater esteem than Sepp Herberger, who reigned as Germany's national coach from 1936 until 1964. 'To have such a player is every coach's dream,' he said. 'Matthews not only has marvellous technique but plays with absolute confidence. I have never seen a player more capable of demoralising the opposition. It is difficult to plan against Matthews because his highly developed dribbling skills and acceleration make opportunities out of nothing. Dedicated, supremely fit, he is, I think, the first modern footballer.' Matthews had joined Stoke City as an office boy straight from school; at fifteen he played two games for the reserves; at sixteen, 22 games; soon after turning professional on his seventeenth birthday in 1932 he was promoted to the first team; and at nineteen he won his first cap for England, against Wales at Ninian Park in September 1934.

Although Matthews netted on his international debut and scored a hat-trick against Czechoslovakia in 1937, a game England won 5–4, he elected to become a maker of goals. Out on the right touchline, he would take the ball down towards the corner flag and cut in on goal. His standard high centre dropped just beyond the far post, out of the goalkeeper's reach; his ground pass was angled back. In both cases supporting players would be moving on to the ball and defenders had to turn. Matthews had such mastery over the ball, he cast so many spells, that he could delay his delivery until a clear opening appeared. Speed off the mark, gained from many hours of sprint training, was Matthews' essential secret. With his other gifts of touch and balance he could still outwit and wrongfoot opponents, but it was the suddenness of his acceleration that left them floundering, or helplessly facing the wrong way. He did this, over and over again, to the best defenders in the world.

Willie Cook was playing at left-back for Ireland in Manchester the day in November 1938 when Matthews made those five goals for Spurs inside-forward Willie Hall in a 7–0 victory. More than twenty years later, Cook was on the training staff at Norwich City when he told me, 'I knew exactly what Stan was going to do, everybody did, but damned if I could do anything to stop him. He shuffled up to you, dropped his shoulder and darted down the line. If you managed to get back at him, the same thing happened. Stan made you feel as useless as an ashtray on a motorbike.'

By the summer of 1939 Matthews was the supreme crowd-puller in English football and known throughout Europe. However, not everybody shared Herberger's admiration; some saw him as self-indulgent, the main criticism being that he overdid the spectacular side of his play, too frequently delaying the final pass until the goalmouth was covered. Matthews never had the full confidence of England's selectors (he was excluded for the whole of 1936), but his value to the team of 1939 was immense. 'It was like having an extra man,' Mercer recalled. 'The opposition thought so hard about stopping Stan that they often failed to give the rest of our attack enough attention.'

None of the England forwards benefited more from this than Tommy Lawton, who had emerged at Everton as the natural successor to their great centre-forward Billy 'Dixie' Dean. In his autobiography *Football Is My Business*, published in 1945, Lawton wrote, 'I'll admit that sometimes I've fumed in the middle of the field when Stan has gone away on a mazy dribble, weaving his way down to the corner flag. But I've lost my irritation when he laid on a perfect pass or centre.' Only seventeen when transferred from Burnley to Everton for £6,500 in December 1936, Lawton was tall and powerfully built, brilliant in the air and with a shell-like shot in both feet. Alex James, mainspring of Arsenal's attack in the 1930s, thought him the lightest mover of any big man he had seen playing football.

However, in Lawton, Matthews, Mercer and the Wolves centre-half Stan Cullis, who was just 22 when he deputised as captain for Hapgood against Romania in the final game of the 1939 tour, England had the nucleus of a team that would never take shape. When the storm gathering over Europe finally broke on 3 September, Lawton, for one, thought his football career was over. 'Surely there couldn't be room for a professional footballer in a world gone crazy,' he told his ghost writer, Roy Peskett. 'Being a young and fit man, still not twenty, I would go into the Services. In the time I had left, I wound up my personal affairs, cursed Adolf Hitler and all his works and wondered about what might have been. I had played for England, all right, I would fight for England. In the future, perhaps, there would come a time when I could pick up the threads of my career. Until then . . . what? I wasn't to know that during the war I was to be far luckier than most, that it would be made possible for me to continue my career in some sort of way, even though I was in uniform.'

English clubs had played only three games in the 1939–40 season when the government, fearing air attacks, banned public assembly. On 6 September the Scottish FA suspended players' contracts, and two days later the English FA followed suit. 'It was a strange time,' Mercer recalled. 'The build-up to a war effort had got people back to work after years of mass unemployment during which professional players had led a fairly comfortable existence. We all expected to be called up [the entire Bolton Wanderers playing staff immediately volunteered], but until then, how were we going to live? Few of us were trained for anything but football and the majority lived in accommodation rented from the clubs.'

When the feared aerial bombardment did not materialise, there was some relief for Mercer and his fellow professionals in the government's decision to lift the ban on organised football for purposes of morale. In October, competitive play resumed with eight regional leagues in England and two in Scotland. English clubs were allowed to pay players 30 shillings a match while, curiously, the Scottish clubs were allowed to pay 40. With contracts suspended, players could turn out for any club they chose. 'You played wherever you could get a game,' Mercer said, and in his case it meant appearing in the colours of Aldershot, a modest Third Division club transformed by the availability of outstanding players stationed at Britain's largest military centre. The Aldershot manager, Bill McCracken, a Newcastle full-back of the 1920s whose cunning had forced a change in the offside law, suddenly had at his disposal some of football's biggest names. Among the men he could call on were Mercer, Lawton and Cliff Britton (Everton), Cullis (Wolves), Copping (Leeds), Denis Compton (Arsenal), Jimmy Hagan (Sheffield United) and Tommy Walker (Heart of Midlothian). Week after week, McCracken was spoilt for choice. 'It was almost as though you could stand at the barrack gate, shout out for a centre-forward, a full-back, whatever, and out would come an international,' he recalled many years later when scouting for Tottenham Hotspur. 'I was like a kid let loose in a chocolate factory.'

During the lull in hostilities, the 'phoney war' that preceded Dunkirk and the blitz, England played three makeshift matches, two against Wales and one against Scotland. Despite the deepening crisis, the success of these fixtures in helping to maintain the nation's morale persuaded the War Office that they should be allowed to go ahead when circumstances permitted. Because service postings made it difficult to muster truly representative teams – a future England star, Stanley Mortensen of Blackpool got his first taste of international football as a replacement for an injured Welsh player at Wembley – it was decided that wartime matches, later to include the Victory internationals of 1946, would not count in the official records. Even so, England had never sent out stronger teams than those of the war years, and they won eleven of sixteen games played against Scotland with a goal record of 53 scored to 21 conceded. On 16 October 1943, England crushed Scotland 8–0 at Maine Road with a team that read: Frank Swift (Manchester City), Laurie Scott (Arsenal), George Hardwick (Middlesbrough), Cliff Britton (Everton), Stan Cullis (Wolves, capt.), Joe Mercer (Everton), Matthews (Stoke), Carter (Sunderland), Lawton (Everton), Hagan (Sheffield United), Compton (Arsenal). 'Let's suppose the war didn't happen and that England had gone back into FIFA in time for a World Cup in 1944,' Mercer pointed out many years later. 'Nobody could have stopped us.'

My friend Brian James, who served the sports pages of the *Daily Mail* with great distinction before moving on to higher things, came across plenty of evidence to substantiate this claim when researching his book *England v. Scotland*, a history of football's oldest fixture. James wrote: 'Those years took great bites out of the career span of some of the greatest players these islands ever produced. The mere fact of the concurrent world conflict should not deprive them of their credit, for it did not disguise the evidence of their talent. By their victory [at Hampden Park] in 1939, England had given notice that a great team was emerging.' The tough Preston and Scotland wing-half Bill Shankly, who went on to become one of Britain's most successful managers, his name synonymous with Liverpool, told James, 'You cannot even *argue* about this. This was a great England team. They had wonderful players in the side, and just as many waiting to get a game. If I had been picking a team from the best players in the country at the time they beat us 8–0, I would have picked that same side . . . it was hard for all of us [in wartime] but it was no harder for the Scots. I can't think of any players that were not available for Scotland because of the war.'

The cessation of hostilities in 1945 brought an opportunity for the four British associations to reassess their role in world football. Virtually bankrupt, FIFA sent a delegation to London in 1946, seeking the benefit of Britain's experience. Flattered by the offer of a vice-presidency and representation on the International Board, the game's law-making body, the home countries rejoined after agreeing that FIFA would receive the proceeds from a celebratory match between Great Britain and the Rest of Europe to be staged at Hampden Park in May 1947.

Simultaneously, England took the unprecedented step of appointing a permanent team manager. The choice fell on Lancashire-born Winterbottom, a physical training graduate of Loughborough College who had turned out at centre-half for Manchester United in the late 1930s until his career was foreshortened by an injury. Winterbottom's organisational ability when head of the RAF's physical training department had come to the attention of the FA secretary Stanley Rous, who first recruited him as director of coaching. Now to Winterbottom fell the task of modernising England's approach to international football.

England's successes in wartime football had been achieved in the traditional manner. The idea that a player good enough to represent his country could be improved by tuition in teamwork and tactics continued to fall on deaf ears. Resistance came from almost every quarter, from players and former players, from managers, the press and also some legislators. 'I was doing this when I was ten years old,' Raich Carter snorted when in the autumn of 1946 Winterbottom introduced passing practice in preparation for the Northern Ireland–England game in Belfast, the first official post-war international match and his first in charge. In his book *Soccer Partnership: Billy Wright and Walter Winterbottom*, a notable football writer of the time Bob Ferrier wrote: 'There was simple basic opposition to the fact of having an England manager, any manager. England international players were selected for their high ability to play the game, and out of the simple experience of playing together they ought to be able to knit quickly and effectively on the field without having anyone to preach to them in advance, and certainly without the need for long sessions of training or preparation. Such was the argument. But it was a fallacious argument, based on false premises. Given the differences in playing techniques and temperaments found in any group of international players, it was clearly necessary to have a third party to bring some unison and directed purpose to the work.'

However, the natural and instinctive reaction of many in positions of influence, managers and players, was to reject Winterbottom's initiative on the grounds that it would suffocate self-expression and flair. Some saw the need for a more scientific approach to training, but the opposition was vehement. Billy Walker, who would manage Nottingham Forest to an FA Cup success in 1959, spoke with the authority of a former England captain. Brought up in a hard school to observe tenets held sacrosanct in British football, he said, 'In my opinion, planned coaching, like any other form of control, gets into a bureaucratic state which not only continues its mistakes, but tends to increase them.'

It was in this atmosphere of doubt and suspicion that Winterbottom attempted to escape from critics who did not share his view that scholarship and sport were congenial cultures. Tall and kindly, Winterbottom inevitably suffered from a vocabulary that was more lecture hall than dressing room. One of the questions put to professional players on a coaching course at Lilleshall was 'Can you give a reason why British players lack environmental awareness?' 'Because we didn't get enough meat during the war,' came the smart-arsed reply. Not the least of Winterbottom's problems was that of being held subservient to a selection committee whose members were not above ludicrous regional bias. 'I quickly learnt that I was there to advise them, not them me,' he said many years later. Discovering that the system led to players being chosen for England on the flimsiest evidence, some for no better reason than that they turned out for a club in an area represented by one of the selectors, Winterbottom was forced to yield in order to get somewhere near the team he wanted. 'Three or four players picked themselves,' he said, 'so I concentrated my arguments on the most important of the others, knowing that I would be outvoted in one or two positions.'

In addition to these difficulties, Winterbottom had to contend with the arrogant belief that English football, secure in its emphasis on vigour, had nothing to learn from abroad. Paradoxically, results worked against him creating an illusion of superiority. The latter war years had seen the emergence of new talent: a brilliant inside-forward, Wilf Mannion of Middlesbrough, had broken into the England team, and from Italy had come word of Tom Finney's prowess in army representative matches. Like so many of his generation, Finney lost several of his most promising years through war service. Only nineteen when he turned out for Preston North End against Arsenal in the 1941 War Cup final at Wembley, he then disappeared to serve with the Eighth Army. Finney's exploits alongside established international players in army teams made it clear that England had found a winger of exceptional ability. Thus, in September 1946 in Belfast, just one month after a belated debut (at 24) for Preston in the First Division, he made the first of 76 appearances for England, understudying the injured Matthews.

When Finney scored the only goal in a hard-fought struggle against the Republic of Ireland in Dublin two days later, it was clear that the maestro Matthews had found serious competition. Matthews was fit for the next game, against Wales at Maine Road in October, but to the astonishment of all who thought his omission unthinkable Finney was retained on the right wing. It has never been clear how Winterbottom stood in the controversy that, to their personal embarrassment, surrounded Matthews and Finney, but the dilemma was resolved by chance. Matthews regained his place in April 1947 against Scotland, lost it again to Finney after a disappointing performance, then returned for a defeat at the hands of Switzerland in Zurich after Finney had played brilliantly in a 3–0 win over France at Highbury in May. Bobby Langton of Blackburn Rovers was injured in the Swiss match, so Winterbottom brought Finney in at outside-left in Lisbon where England routed the Portuguese 10–0, Lawton and Mortensen each scoring four times.

Unquestionably, a World Cup in 1948 would have seen England installed as firm favourites. Scepticism over the appointment of a team manager had given way to growing support for Winterbottom's influence. In spite of his struggles with the selection committee, a strong team had taken shape under the captaincy of the Wolverhampton Wanderers wing-half Billy Wright, another product of wartime football. Of eighteen matches played between the resumption of international football in 1946 and December 1948, England's record was fifteen victories with two draws and only one defeat, with 66 goals against fourteen. 'Of course, you can't be sure,' Winterbottom would say, 'but the England team of that period, if properly prepared for a World Cup, would have taken some beating. We had a very good blend of youth and experience, outstanding defenders and forwards who could make and score goals against any opposition.'

Unfortunately, the 1950 World Cup came too late for such notable figures as the giant Manchester City goalkeeper Frank Swift, full-back Laurie Scott and two of the best forwards to wear England's colours, Carter and Lawton, their international careers over by the time of FIFA's decision to leave places open for the first- and second-placed teams in the British Championship of 1949–50. Petulantly, Scotland decided that they would go only as champions of Great Britain. Later pleas were ignored, so for Scotland it came down to a decider at Hampden Park on 15 April 1950, England having already announced that they would take part in Brazil regardless of the game's outcome.

Among the players selected by England was a 24-year-old West Countryman, Roy Bentley, who had come to the fore with Newcastle United before a transfer to Chelsea. Five years later Bentley's name would be on 21 of the 81 goals that brought Chelsea their only League Championship, but never on one that carried more significance than the match-winner at Hampden that spring day. Quartered at Troon on the Ayrshire coast, Bentley and his team-mates were no less confused by what the future held than their Scots counterparts. 'We knew that England would be going to the World Cup no matter what, and naturally we all wanted to be a part of it,' Bentley recalled when we spoke at his home in Reading. 'But the World Cup was as much a mystery to us as it was to the public. Because of the war it hadn't taken place for twelve years, since we were boys. I don't think many in our team were sure who held it. I certainly wasn't.' As the game grew closer it became clear to the England players that an opportunity to play in the World Cup mattered less to Scotland's supporters than the prospect of putting one over on their oldest adversary. 'I don't remember reading much in the papers about what a Scottish victory would mean in the long term,' Bentley added. 'Of course, things are a great deal different now. Television has long since given football supporters a much wider perspective, and just to qualify for a major international championship is worth millions of pounds.'

Bentley's thoughts that week centred on what it would be like to play at Hampden, to experience the most famous roar in football. 'I didn't think I would be put off by it because I'd grown used to playing in front of big crowds for Newcastle and Chelsea,' he said. 'On the other hand it was only my second appearance for England and some of our players who were going back to Hampden, such as Billy Wright, Tom Finney, Neil Franklin and Stan Mortensen, warned that I hadn't heard anything yet.' When called upon the previous year against Sweden in Stockholm, the first of his twelve caps, Bentley had learnt something about England's dressing-room hierarchy and the difficulties under which Winterbottom was forced to work. 'The Chelsea chairman, Joe Mears, had been appointed to the selection committee and he told me a story I found hard to believe. At the first meeting Joe attended he was asked for his team. He thought selection was the manager's responsibility and said so, but that wasn't the way they did things at the Football Association.' Bentley also became aware that established members of the team felt threatened by newcomers. 'You could sense it in the attitude of some, but others were terrific, especially Tom Finney, who has always been one of my heroes both as a player and as a man.'

As the teams emerged from the dressing-room tunnel, another of Bentley's idols, Stoke City centre-half Neil Franklin ('perhaps the best I've ever seen'), looked out at the vast crowd and reflected on the working conditions under which English professional players were then held. 'Look at this,' he said to Bentley. 'All these people, and here we are, twelve quid a week [then the maximum wage] for playing in a match like this.' Franklin, still only 27, was about to make his last appearance for England. Bentley might have become one of his successors, his play at centre-half after moving from

Chelsea to Fulham so impressive that the possibility of selection was put to him by Winterbottom. 'I turned it down,' he said. 'I could still cope with First Division but I was well into my thirties and past playing international football.'

But Hampden in 1950 was something else. Bentley found the atmosphere invigorating, not frightening at all. 'Not so much a roar as a swirl of sound all around you. Officially, the attendance was around 130,000, but when I look at old photographs it's easy to believe the speculation that as many as 200,000 got in.' And the opposition was strong. For once setting aside the pathetic prejudice that had frequently prompted the rejection of players who had moved south, Scotland chose four from English clubs: Alex Forbes of Arsenal, Derby County inside-forward and record transfer holder Billy Steel, Willie Moir of Bolton and the powerful Liverpool left-winger Billy Liddell. Apart from the Morton goalkeeper, Jimmy Cowans, and Alex Bauld of Hearts at centre-forward, the rest – George Young, Sammy Cox, Willie Woodburn, Ian McColl and Willie Waddell – reflected the domination of Rangers in Scottish football.

The *Daily Herald*'s football correspondent, Clifford Webb, wrote of the match: 'There was grand approach work by the England forwards and half-backs, typically dour defence by the Scots, and occasional spasms of Scottish genius in attack, which actually gave them more chances (with the score 0–0, Bauld hit the crossbar) than their opponents.' The chance that mattered fell to Bentley midway through the second half. 'From the photograph of me scoring it looks as though I have headed the ball close in,' Bentley said, his West Country burr still distinctive. 'It was a pass from Bobby Langton that I took just inside the penalty area and sent past Cowans.'

While waiting that night to board the London sleeper, Bentley wandered into a bar across from the main Glasgow railway station. 'After ordering a shandy – I seldom touched much more in those days – I became aware of a man looking directly at me from across the room,' he recalled. 'He had on the full Scots gear. Kilt, sporran, the lot. He came over and spoke. "Aren't you the one who scored against us today?" he asked. I nodded nervously. "Well, now, you'd better have a real drink with me, then," he said, going off to bring back a large whisky. Funny thing, but he never mentioned the World Cup.'

2. BRAZIL 1950

By the spring of 1950 tremors of discontent were being felt in English football. The post-war boom – attendances in the 1949–50 season had risen above 40 million, generating revenue of more than £4 million – held nothing to persuade the clubs that a drastic review of working conditions was overdue. Transfer fees had risen above £20,000, a landmark established in 1948 when Lawton agreed a sensational move from Chelsea to Notts County of the Third Division, but apart from the introduction of a Provident Fund to provide players with a modest nest egg on retirement the Management Committee of the Football League maintained its Victorian business ethic.

'Enough is enough,' the Players Union chairman Jimmy Guthrie growled after consulting with members of his management committee following the League's second refusal to discuss and increase the maximum and minimum wage. A former Portsmouth captain who had led the club to victory over Wolverhampton Wanderers in the 1939 FA Cup final, Guthrie notified the Ministry of Labour of an industrial dispute and went to court. The Players Union pressed for a pay increase to keep pace with a rise in the cost of living, longer contracts, abolishment of the maximum wage and the right of players to move on at the completion of existing agreements. Guthrie reflected in his autobiography *Soccer Rebel*: 'We made some progress, but not enough. The maximum went up to £15 but there was no give to the other issues. The player was bound to his club for life whilst the employers could, if they so wished, kick out the injured or unsatisfactory man with only fourteen days' notice.'

One or two, most notably the gifted Middlesbrough and England inside-forward Wilf Mannion, had struck against the system only to be forced into submission. In 1948, Mannion had fallen into a bitter row with Middlesbrough when he refused to re-sign. He took a demonstrating job outside football but soon gave up the fight, having lost a considerable amount in wages and having missed six international matches. The failure of Mannion's protest and the League's confidence that international players would always draw back from supporting Guthrie in concerted strike action left English football ill-prepared for the shock it awakened to in early May 1950, when a Sunday newspaper revealed that clubs in Colombia had made offers to a number of players in the Football League, including the England centre-half Neil Franklin. Franklin's remarks to Roy Bentley at Hampden Park a few weeks earlier now took on greater significance. 'At the time I didn't give them a second thought,' Bentley said. 'After all, it wasn't unusual to hear players moaning about wages, we all did. But I was staggered to discover that Neil was prepared to take such a huge gamble with his career.'

Citing his wife's difficult pregnancy, Franklin had been granted the FA's permission to miss matches against Portugal and Belgium played between the victory in Scotland and England's departure for the World Cup; it was a deception to conceal clandestine negotiations with two former internationals, Jock Dodds of Scotland and George Eastham of England, who were acting for clubs in Colombia. Because Colombia had left FIFA, its clubs were free to poach players from wherever they wished without paying a transfer fee. Up to this time the poaching had been confined to Argentina and had involved a number of famous players, among them a young Alfredo di Stefano, who had deserted their homeland to take advantage of better terms. Now temptation was put in the way of British players. Several fell for the Colombian bait: Franklin, his Stoke team-mate George Mount-ford, the Welsh international Roy Paul of Swansea, Bobby Flavell of Hearts, and Jack Hedley. Franklin and Mountford, accompanied by their families, left to play for Santa Fe after failing to inform Stoke or the FA, leaving the disciplinary committee with no option but to suspend them. The go-between Dodds, then playing for Lincoln City, was found to be an agent of the Millionarios club and was expelled from the League.

Most of the defectors quickly returned without signing. A couple of months later, to the fury of the Santa Fe director Luis Robledo who had engineered the coup, Franklin flew home. Mountford also came back. Only Charlie Mitten of Manchester United, typically slipping into Bogotá just when the whole affair seemed over, stayed, made money and came back in his own time. Ironically, Mitten was the manager of Newcastle United in 1960 when George Eastham junior refused to re-sign for the club, his stubborn action setting off a train of events that put paid to the maximum wage and the retain and transfer system.

The loss of Franklin was a heavy blow to England's prospects in their first World Cup venture. Born in Stoke, he had come to attention during the latter war years playing for a powerful RAF representative team, bringing poise to a position that had been dominated in British football by players primarily chosen for their strength and aerial ability. Although standing barely 5ft 11in and weighing around only eleven stones, Franklin's outstanding positional sense enabled him to cope with all forms of attack, whether it was the close passing then favoured by foreign opposition or the more direct method commonly employed in Britain. When Bentley dropped back to centre-half towards the end of his career, he had Franklin's example in mind. 'I'm sure Neil never found the game as easy as he made it look, but when coming up against him in club matches or for England I never saw him flustered.'

Later, I struck up a friendship with Franklin which began shortly after he took up a coaching appointment in Cyprus. Looking back on the Bogotá affair, he said, 'It turned out to be a huge mistake, one I've regretted ever since. But at the time it seemed like a marvellous opportunity to build up something for the future. If Stoke had sold me [Arsenal, Chelsea, Manchester United and Wolves made offers in the region of £30,000] I would have got only a £10 signing-on fee and a miserly accrued share of benefit. In three post-war seasons with Stoke I hadn't made £2,000. Santa Fe promised to immediately pay that much into a bank account. My wages would be £120 per week, ten times what I was making in England, plus bonuses. For the first time in my career I was looking at real money. It hurt me to think that I was unlikely again to pull on an England shirt, but I'd seen plenty of terrific players reach the end of their time in the game with little to show for it but memories. Take Stan Matthews. He was a world star who put thousands on the gate wherever he played, yet his future, financially, wasn't much brighter than that of the average player. The people running English football didn't seem to be interested in the welfare of players, and most of the men who progressed into management were careful not to rock the boat, running scared of directors. If you picked up a serious injury, that was it, they didn't want to know you – very little compensation. At thirty-five years old, the majority of players were thrown on the scrap heap, left to run corner shops and pubs, to work in factories.'

It was in this atmosphere of uncertainty that Franklin agonised over Santa Fe's offer, the need for secrecy making it difficult for him and Mountford to discuss it even with trusted friends. 'We first tested the ground by asking for Stoke's permission to spend part of the close season coaching in South America,' he added. 'The manager [Bob McGrory] turned us down flat. We didn't know who else was involved [it was later revealed that John Aston and Henry Cockburn of Manchester United, both subsequently included in England's World Cup squad, had rejected offers] but a decision had to be made. We chose Bogotá.' Despite intervention by Stanley Rous, who contacted Santa Fe in a belated attempt to block the move, Franklin was out of the World Cup and lost to the England team. When Franklin's suspension was lifted in 1951, he joined Hull City but was never again the same player, his career going swiftly into decline.

Franklin's request to miss the matches against Portugal and Belgium in May had at least provided Winterbottom and the England selectors with an opportunity to look at an alternative centre-half, the choice falling on Bill Jones of Liverpool, a resolute defender but hardly in Franklin's class. 'Replacing a defender of Neil's calibre was an impossible task,' Winterbottom later confirmed, a task made more difficult by FIFA's ridiculous decision to demand the posting of World Cup squads 21 days before the opening game, between Brazil and Mexico on 24 June. Hesitant on his debut, Jones was given a second chance four days later in Brussels but again failed to impress. 'Given more time to adapt, Bill might have come through,' Winterbottom said, 'but we didn't have time on our side.'

And never had the perversity of the FA been more evident than when they selected Stanley Matthews for a tour of Canada along with the Fulham centre-half Jim Taylor, one of the men Winterbottom had earmarked as a possible replacement for Franklin. Matthews had not been called on for more than a year, but such was the outcry caused by his omission from the most important challenge ever undertaken by the England team that once his fitness was confirmed he was given the option of breaking off from the Canadian tour to join the adventure in Brazil. Eventually, Matthews and Taylor would link up in New York with Aston and Cockburn, who had been released to play for Manchester United in North America. From New York they made a fifteen-hour journey via Port of Spain, Trinidad, arriving in Rio just three days before England's first match.

Although England were able to send out some of the leading figures in world football, as a consequence of the war they were not, on average of age and international appearances, blessed either with youth or experience. Only three members of the 21-strong squad – the captain Billy Wright (29), Matthews (30) and Finney (25) – possessed more than twenty caps; five, including Eddie Baily and Bill Nicholson, whose selection along with Alf Ramsey and Ted Ditchburn meant that Tottenham were the best represented club, had yet to appear in the national team.

The choice of four members of the Tottenham team that had cantered away with the 1949–50 Second Division championship, finishing eleven points clear of second-placed Sheffield Wednesday, was a tribute to the influence of their manager Arthur Rowe. The club's centre-half in the troubled 1930s, his return to White Hart Lane in 1948 began a period of mature and articulate football that would make style and Tottenham synonymous. In a few glorious years, before illness led to his departure in 1955, Rowe promoted a brilliant formula for success. Emphasising the importance of simplicity, he instilled in all his men a desire for possession and the need for an absolute minimum of ball-play. The essence of Rowe's instruction was speed, speed in transferring the ball from man to man in as short a route as possible to goal. Ahead of his time, Rowe saw that intelligent movement was fundamental to any strategy, his beliefs embodied in the phrase 'Keep it simple, make it quick.'

No member of Rowe's team responded more enthusiastically to the principles that brought Tottenham the Second and First Division championships in successive seasons than Baily. Born and raised in Hackney, north London, a neat and intelligent inside-forward with an ebullient personality, Baily's willingness to suppress natural instincts in the team's cause became such a key factor in Tottenham's heady progress that his inclusion in the World Cup party had been widely predicted. Baily, who at 75 still works in football as an Ipswich scout, learnt that he would be going to Brazil when he was met by his wife Elsie after flying home from a short club tour of Switzerland. The excitement Baily felt when his selection was confirmed quickly dissolved when the reality of England's disorganisation hit home. Left with only a week before the squad's departure, a harassed Winterbottom hastily arranged training at the Dulwich Hamlet football ground in south-east London. 'The dream of every footballer is to have a chance of playing for his country, but I was quickly disillusioned,' Baily said. 'The training was a joke.

Walter did the best he could in the circumstances, but the FA was either too mean or didn't think it important enough to keep us together. Players were expected to make their own arrangements, as cheaply as possible. When Willie Watson came first class from Sunderland because the train was full he was ticked off and had the extra amount deducted from his expenses. Not many footballers owned cars in those days, but Ted [Ditchburn] had this old American job, a Cadillac I think it was, and he came round to pick us up, otherwise it would have meant crossing London by bus and tube. That's how we normally got about, but it was no way to get ready for the World Cup. There was no planning to speak of, and some of the officials seemed to think that all we had to do was turn up in Brazil and collect the trophy.'

Baily was entering the unknown. He was completely ignorant of Brazilian culture, their style of football, even what the people looked like. 'I didn't know whether they were tall or small, or what colour. The only Brazilian I'd ever heard of was the Hollywood star Carmen Miranda, who jumped around in films with fruit piled up on her head.' Only Ramsey, who had gone to Brazil with Southampton in 1948, and Laurie Scott, who had played there for Arsenal a year later, knew what to expect, although neither had seen much of the country. 'Alf didn't have a lot to tell us,' Baily revealed. 'Warned us about the food, the heat, the dust – all the usual complaints. He had, however, returned from Brazil with a great deal of respect for their football, and he warned us that it was different from any we had come up against.'

Ironically, one of the FA's biggest mistakes was to set aside their traditional insularity and consult with the Arsenal manager Tom Whittaker about accommodation in Rio de Janeiro. When playing four matches in Brazil during the summer of 1949, Arsenal had stayed at the Hotel Luxor, located alongside Copacabana beach. But when Winterbottom saw the accommodation, he was horrified. 'Probably it was my fault because we should have gone into things more thoroughly, but the Luxor was hopeless for our needs,' he said. 'Arsenal went there in different circumstances. They were on a close-season tour with nothing much at stake, so being so close to the beach added to the enjoyment. As soon as we arrived I knew there would be problems. When I inspected the kitchens I was almost sick; the smell went up into the bedrooms, the food was swimming in oil and it was practically impossible to arrange suitable meals. Nearly all the players went down with tummy upsets at one time or another. We had to share the hotel with other guests and it was always swarming with journalists. The players, especially the older ones, were discontented, making it difficult for us to settle down in the short time available. They were nervous, too, worried about the Brazilian supporters, not understanding that the noisy crowds were simply people having fun.'

But before all that, the players had to get there. The thought of a long, tedious journey weighed heavily on their minds, as Baily confirmed. 'The longest I'd been in the air was a couple of hours. I didn't know how the flight would effect me, hadn't got a clue about time zones.' The propeller-driven airliner that carried England to Rio left London on 19 June, routed via Paris, Lisbon, Dakar and Recife, and arrived an exhausting 31 hours later. 'By the time we stepped off the plane in Rio everyone was knackered,' Baily recalled. 'The journey seemed to have taken for ever, hour after boring hour, slumped in a seat trying to sleep.' Rous and the chairman of selectors Arthur Drewry travelled with the party, but no place had been reserved for a doctor; running repairs and simple ailments were left to the Charlton trainer Jimmy Trotter. 'Can you believe it?' Baily added. 'All that way across the world and no bleedin' doctor! I was a new boy, only 23, so it made sense to keep my eyes and ears open and mouth shut, but it was unbelievable that the senior players never made a fuss.'

Going from a mild English summer to the soaring temperatures of Brazil was just one of England's problems. Another, as Ramsey had warned them, was their ignorance of South American football. 'It was pretty much a mystery to us,' Finney recalled. 'There was no television, very little to go on apart from what Alf Ramsey and Laurie Scott had learnt from tours to Brazil. They'd both been impressed by the level of skill and warned us about the quick inter-passing style, one our defenders rarely came up against.' Apprehension set in when England watched Brazil defeat Mexico 4–0 in the opening game of the tournament. 'I fancied myself at the ball skills,' Baily said, 'but these people were a different class. We'd got a good thing going at Tottenham, moving the ball quickly, going for the return pass, and it paid off the following season when we won the First Division championship. This, though, was something else. We came away from that game hugely impressed and more than a little concerned. Of course, we had our strengths – players among the best you could think of, and a big tradition – but my impression was that Brazil were way ahead of us in development.'

Something similar could have been said about Maracana, a vast new stadium erected in a suburb of Rio with an intended capacity of nearly 200,000. 'At the time it seemed to us like something from another planet,' Baily recalled. 'They were still working on it, cranes everywhere, some of the plaster still damp. You could see hundreds of people trying to jib in over fences. The noise when Brazil scored their first goal was frightening. Fireworks, even a cannon went off. We had players – Stan Matthews, Tom Finney, Billy Wright, Wilf Mannion – who were used to the atmosphere of international matches at Wembley, Hampden Park and across Europe, but they'd never heard anything like this. I remember saying to Ted [Ditchburn] that we wouldn't be playing against the crowd, but from the expression on his face he didn't appear to be convinced.'

Some of the press coverage did nothing to assuage the England players' feelings of trepidation. The 1950 World Cup presented the sports editors of England's newspapers with problems none had previously encountered. The post-war football boom and the novelty of England's debut in the tournament called for comprehensive coverage regardless of the time difference and difficulties in communication. The press corps was made up mostly of establishment men who stood nervously in Rous's presence. Of one or two exceptions, the most notable was John Macadam of the *Daily Express*. A flamboyant, rebellious Cumbrian who frequently fell out with sporting authorities, his first cable from the front raised a storm in Rio, causing England, by association, much embarrassment. In a book published some years later, Macadam wrote: 'By 1950, I thought myself wiser in the ways of the football world and well past the days of rebelling for the sake of rebellion. I was sweet reasonableness itself. I had the confidence of Arthur Drewry, leader of the party of English ambassadors, and Stanley Rous, who had wiped out old scores like the sportsman he is; the players were my friends. The Equator, even at my first crossing, had treated me right, and I was prepared to be the best friend Brazil had ever had. In the middle of filing stories about the general well-being and world-beating quality of the England team, I wrote what I regarded as a highly complimentary piece about the little I had seen and the great deal I had been told about Rio and its hinterland. It was given full treatment in my newspaper, and the significant part of it was: "You could stroll for ten minutes from the players' hotel on Copacabana Beach and find yourself in trackless jungle filled with crocodile-ridden swamps fringed with wild banana trees . . ." No sooner had the Brazilian staffmen in London read that on the morning after I sent it than they cabled it straight back, and by the time the evening newspapers had been delivered on the streets of Rio I was splashed all over the front pages with exclamation marks. My knowledge of Portuguese was nil, but the hurried translations given me by English-speaking Brazilian acquaintances, particularly the way in which they pronounced the exclamation marks, told me that all was not well with my well-intentioned piece.'

All was not well with England, either. If Brazil's virtuosity was not enough to be going on with, Winterbottom had to contend with the rash presumptions of superiority – Macadam's careless phrase 'world-beating' was typical – in the reports sent back to London. 'It didn't help that the press were very blinkered,' Winterbottom said. 'Nobody had seen Brazil play, even I hadn't, which was a big mistake. As soon as I watched them I knew we would find it extremely difficult to reach the latter stages of the tournament, never mind win it. It wasn't just their exceptional touch. The combination play was better than any I'd seen before. One of the moves I knew would cause us trouble involved an attacker coming away from his marker to receive the ball, then returning it for a pass sent through to a third man moving on the blindside of the defence. We were still operating a swivel defence, the full-backs swinging around the centre-half to provide cover, which meant that runners coming at us on a diagonal weren't running the risk of being caught offside. I spoke to the players about this, but it was no time to experiment with an alternative system.'

Interestingly, Winterbottom's concern was not entirely shared by the players. Ramsey admired the technical dexterity of South American footballers he'd first come across two years earlier but felt that England, at their best, could handle it. 'Alf's argument was that they had their method of play and we had ours, and nobody could say which was better,' Baily said. 'Like Stan Matthews, he believed that we had qualities no other country could match, that if we made the very best use of them we had little to fear. I wasn't so sure.' Baily's doubts sprang from the success he had recently enjoyed with Rowe's 'push and run' method, similar to the South Americans' style, which had swept away Second Division defences. 'Second Division maybe,' Baily added, 'but, as we proved by immediately going on to win the championship itself [in 1951], even the most experienced defenders in English football had a problem with quick interplay around the penalty area. They just weren't used to it. On top of that, the best centre-half in Britain, and probably the world, had legged it to Bogotá.'

At least England would avoid the most dangerous teams until the latter stages of the tournament. In perhaps the most chaotic of all World Cups, the host country relied heavily on nations from its own continent – though Argentina was a notable absentee – refusing to take part because of an unresolved dispute with the Brazilian Federation. Germany were excluded following the Second World War, Hungary and the Soviet Union remained in isolation, and Austria and Czechoslovakia opted out. Although only thirteen countries took part, it was decided that four teams would come through from four qualifying groups. Farcically, Group 4 contained only two teams, allowing Uruguay, who defeated Bolivia 8–0, a virtual walkover.

England were drawn in a group with Chile, Spain and the USA – hardly a daunting proposition for such notables as Matthews, Finney, Wright, Mannion and Mortensen who were hailed in Brazil as masters of the game. Soon, however, Winterbottom sensed trouble. He had no complaints about the training facilities provided by Botafogo, one of Rio's leading football clubs, but it was clear that several players, including Alf Ramsey, were finding it difficult to adapt to the conditions, complaining of exhaustion after the gentlest of workouts. When the lightweight boots ordered by Winterbottom arrived they were made of rubber, more suitable for gardening than football.

The loss of Franklin had left England with a problem that would persist until Wright took over at centre-half for the 1954 World Cup in Switzerland. Some eight men – Allenby Chilton (Manchester United), Leslie Compton (Arsenal), Jack Froggart (Portsmouth), Malcolm Barrass (Bolton), Harry Johnston (Blackpool), Derek Ufton (Charlton), Harry Clarke (Tottenham) and Syd Owen (Luton) – were tried out to that point, but the duties in Brazil fell to one of the squad's five uncapped players, Laurie Hughes of Liverpool. It was generally felt that Matthews should be selected, but apart from Hughes the team to play Chile at Maracana on 25 June showed only one change from the match against Scotland two months earlier, Jimmy Mullen of Wolves replacing the Blackburn outside-left Harry Langton. 'As it turned out, the heat and humidity were a bigger problem than the Chileans,' Bentley recalled. 'Although we didn't play all that well, they weren't up to much and in the end we won quite easily.' England had their first points on the board, but a comfortable 2–0 victory had its downside: tiredness. 'Even a relatively easy match took a lot out of us,' Bentley said. 'Breathing was an effort, and the thick grass took its toll on our legs.' Wright's faith in his fitness was dented. 'For the first time in my life I felt weary long before the end of a game,' he told Winterbottom.

Back home, England's second match, against the USA in Belo Horizonte, an hour's flight from Rio, was assessed as a formality, merely a run-out before a stiffer test against Spain. 'Even though one of the reporters pointed out that they had reached the semi-finals of the World Cup in 1930 [which England were not to do for another sixteen years] and hadn't done at all badly when losing 3–1 to Spain in their opening game, it was easy to take the Yanks lightly,' Baily said. 'Nobody gave them a prayer. You could have laid them at 100–1 and not found any takers.'

England's arrangements in Brazil in 1950 set the tone for years of muddled planning, culminating in the embarrassment of 1970 when no provision was made for accommodation in Leon should Ramsey's team qualify in second place for the quarter-finals. If relieved to be leaving the Luxor ('You can only eat so many bananas,' Jackie Milburn said), it was with some trepidation that the England players travelled to the British-owned Morro Velho gold mine in the mountains, sixteen miles from Belo Horizonte, and getting there from the airport turned out to be a hair-raising experience. In places, the precipitous road to Morro Velho was little better than a dusty track, its many hairpin bends looked upon as a challenge by the Mexican bus driver. Already unnerved by the turbulent flight from Rio, the England party found no humour in the situation, fearing that an error in the driver's judgement would send them plunging hundreds of feet down the mountainside. 'I vowed that if I ever became a manager

I would never put players through an ordeal like that, especially so close to an important match,' the normally phlegmatic Bill Nicholson said.

Difficult as he found it to concentrate, Winterbottom went over the events of the past week in preparation for a meeting with Drewry, who had the final say in team selection. Aware that a number of players needed more time to acclimatise – Wright was the last man he had expected to hear complaining about fatigue – Winterbottom, with the support of Stanley Rous, intended to press for changes in personnel. 'From what we'd been told about the Americans [if anyone was sent to watch the match between USA and Spain he was never identified] they played with great spirit but weren't up to much technically, so it seemed like a good opportunity to give key men a rest and look at some of the others,' the England manager said. 'Rous felt that we should bring in Stan Matthews, who had adapted well to the conditions, and I agreed that he might be just the man to unsettle a team that had very little international experience.' But Drewry would have none of it. 'Never change a winning team,' he said, repeating the hoary adage to Rous when the FA secretary intervened on Winterbottom's behalf.

Thwarted by Drewry's obdurate refusal even to discuss the matter, the England manager now had to guard against complacency. USA might be the weakest team in the tournament, a carefree collection of novice professionals with no sporting status in their homeland, but Winterbottom sensed danger in taking them too lightly. 'It was easy for our players to think they would have an easy game, no more than match practice, which in fact was how Drewry saw it,' he said. There were stories about the Americans staying up late drinking. Their coach Bill Jeffrey, a Scot from the Pennsylvania State University, announced that he was expecting a heavy defeat. Writers travelling with the England party organised a sweep on how many goals England would score. 'Double figures weren't thought to be out of the question,' John Thompson of the *Daily Mirror* recalled.

The newly constructed stadium in Belo Horizonte gave Winterbottom fresh cause for concern. The narrow pitch was rutted and strewn with stones, completely unsuitable for a World Cup tie, and a rat was seen scampering from the small, dimly lit dressing rooms. 'I'd known better playing as a kid on the marshes,' was Baily's view. But Winterbottom saw no gain in protest. 'We were rated one of the strongest teams, USA the weakest, so what would the football world make of us if we complained about the conditions?' he stated. Nevertheless, he refused to let his players use the slum-like facilities; instead, the team changed at the Minas Athletic Club, ten minutes' coach drive away.

With no dramas to report, the English press turned to the American team for inspiration. The USA were fielding a Belgian left-back, Marca, a Scottish wing-half, Eddie McIlvenny, who had recently been given a free transfer by Wrexham, and a Haitian-born centre-forward, Joe Gaetjens; in goal they had a former baseball player, Borghi, and their centre-half, Colombo, played in leather gloves. 'It would be fair to give them three goals of a start,' the *Daily Express* opined.

It was still a time of spontaneity in English football; if they were held at all, team-talks were brief and concentrated on effort. Winterbottom kept his simple. 'In those days, tactics seldom came into it,' Bentley said. 'Managers might tinker here and there to deal with a particular threat, but in the main players were expected to work things out for themselves, to use their experience. I think Walter might have been concerned over how we would react to the pitch. He told us not to be put off by bad bounces of the ball, to make sure that we concentrated at all times. From what we'd been told the Americans would put up a fight so it was essential to get on top of them from the start. Looking around at the talent in our dressing room I couldn't imagine anything other than a comfortable win. On the other hand, it was a bit like a big team playing away to a small team in the FA Cup. Shocks are never out of the question.'

Above the twelve-foot-high wall that surrounded the cramped playing area a mainly local audience of around 20,000 raised great support for the underdogs. 'It felt as though we were playing in a prison,' goalkeeper Bert Williams recalled. Nevertheless, England found it easy to cut through the USA's defence and mounted attack after attack, but with half an hour played they still hadn't scored. Watching from the stands, Baily had a premonition. 'I had a sense of it being one of those games where you have all the game, make loads of chances, and end up losing. Despite being completely outclassed, the Yanks were hanging on. Goodness knows how many goals we missed. The ball just wouldn't go in. For a while, it made us laugh to see the American goalkeeper scrambling about on his line, even saving a couple of shots with his face, but the longer it went on the more worried we became.'

The pattern had been set within a minute of the kick-off when a bad bounce caused Mullen to lift a simple chance over the crossbar. It was the first of many lamentable efforts on goal. Mullen again misfired; Mortensen hit a post. 'It was simply unbelievable that our finishing could be so poor,' Wright recalled. 'We should have been four up inside twenty minutes.' Instead, England sensationally fell behind. In a pre-coverage era, the game was not filmed, so Winterbottom had nothing against which to check his memory of what caused England to give up a goal eight minutes before half-time. One or two reports saddled Williams with the blame, suggesting that his concentration had wavered after a long spell of comparative inactivity; others questioned the defenders in front of him. To Wright's mind, a cross-shot by the American left-half Bahr from outside the penalty area struck the scorer, Gaetjens, on the back of the head when Williams had it covered. The Americans claimed that Gaetjens had hurled himself at Bahr's drive, deflecting the ball past Williams with a courageous diving header. Either way, England had a problem. 'Walter tried to calm things down during the interval, telling us to be patient,' Bentley said, 'but it had begun to feel as though we could play for a week and not score. It wasn't a happy dressing room.'

With the crowd right behind them, and no longer in awe of England's status, the Americans gave everything in defence of their lead, the foul count rising against them. When Mullen sent another shot wide, Thompson of the *Daily Mirror* noted that England had by then squandered ten good chances. 'It didn't seem possible,' he said. 'Time and time again our forwards opened up the American defence only to make a mess of things. And the further the game went the more you began to think about a sensational defeat.'

After being told to switch positions with Finney, who was brought into the middle, Bentley became involved in an incident that completely summed up England's shortcomings in front of goal that day. 'Finney went through on his own and sent the ball to me across an open goal,' Bentley recalled. 'Hearing a shout of "Leave it!" I let the pass run through. The call had come from Mortensen, and he shot wide. It was that sort of game.' When the Italian referee Generoso Dattilo rejected Mortensen's claim that his header from Mullen's centre had been scooped up from behind the line, England were finished. 'We'd gone to the game expecting to file a routine report,' Thompson said, 'instead we found ourselves writing about a defeat like no other in English sporting history.'

Together with a small group of colleagues, Thompson, five hours behind London time with a hot story to deliver, was up against it. News of England's humiliation was already on the wires, sent by the Reuters correspondent, who alone of eight men covering the game had a telephone link with Rio and the outside world. When the 'flash' result was passed to a sub-editor in London he smiled, understandably assuming an error in transmission; he reached for a pen to correct the score – surely, England 10 USA 1. Still smiling, he turned to a colleague and said, 'England defeated by the United States. Now, that *would* have been some story.'

Back in Belo Horizonte, his work done, the man from Reuters handed over his telephone to the grateful English pressmen. 'How are we going to do this?' one of them anxiously asked. Maurice Smith of the *People* took over. As the representative of a Sunday publication, Smith, for once, had time on his side. Putting it to comradely use, he spent the next hour telephoning reports to Rio for cabling to London, page after page, for the daily newspapers. When the stadium was plunged into darkness he read by the light of burning newspapers. 'Typical of Maurice, it was a heroic performance,' Macadam of the *Express* said later. The sole American journalist present had been assigned to the match simply because it coincided with his vacation in Rio. Told to file only if there was something interesting to report, bemused by the excitement, and not fully appreciating the impact of his nation's victory, he scampered off in search of a cable office.

Thompson's racy report arrived at the *Mirror* offices in Fetter Lane in time to sit beneath the headline BOMBSHELL FOR OUR WORLD CUP HOPES – ENGLAND FALL TO U.S. AMATEURS (which was not strictly true). It began: 'English soccer was humbled as it has never been before in the little stadium here today, when America beat us 1–0 in the World Cup match. The Americans, who entered the competition on a "hiding-to-nothing" basis and completely unfancied, were the better team, and fully deserved their victory . . .' In more considered follow-up articles the press were not as one in apportioning blame for England's humiliation: one or two correspondents questioned Winterbottom's stewardship, wondering whether a firmer hand was needed on the tiller, and several called the players to account, but none pointed a finger at Drewry who had declared himself 'speechless' before flying to Rio while the England party returned shamefaced to Morro Velho.

This reluctance to hold the establishment responsible would persist, to the detriment of English football. 'When I started covering England for the *Daily Mirror* it was made clear to me that officials of the Football Association were not fair game,' Frank McGhee revealed. 'The older guys wanted to keep things cosy. Anybody who dared to step out of line was jumped on by Stanley Rous.' In 1959, McGhee was among five reporters named by the Football Association in a complaint to the Press Council over comments passed about defeats on a close-season tour of South America. 'The FA simply couldn't accept that they weren't running the game for their own benefit,' McGhee said. 'England played poorly on that tour, losing three successive games [2–0 to Brazil, 4–1 to Peru and 2–1 to Mexico], but still the FA took exception to criticism, claiming that it adversely affected the attendance at the game against the USA in Los Angeles [which England, thankfully, won 8–1]. I don't know what the FA hoped to achieve by reporting us to the Press Council, but it didn't get them anywhere.'

In 1950, Drewry saw no reason why he should be saddled with any of the responsibility for the most ignominious defeat England had ever suffered on a football field. 'I ruled against the changes Winterbottom and Rous wanted to make against the USA because I'd been brought up to believe that you never altered a winning team,' he later claimed. 'The Americans obviously weren't up to much, and from what I'd seen in the first game our players needed match practice. I didn't miss all those chances.' But there had been good, sound reasons for the changes Winterbottom had wanted to make. He was worried that one or two key players were not properly rested after the game against Chile, which had come so soon after the long journey from England. Also, it occurred to him that eager reserves might be less troubled by the thought of picking up an injury on a rough playing surface.

'I didn't once imagine that we'd lose to the Americans,' Winterbottom said. 'However, there was this niggling at the back of my mind. Then, as chance after chance went begging I sensed that something bad was going to happen.' Afterwards, the manager was as near to despair as he could be. 'What can you say about a result like that?'

he gasped. 'If just one of our efforts had counted it could have been a massacre.' Back at the gold mine, the dejected England players sat around in small groups. 'Tell me it didn't happen,' Mannion remarked to Bentley. 'It was bloody ridiculous.' 'When we beat Chile last Saturday I thought we were going to win the World Cup,' Mortensen said gloomily. 'Now it's going to be difficult even to reach the next round.'

A knee-jerk reaction to England's defeat meant that changes were inevitable. England had to beat Spain to gain a play-off place. Matthews was brought in, Finney switching to the left wing in place of Mullen; winning his first cap, Baily took over from Mannion; Bill Eckersley, another debutant, replaced John Aston at left-back; and Bentley's place in attack went to the Newcastle speed merchant Jackie Milburn. 'Just my luck to get into the team when we were up against it,' Baily said. In fact, England at last lived up to something like their reputation, the football they played against Spain later described as among the best seen in the tournament. 'We did play well,' Baily agreed. 'We got the ball moving, built up a lot of pressure and kept our heads, which wasn't easy. The referee [again an Italian, Giovanni Galeati] allowed an unbelievable amount of obstruction and shirt-pulling. I remember Alf [Ramsey], who had this thing about fair-play, being furious.' With fifteen minutes on the clock, Milburn was ludicrously given offside after sending a header past Ramallets, who had an outstanding match in the Spanish goal. Shortly after half-time, Spain's centre-forward ended England's adventure. Hailed on arrival as the masters of world football, England had failed even to get beyond the first round of matches.

Accompanied by all but one of the reporters, England immediately returned home, leaving no one behind to study other methods of play. 'I should have stayed,' Winterbottom admitted later. 'I was already convinced there was no future in just selecting teams. We needed to build one. In 1950, I was as much to blame as anyone in thinking that we were good enough to win the World Cup despite losing our best defender [Franklin]. I soon realised that some of the other countries were much better prepared, while our players didn't have the experience of playing abroad their successors would get from international club competitions.'

Shortly before the 1950 World Cup began, a distinguished Swedish critic, Ceve Linde, wrote about the England team: 'The remarkable thing is that England competes in a soccer world championship for the first time. For the first time she tests herself in a fight for football world supremacy. England has always claimed to be the first. Now she has to prove it on the playing-field, not round the committee table . . . It is very courageous of England to try. The world knows that English soccer has deteriorated . . . that British club teams lose many a match when travelling abroad. Nevertheless, the English will travel to Rio. All honour to them! England *has* to win. For her own and for the entire world's sake.' Fearing that a South American victory could seriously undermine Europe's influence, Linde added, 'We should remember that the game has been built up by the English, that the English Laws of the Game gave football its solid shape no other sport can rival. The British have been hard and conservative like granite, but that was necessary. They were able to maintain their commanding position on account of their playing supremacy . . . How will it go, however, if England fails in Brazil?' Within weeks, Linde was writing, 'England returns from the World Cup with the same number of points as Chile and the USA, knocked out and with plenty of bitter experiences . . . the unpalatable truth is that English soccer has gradually deteriorated, finally fallen off its pedestal, and now keeps rolling downwards. No longer does it impress by its quality, but only by its breadth . . . the sorriest feature in this drama is that the English, with very few exceptions, cannot get themselves to recognise what has happened. In their self-satisfaction and conceit they still fancy themselves the first in the football world and their defeats sheer accidents. The fact is that English soccer has an enormous amount to learn from the rest of the world, about training, tactics, organisation and strategy.'

As far as they went, Linde's remarks barely dented the insularity of English football. Once the disappointment passed, excuses were found for the poor showing in Brazil: distance, climate, dodgy decisions, Franklin's defection, the fact that England's first appearance in the World Cup came a few years too late for such stalwarts as Swift, Lawton, Carter and Mercer. Bob Jackson, whose uncomplicated management skills had put Portsmouth's name on the League Championship trophy for the second successive season, warned that it would be a big mistake to abandon the traditional virtues of British football for a more scientific approach. 'What suits the Continentals and South Americans doesn't necessarily suit us,' he argued. 'We have a way of playing that has stood the test of time. Given more favourable conditions and a fair crack of the whip, England can beat anybody.'

With the national team back home, the World Cup was no longer a priority for English newspapers. George Casey, whose career as sports editor of the *Sunday Pictorial*, today's *Sunday Mirror*, had spanned 40 years by the time of his retirement in 1972, recalled, 'From reader reaction, it was pretty obvious that the public lost interest in the World Cup once England were out. The World Cup was something new for us and in those days there was very little interest in foreign football unless England were involved.' With every day that passed, then, Winterbottom's regret at his decision not to remain in Rio increased. 'There was no television coverage, and newspapers carried only the barest details,' he said. 'I'd passed up an opportunity to be better informed about developments in the game.'

Had Winterbottom stayed, he would have seen football the like of which had never been witnessed in Europe. No wonder Brazil became hot favourites to win the tournament as they stormed through the final pool. The combination play between their three gifted forwards, Zizinho, Ademir and Jair, was breathtaking. Sweden, the 1948 Olympic champions who had reached the final pool by beating Italy and topping Group 3, were crushed 7–1 at Maracana, four of the goals coming from the rapacious Ademir. Spain, softened up by Uruguay's hard response to the fouling that had unsettled England, were also bewildered by Brazil's virtuosity and lost 6–1.

Consumed by a passion for football, all Brazil prepared for a coronation at Maracana. A draw against Uruguay, the winners in 1930, would be enough to secure the World Cup, but Brazil wanted a result that would establish clear superiority over their neighbours. Failure was unthinkable, yet George Raynor, the Englishman who managed Sweden, could see it happening. 'In the circumstances, I just wasn't sure about Brazil,' he confided to Rous. 'I kept thinking about how nervously they played against my team until they got on top – we had two chances to score before their first attack. At Maracana, with all that expectation bearing down on them, I thought Brazil might struggle to find their best form against a team that wouldn't be intimidated by the atmosphere.' Raynor was proved right. Against the odds, Uruguay won 2–1 to send Brazil into deep mourning. It was said that more than 30 people committed suicide that day, and in the railway junction of Bauru a nine-year-old boy could not believe what he was being told. But Pele's time would come.

3. 1950 TO SWITZERLAND 1954

As the 1950 World Cup passed into history, the FA began to explore ways in which the standard of the England team could be improved. Prompted by Rous, a 'Technical Sub-Committee' was formed. Comprising the chairmen of each selection committee – Senior, Intermediate, Amateur, Youth – it was given the authority to consult directors, managers and players. It first met on 8 November 1950, its function 'To examine by what means the work of the International Committee and its Selection Sub-Committee could be made more effective'.

Arthur Rowe left the second of these meetings with a heavy heart. 'As much as anyone I wanted the England team to be on top, but I was left with the impression that nothing had really changed,' the Tottenham manager said. 'When my World Cup players [Baily, Ditchburn, Nicholson and Ramsey] came back from Brazil they told me that despite the difficulties England should have done much better. As I suspected, England suffered most from poor organisation. My view was that the bulk of preparation for future foreign tours and World Cups should be done at home.'

The views of managers and former international players conflicted. Raich Carter, an opponent of concentrated coaching, felt that players not already in possession of the basic skills had no business being in professional football. Joe Mercer agreed. 'I would have second thoughts,' he said, 'but at the time I felt our League system would continue to produce players of outstanding ability. The idea of putting international players to work on ball control was worthless, and insulting.' Tommy Lawton and Laurie Scott argued that pre-match training should be as long and as thorough as possible; Jimmy Hagan thought that match practice was essential.

All were startled to discover that Brazil had trained together for four months prior to the World Cup, an advantage made possible by the suspension of domestic league matches. Uruguay were thought to have spent even longer in preparation. 'It wasn't worth one minute's discussion,' Stan Cullis snorted. 'In principle I agree absolutely that the England manager should have more time with the team, but any idea of intruding on the League programme simply isn't practical. The clubs would never stand for it.' Having success-fully made the transition from player to manager, Cullis had grown in reputation when Wolves defeated Leicester City in the 1949 FA Cup final. A man of unswerving high principle, he was and would remain a devotee of forceful attacking football, not the crude method that became damagingly fashionable three decades later, but raking crossfield passes to hard-running wingers.

Some time afterwards, when I was the 'ghost writer' of Cullis's syndicated newspaper column, I asked him whether the events of 1950 had undermined his faith in the essential vigour of British football. 'Not for a moment,' he replied. 'I was at a disadvantage because I had nothing to go on apart from reports in newspapers and what I'd been told by Billy Wright and Jimmy Mullen, who returned to us full of praise for South American football. I pointed out to them that one style wasn't necessarily superior to another. It seemed to me that a country's football reflected national characteristics. We didn't lack skill, far from it, but few could match us for spirit.' Although disappointed by England's World Cup performance, Cullis saw no reason for a radical change in policy. 'Our national team had never before travelled further than Europe,' he told the FA committee. 'The World Cup was a new experience. Maybe we should look more closely at developments in other countries, but the important thing is to restore faith in the British style of play.'

Rowe didn't share Cullis's unshakeable faith in the traditional virtues of the English game. Having unearthed a brilliant formula for success at Tottenham, he saw the failure in Brazil as the inevitable result of resistance to change. 'If the Football Association don't understand that, they don't understand anything,' Rowe confided to close friends in the game.

While the meetings went on, Winterbottom set about repairing England's reputation. 'Apart from the freak loss to the United States, on reflection I didn't think we'd done all that badly in the World Cup,' he said. 'The game against the Americans was a disaster, a freak result, but with a bit of luck we could have beaten Spain and played off for a place in the final pool where anything might have happened. However, this didn't blind me to our shortcomings. If we were going to do anything in the next World Cup there would have to be a big improvement both in the way we prepared for games and in how we dealt with the more refined techniques of foreign teams.' But, helped on one hand, hindered on the other, Winterbottom was still subject to the whims of a selection committee whose members were not above striking deals with one another to suit regional interests. 'As far as we could tell, it was the same old story,' Mortensen told me one night at a dinner in Blackpool. 'Walter was very thorough, but what chance did he have when they wouldn't give him a free hand?'

During the next eighteen months, twelve England players, including the gifted Wilf Mannion, disappeared from international football. This did not, however, prevent England from putting together an impressive sequence of results that saw them beaten only once – 3–2 by Scotland at Wembley in April 1951 – in twenty games. Yet for reasons of injury, loss of form, or sheer perversity on the part of the selectors, only once in 42 matches played between the beginning of the 1950 World Cup and the end of a summer tour in 1955 did the England team remain unchanged. As Malcolm Allison stressed in his book *Soccer for Thinkers*, almost everything in football – results, standard of skill, attraction, strength and even behaviour – comes through the team. 'Individual players stick in the memory,' he wrote, 'but the greatest of them could not make a school 2nd XI without the support of ten others.'

Gutsy teamwork was the essence of a famous victory over Austria in May 1952, one that gave Nat Lofthouse of Bolton Wanderers the heroic sobriquet 'Lion of Vienna'. Lofthouse had won his first cap six months earlier, when he scored both goals in a 2–2 draw with Yugoslavia at Highbury. With the arms and shoulders of a navvy, Lofthouse met the popular image of a centre-forward; he made no demands upon the audience, and it wasn't necessary to probe for hidden qualities in his game or to appreciate some subtle role in the tactical scheme of things. Lofthouse was, quite simply, strong and fearless, and a ferocious goalscorer.

Though unbeaten over eight games when arriving in Vienna for the second game of a summer tour, England's form was poor and subject to the criticism of football writers who had begun to operate on the principle that admiration could be wrung from them only by the supreme artistry of a great performance. 'Since the World Cup I had noticed a big difference in the approach of reporters who travelled with the England team,' Baily said. 'Where they had been prepared to give us the benefit of the doubt, when we didn't quite come up to scratch they wrote harder things. To my mind it was all to do with the World Cup. They'd given us this big build-up and when things went wrong they felt let down. After that it was never the same.' England's tour that summer had begun with a 1–1 draw against Italy in Florence, the result more satisfactory than the performance. Austria had further cause for optimism: of sixteen previous games, ten had been won convincingly with only two defeats.

Urged on by a capacity crowd of 65,000, the Austrians hurled themselves at England's defence. Lofthouse scored against the run of play. Huber equalised. Jackie Sewell of Sheffield Wednesday put England back in front. Dienst brought Austria level again. 'It was ding-dong stuff,' Baily recalled. 'The important thing was that we were never behind because that really would have fired up the crowd. Our winner came when Gil Merrick [England's goalkeeper] threw the ball upfield to Tom Finney. As I ran to support Tom he checked inside and sent Nat through the middle. You had to be brave to do what Nat then did.' Bursting clear, Lofthouse slid the ball under the advancing goalkeeper before going down under a heavy challenge. 'It was the best goal I ever scored,' Lofthouse told me long after his retirement from the game. Carried shoulder high from the field by British troops (Vienna was still an occupied city), Lofthouse was made. He went on to reach 30 England goals, a tally surpassed only by Bobby Charlton (49), Gary Lineker (48) and Jimmy Greaves (44), and equal to that of Alan Shearer, who in terms of style most closely resembled him.

The irony of Lofthouse's effectiveness – 50 per cent of his goals for England were scored overseas – was that it decelerated the movement towards accepting that the reputation of English football could be restored only by making better use of its resources. With Lofthouse in unstoppable form, the clamour for change faded to a whisper, especially when England thumped Belgium 5–0 at Wembley in November 1952. RECOVERY COMPLETE: ENGLAND ON TOP AGAIN, trumpeted one headline.

A few days later, it was announced that Hungary, the recently crowned Olympic champions, had agreed to play England at Wembley in November of the following year. Initiated by Stanley Rous following the Olympic final in Helsinki, it had not been easy to arrange. Hungarian football was state-controlled through a Sports Ministry answerable to the Central Committee of the Communist Party. First, the party bosses had to be persuaded that Hungary had at least a reasonable chance of victory in London. 'Prestige, or rather loss of it, was very important to them,' Sandor Barcs, then president of the Hungarian FA, pointed out in a radio interview conducted many years later. 'I said no one could guarantee such a thing in football, but I felt we could guarantee a sensational game with world coverage of the event.' When official sanction came, Hungary's coach Gustav Sebes was quietly confident. No foreign team had ever returned from Wembley victorious, but nothing was for ever. Still, he had mixed emotions about taking his team to Wembley. 'We had a number of outstanding players – Puskas, Hidegkuti, Bozsik, Kocsis – players good enough to win any match. However, I felt England were bound to be stronger at home than they were in the 1950 World Championship, especially because they were defending a record. We'd been told that British football was living in the past, but England's recent record against foreign opposition, home and away, was good.'

If good enough to restore England's confidence, it was misleading; the shortcomings so obvious in the 1950 World Cup continued to trouble Winterbottom and other forward thinkers, and resistance to change was stronger than ever, forward planning rare. Players who expressed an interest in coaching were talked down by their team-mates. Tales of players dozing off in team meetings were gleefully told.

In May 1953, three months after his 38th birthday, Stanley Matthews starred in a sensational FA Cup final that saw Blackpool come from 3–1 down to beat Bolton Wanderers 4–3. Quiet for most of the match, Matthews came into his own when Bolton naively sent their injured left-half Bell to the left wing, moving Bobby Langton inside. Seeing that Bolton's left-back was now without Langton's harassing support, Blackpool's inside-right Ernie Taylor brought Matthews into the game. 'I don't think we would have won without Bolton making that switch,' Mortensen recalled. 'Stan hated it when the opposing winger on his side of the field worked hard to prevent him receiving the ball. I think he thought it unfair, not in the spirit of the game.' Many years later, Don Revie sat through a video of that 1953 final. 'I'd read plenty about the game, how Stan had taken Bolton apart, but I'd never seen it,' he said. 'Seeing how Bolton reacted to Bell's injury reminded me of how tactically naive most managers were in those days.' Typical of that time, the Bolton manager Bill Ridding had not approached the final in any great detail. 'Go out and play your own game,' he'd told his players.

Taking no chances with public opinion, the England selectors recalled Matthews after an absence of more than two years, inviting him to join a tour of South America, the most ambitious ever undertaken by the national team. But, after allowing it to slip out that he'd been given an injection for a leg strain immediately prior to the final, Matthews declined. In truth, his reputation already enhanced, Matthews was not prepared to run the risk of an injury that might prevent him from starting the 1953–54 season. Already past the age when footballers must confront the anti-climax of retirement, Matthews, still as fit as a flea, was planning the next phase of a career astonishing for its longevity; in future, the harder northern locations of English football, places where his reputation mattered less to the home supporters than it did in the south, would seldom figure on the Blackpool winger's agenda. As for South America, he saw only an exhausting journey, unfamiliar conditions, hostile crowds and the attention of ruthless defenders.

Newspaper reports sent back from the England tour soon confirmed to Matthews that he had made the right decision. According to one writer, the opening match against Argentina in Buenos Aires on 17 May had the makings of a riot when it was abandoned after just 23 minutes because of atrocious weather conditions. Even in that short period of play a conflict of different football cultures was again evident. On a pitch made heavy by torrential rain, England found it easier to break up Argentina's moves with forceful tackling. 'Conditions were in our favour, and they didn't like it,' Billy Wright reflected. 'They began elbowing and tripping, shirt pulling whenever one of our players looked like breaking clear.' If Wright was prepared to concede that English football needed to address tactical shortcomings, it was clear that his loyalty to the English style was as strong as ever. 'Since the World Cup, I think we have shown that there isn't a great deal wrong with our game,' he said. 'Foreign teams still fear us.'

They would certainly come to fear Tommy Taylor, the powerful Manchester United centre-forward who made his international debut in Buenos Aires that day along with the United outside-right John Berry and the Blackpool centre-half Harry Johnston. Signed from Barnsley for what was then a record fee of £29,999 – Matt Busby did not want him burdened with the first £30,000 tag – Taylor represented the next generation of England players.

Keeping the same team, England moved westward to defeat Chile 2–1 in Santiago, then back again to face world champions Uruguay in Montevideo, where Taylor scored his second goal of the tour in a 2–1 loss. Ugly scenes on and off the field marred both matches. 'It was only our second experience of South American crowds, and even the players who were with us in 1950 found it disturbing,' Winterbottom recalled. 'We were never in any real danger, but it was difficult to get that across when the team bus was being bombarded with oranges.'

After concluding the tour on 8 June with a 6–3 victory over the USA in New York that erased some of the memories of humiliation three years earlier, the English team had done well enough to obscure its limitations. 'Some good players are coming through, but in team play we are way behind,' Winterbottom confided to his coaching disciples. 'I'm still being prevented [by the selectors] from building a team. From match to match, there are too many changes to make planning possible. Stanley Rous is with me on this, but he can't get through to the International Committee.'

When Winterbottom met with the International Committee in late September 1953, continuity was uppermost in his mind. As in 1950, the first- and second-placed teams in the British Championship would qualify for the forthcoming World Cup in Switzerland, making it imperative that England did not slip up against Wales in Cardiff. Winterbottom pointed out that heartening results in South America had been achieved with a rare unchanged team. 'Yes, but some of those players have not started the season well,' grunted one of the selectors. Deaf to the manager's counsel, the selectors made three changes in attack, bringing in the Sheffield Wednesday prodigy Albert Quixall and the Wolves left-wing pair Denis Wilshaw and Mullen. A 4–1 victory at Ninian Park put the selectors in a mood of smug contentment.

Later that October, to celebrate the Football Association's 90th anniversary, a team selected by FIFA, playing as the Rest of Europe, met England at Wembley. Soon, the truth was out. Matthews had been recalled at outside-right, but compared with that of their opponents England's football looked banal and pedestrian. The eye-catchers were all foreign: Ladislav Kubala, who in his time would wear the colours of Hungary, Czechoslovakia and Spain; Vukas and

Cajkovski of Yugoslavia; the imperious Austrian midfielder Ocwirk; and the suave Italian winger Boniperti, later to become president of Juventus. In the summer of 1967, when I was acting as consultant to Toronto Falcons in the newly formed but doomed North American Soccer League, I was thrilled when Kubala agreed to sign for us. Although past his best, he could still delight with his effortless control of the ball and studiously placed passes. One night, during a long coach journey, he spoke about that match at Wembley. 'We could have won it easily,' he said, 'but it was an exhibition game, not serious, and none of us wanted to return to our clubs injured. As we expected, England played flat out, gave it everything. We hardly knew each other, but as soon as we got together, really there was only one team in it.'

With only a minute left to play, England were down 4–3, their unbeaten home record seemingly gone until Mortensen was fouled in the penalty area by Cajkovski. Ramsey strode forward to level the score. Among the audience was West Bromwich Albion manager Vic Buckingham, who went on to win the FA Cup that season and later the Spanish Cup with Barcelona. A flamboyant figure, Buckingham had spent most of his playing career with Tottenham Hotspur before being drawn into Winterbottom's coaching structure. He winced at the shredding of England's defence, agreeing with Kubala that England 'weren't at the races'. 'Against players who were introduced to each other only a day before the game, England were lucky to get away with a draw,' he continued. 'The idea that we were still among the best in the world was absolute rubbish. Unfortunately, not many people were alive to the problems. There's none so blind as those who cannot see.' And several players suffered as a result of this blindness. A few hours after the game, I came across Derek Ufton at London's Charing Cross railway station. In his only appearance for England, yet another to be tried in the troublesome centre-half position, the Charlton Athletic defender had been repeatedly drawn out of position by swift inter-passing and intelligent movement. With little support coming from England's wing-half backs Wright and Jimmy Dickinson, he literally hadn't known whether he was coming or going. 'Nobody said anything,' he grumbled. 'I was left to work things out for myself.' He would never get another chance.

The next day, a lone figure could be seen prodding the Wembley turf. Dressed in a sober suit and football boots, and carrying a football beneath one arm, he paced out the pitch, end to end, side to side. Watched quizzically by the ground staff, he then began to volley the ball up out of his hands. After watching it bounce on various parts of the pitch he took a piece of paper from his pocket and made notes. With typical thoroughness, Hungary's coach Sebes was preparing for a game that would finally disperse the illusion of English superiority. Through Stanley Rous, he had obtained permission to return alone to the stadium; when Sebes checked in for a flight back to Budapest his luggage contained three footballs given to him by the FA secretary and a file of vital information. He knew all there was worth knowing about England's key players and their system of play; he had the measurements of the pitch, knew roughly where the sun would be if it shone on the afternoon of the match, knew even that high balls didn't bounce much more than a metre at Wembley. Back home, Sebes found a pitch of approximately Wembley's dimensions on which Hungary trained for three weeks against teams sent out to imitate England's way of playing, rather like a sparring partner apes the style of his employer's next opponent. The footballs – harder, less sensitive – used were those Sebes had brought back from London.

Although Sebes was answerable to the Sports Ministry, he had complete control of the national team's preparation and selection. The post-war years had seen a remarkable transformation in Hungarian football: from 15,000 registered players in 1939, the figure had risen to more than 100,000; and while Winterbottom was still struggling to establish a coherent development structure, Hungary had more than 900 qualified coaches. As the most promising players progressed, every aspect of their potential was checked. On a visit to Lilleshall eight years later, Sebes startled Winterbottom's students by stating that when Ferenc Puskas was in the fifteen-year-old age group, four of his contemporaries were more technically advanced. 'We went with Puskas because of his temperament,' Sebes revealed. 'The play of the others could range between brilliant and mediocre. We knew that even on the worst day of his life Puskas's form would not drop below an acceptable level.'

Fully aware of Hungary's progress, and still obliged to accept limited authority, Winterbottom became apprehensive about a fixture that had captured the public's imagination. 'There was no doubt in my mind that Hungary would be formidable opposition,' he said.

'They'd made a big impression in the 1952 Olympics and were unbeaten anywhere in the past four seasons.' Apart from the 1950 World Cup and on summer tours, the England team had never been together for more than two days prior to a game. It was as much time as Winterbottom could expect.

First, he had to concentrate on a match against Northern Ireland at Goodison Park that took place two weeks before Hungary's visit. Harold Hassall of Huddersfield, who was recalled for the last of his five caps, scored twice in a 3–1 victory that simplified qualification for the World Cup, but the overall performance was not encouraging. Two days later, Winterbottom flew to Budapest to watch Hungary play Sweden accompanied by a small group of sportswriters, among them Alan Hoby, later of the *Sunday Express* but then working for the *Sunday People*. Hoby was 88 years old when we spoke at his home in Hove in September 2002. Tall, still erect, a Royal Marine veteran of the Second World War, he looked years younger. 'Ever since the 1952 Olympics, I'd been convinced that Hungary would be the big team of the 1954 World Cup,' he said. 'They had terrific individuals, but the most impressive thing was their teamwork. Players were always on the move, opening up spaces. They used long and short passes, and they could shoot – my goodness, they could shoot! When it was announced that Hungary had agreed to a match at Wembley I feared for England. The England team was always being changed, hardly ever the same from one match to the next, and there was little to suggest that English football was moving forward.'

By holding Hungary to a 2–2 draw, Sweden fired up all but a handful of Hoby's colleagues. 'Where's your fantasy team now?' he was asked. The consensus of opinion was that if Hungary could not beat Sweden at home then surely they had little chance of defeating England at Wembley. England, in fact, were following a false trail, not one laid by the wily Sebes but by the rare inadequacy of his team. Consumed by the great task ahead, Sebes had taken the Swedes too lightly, making it easier for their English coach George Raynor to plan against him. Raynor was one of the most interesting figures in European football. Scorned in his homeland – even after he took Sweden to the 1958 World Cup final against Brazil the only offer of work in England came from a non-League club – Raynor made his name abroad. Frustrated by the clever little Yorkshireman's defensive tactics, Hungary were disappointing. Sebes's only consolation was that Winterbottom had seen nothing of the strategy he intended to employ in London.

In order to create exceptionally strong club teams, leading players in Hungary had been ordered to join either MTK or the army side Honved. (Ostensibly soldiers, Puskas and his team-mates in fact did very little military training. Puskas rose to the rank of major without ever lifting a firearm.) It was a state-driven policy that brought the added benefit of centralising the national team's resources. But the advantage this gave to Hungary failed to register with the majority of English sportswriters, who took the result in Budapest as proof that there was little to fear. 'It astonished me,' Winterbottom said. 'They had been unable to see what was before their eyes, taking everything at face value. It was obvious to me that if Hungary got into their stride they were capable of murdering any team. They had, more or less, the same players who won the Olympic tournament. They all knew each other. They all played for clubs in Budapest and frequently trained together as a team, knitting to perfection. We barely had enough time to work at free-kicks, corners and throw-ins; they had the time to rehearse whole movements.'

Before leaving for home, Winterbottom had a long conversation with Raynor, who urged tactics similar to his own. A defensive policy, however, was unlikely to meet with approval in England's dressing room or in the selection chamber; also, there was the thought of what could result from conceding the initiative to such a talented team as Hungary.

Hungary made their way across Europe by train, stopping off in Paris to warm up against a team from the Renault car plant, where Sebes had worked before the war. In his column, Hoby sounded a warning note. 'It was only a practice match, but Hungary scored seventeen goals. They are very good.' Few shared his fears. Even Raynor believed that England had the means to defeat Hungary. Commissioned to preview the game for a Sunday newspaper, he wrote: 'I'm convinced that playing in the old British style and spirit, England's footballers can win at Wembley on Wednesday.' The British style was also close to the heart of Charles Buchan. Prominent in sports journalism after a distinguished pre-war playing career with Sunderland and Arsenal, he wrote: 'I think we have the men to beat the brilliant Hungarians. The clever ball control and close passing of the Hungarians do not alarm me in any way. Close marking by the half-backs is the answer. Our defenders should prove equal to the task.' Unable to accept that England no longer enjoyed a pre-eminent role in the game, Buchan could not bring himself to imagine a Hungarian victory; he saw only what he wanted to see – further proof that little had been learnt from the events of 1950. HARD TACKLING THE WAY TO BEAT HUNGARY; MAKE 'EM RUN, ENGLAND; and TEAR IN, ENGLAND, AND WIN were typical headlines. It was 1934 all over again. When Rous warned against complacency, one critic accused him of being defeatist. Rous's foreboding was, however, shared by Geoffrey Green of *The Times*. As David Miller recalled in his excellent biography of Stanley Matthews, the warning issued by Green in a BBC discussion was remarkable in its prescience. 'Green, who had not seen the Hungarians yet but was alert to England's tactical and technical shortcomings during the FIFA match, said that "one of these days we shall wake up and find six goals in the back of our net. I believe Hungary will beat us 4–2." '

Refused permission to train at Wembley, the Hungarians worked out at the Queens Park Rangers ground in west London. Sebes gave nothing away, the practice sessions consisting mainly of light ball work. Hungary had no set way of playing. What worked against one team might not work against another. Expecting England to be strong in defence, Sebes decided to attack with a fluid formation that had his centre-forward Hidegkuti dropping deep to link up with Bozsik in midfield. The wingers Budai and Czibor were given the responsibility of assisting in defence, leaving Puskas, Kocsis and Hidegkuti to attack at will. 'From what I saw last month, the England defenders will follow you,' Sebes said.

Even by their own towering standards of ineptitude, the England selectors excelled themselves: three of the forwards were changed, and when Finney withdrew with an injury his place, quite astonishingly, was given to George Robb of Tottenham Hotspur; a member of the British Olympic team in 1952. Robb had spent only one season in professional football; a year before, he had been an amateur international playing with Finchley in the Athenian League. Much as Arthur Rowe was pleased for his outside-left, he feared for him. 'George was doing well for us, and had a good temperament,' he said, 'but it was too big a step.'

Jingoistic appraisal left the public unprepared for the storm that was about to break over English football. Much was made of

England's unbeaten home record against foreign teams (defeat by the Republic of Ireland in 1949 was again conveniently overlooked), but even that was an exaggeration: since the first international match was held in 1872, England had met only 23 foreign teams on home soil, and Wembley hardly came into it. Hungary were only the fourth foreign team to play there.

Dave Sexton, later to manage Chelsea, Manchester United and Queens Park Rangers, and to assist five England managers, was in a party of West Ham players who made their way to Wembley for the game. 'There wasn't much football on television in those days, so all we knew about the Hungarians had come from the press,' he said. 'We got there early, and one of our players, Jimmy Andrews [a future Chelsea coach], wandered off. Jimmy came back chuckling. He'd seen the Hungarians warming up on a terrace underneath the stadium. "I don't think they're going to give England much of a problem," he said. "They've got a little fat fella, all left foot, who's down there doing tricks with the ball." ' It was Andrews's first glimpse of a player who would become known as one of the greatest in football history – Ferenc Puskas. 'We teased Jimmy for days afterwards,' Sexton added. 'We'd shout at him in training, "Hey, Jimmy, show us how the little fat fella does it," and he'd reply, "All right, all right, but how was I to know?" ' How was anybody to know? 'We'd been fed the idea that foreign teams wanted to walk the ball into the net,' Sexton continued. 'The Hungarians put that one to rest. One of the things that impressed us was the power of their shooting. They clubbed the ball. People blamed Gil Merrick for not getting to shots struck from outside the penalty area – our goalkeeper, Ernie Gregory, reckoned that he might have got to a couple – but I wasn't so sure. Then there was the movement. Because we were still operating with full-backs swinging around the centre-half to provide cover, the Hungarian forwards didn't have to worry about being caught offside. They cut us to pieces.'

Nobody suffered more embarrassment that day than England's centre-half Harry Johnston. Six months before, Johnston had tasted success at Wembley in the FA Cup final with Blackpool; now, Wembley was the scene of his worst moments in football, and he would never play for England again. Johnston's problem was precisely that experienced by Ufton in the match against the Rest of Europe: left to work things out for himself, Johnston did not know whether to track Hidegkuti when the Hungarian centre-forward dropped deep or to hold his position.

Before Johnston could address the dilemma with any certainty, in less than a minute Hungary scored. From a throw-in conceded by Dickinson the ball reached Bozsik who immediately established the planned link with Hidegkuti. Catching Johnston in two minds, the Hungarian centre-forward arrowed at England's penalty area and sent an unstoppable drive past Merrick. 'It was like a flash of lightning,' Sexton recalled. 'Hidegkuti's pace, that was the thing – and the finish. Clinical.' Johnston's confidence rose when he broke up an attack to start the move that saw Jackie Sewell equalise after a quarter of an hour's play, but before ten more minutes had passed England's defence lay in ruins. That exhilarating passage of Hungarian ascendancy was vividly described by Green in his report for *The Times*: 'However disturbing it might have been, it was breathtaking. At the twentieth minute, for instance, Puskas sent Czibor racing down the left [Sexton still speaks of the many devastating passes Hungary sent inside England's full-backs] and from Kocsis's flick Hidegkuti put Hungary ahead again at close range, the ball hitting Eckersley as he tried a desperate intervention. Almost at once Kocsis sent the fast-moving Czibor, who entered the attack time after time down the right flank, past Eckersley. A diagonal ground pass was pulled back by Puskas, evading a tackle in the inside-right position – sheer jugglery, this – and he finished off with a fizzing left-foot shot inside the near post: 3–1. Minutes later a free-kick by the progressive Bozsik was diverted by Puskas's left heel past the diving Merrick, and England, 4–1 down with the half-hour not yet struck, were an army in retreat and disorder.'

Encapsulating the marvellous flourish of Hungary's skill and confidence, the second of Puskas's two goals entered the lore of football as a classic of opportunism. Puskas was facing away from England's goal and had no apparent angle for a shot when he darted diagonally on to Czibor's pass as Wright closed on him. One of Wright's strengths was swiftness in the tackle. He had been in similar situations many times and come out on top. This time he was made to look foolish as Puskas dragged the ball back with the sole of his left boot then pivoted to strike a ferocious shot over Merrick's left shoulder. Wright recovered only just in time to see the ball hit the net. The sheer audacity of it stunned England's supporters. Wright was more than just England's captain; sturdy, uncompromising but unswervingly fair, he epitomised the best type of British professional player. To see him left helpless, utterly bemused, by Puskas's trickery was a telling moment for the English game.

Although Mortensen pulled a goal back for England, and Grosics made a point-blank save from a Robb header, it was clearly only a matter of time before Hungary further emphasised their superiority. Both Bozsik and Hidegkuti struck home before Ramsey scored a penalty to complete the score of 6–3.

Johnston's overriding memory of the game was one of helplessness. Walking off at half-time, he'd turned to Matthews and said, 'I don't know what to do [about Hidegkuti]. Do I go with him or stay?' Matthews told his biographer, 'I can't remember Walter Winterbottom saying anything to Harry Johnston. He seemed to spend most of his time talking to Robb. After the first five minutes you could see that our defence was getting in a mess and that it made sense for one of our inside-forwards to drop back and pick up Hidegkuti whenever he came deep for the ball. But nothing was changed.' The burden of failure sat heavily on Winterbottom, who tried to console himself with the thought that no team in the world could have withstood the brilliance of Hungary's attacking play. 'They had six players in the highest class,' he said. 'They knew each other's play inside out. Even if we had altered our system to deal with a deep-lying centre-forward I'm sure Hungary would have come up with something different of their own.'

Malcolm Allison was another of the West Ham players watching at Wembley. 'We'd completely lost our way,' he said. 'There was no direction in English football. We were blind to developments elsewhere in the world, stuck with the old ways. It was the same old routine. Training from ten until twelve, a dozen laps, a few sprints, a bit of five-a- side or head tennis. At West Ham we talked a lot about the game, offered up ideas, but from talking to players at other clubs I knew they were discouraged from putting in extra work simply because the training staff couldn't be bothered to put out kit for them. There were still managers who believed that if players didn't see a ball all week they would be hungry for it on matchdays.'

When Alf Ramsey returned to Tottenham the following day, he had little to say about the game. 'Alf knew that he'd played his last match for England, but there was more to it than that,' Eddie Baily recalled. 'He was a patriot who believed in English football, and I sensed that such a heavy defeat hurt him more than anybody else in the team.' Ramsey, in fact, was furious, not only because he felt that Merrick should have stopped three of Hungary's scoring efforts but at the fact that English football had got itself in such a hopeless position. 'It was still hit or miss,' he recalled. 'The England team stumbled from one game to the next, change after change to suit the whims of the selectors, few of whom had a clue about football. I had no thoughts about managing England; however, I could see that unless one man was given absolute control over policy and selection there was little hope for the future.'

Arthur Rowe, lost in admiration for England's conquerors, told Ramsey that he was astonished by the progress they'd made in the fourteen years since he'd coached in Hungary. 'I saw nothing then to suggest that they could become a power in the game,' he said. 'It's too easy to say that Hungary are simply fortunate to have found so many gifted individuals in one generation. That sometimes happens in football, but my guess is that they have a system of development far in advance of our own.'

Despite the drubbing, England's selectors continued to put club form over Winterbottom's plea for a team-building process. By the time Scotland and England met at Hampden Park in the spring of 1954 to settle the British Championship, both countries were assured of qualification for the World Cup finals in Switzerland. Still, eight changes were made to the national line-up, including five new caps. Attracted by West Bromwich Albion's strong challenge for League and Cup honours, the selectors chose two of the club's forwards, Ronnie Allen and John Nicholls; the hapless Johnston gave way to Harry Clarke of Tottenham – yet another attempt to solve the problem at centre-half; Roger Byrne of Manchester United made his international debut at left-back; Finney once more replaced Matthews on the right wing; and Mullen was restored on the left flank. Allen and Nicholls both scored in a 4–2 victory, but neither would make it into a seventeen-strong World Cup squad; they weren't even included among the five players on standby.

The fate of Allen and Nicholls was settled in mid-May by a 1–0 loss to Yugoslavia in Belgrade a week before a return match against Hungary. Finney, lucky to have missed the Wembley débâcle through injury, travelled on to Budapest fearing the worst. 'We hadn't played with any confidence against Yugoslavia, and there we were in our last game before the World Cup finals coming up against the favourites, who had slaughtered us at home. It wasn't the best of planning. You can imagine how we felt when one of the reporters told us that the match had been arranged the day after Hungary's victory at Wembley.'

In their now desperate search for a centre-half, the selectors turned to Syd Owen of Luton Town, who was given the thankless task of trying to deal with Hidegkuti. An intelligent footballer who would have a prominent role to play on the coaching staff at Leeds under Don Revie's management, Owen was determined not to make Johnston's mistake of being caught in no-man's land. 'Walter agreed with me that the best way of trying to cope with Hidegkuti's movement was to react to situations as I saw them. But we didn't have a cat in hell's chance of holding Hungary. They came at us in waves; their combination and support play were sensational.' It astonished Sebes to discover that England had made no attempt to alter their tactics from the first game. 'All they did was make changes,' he said. Eight in all, to be exact, four among the forwards, bringing the total to 22 in seven matches. 'We were ready for England to do something about holding Hidegkuti, but we didn't really have to do anything different. The centre-half [Owen] followed him everywhere and we poured into the gap.'

Finney remembered one of England's selectors visiting the dressing room before the game. 'He went on about the Hungarians being worried because our team included players who hadn't appeared in the first match,' Finney said. 'Ivor Broadis gave me a nudge, and when I looked around he winked and whispered, "Yeah, I can imagine it. Who does he think he's kidding? If the Hungarians are worried, what about us?" ' Sure enough, as at Wembley six months earlier, England found themselves chasing shadows. 'We were never in it,' Finney recalled. 'The Hungarians were far too quick for us and their combination play was even better than in the first match. They had fantastic players and tremendous confidence. At one time I thought they might get into double figures. I'd never played in such a one-sided match. In an odd sort of way, I took pleasure from being out there. Hungary had proved what nobody had thought possible – the blending of great individuals into a team. Five or six of their players deserve to rank among the best the game has ever seen, but the team came first. They seemed capable of reading each other's minds.'

Having scored three times in ten minutes midway through the second half, Hungary were 6–0 ahead when England mounted their first decent attack. 'Defensively, we'd learnt nothing since 1950,' Billy Wright said. 'We were still defending as individuals, not as a unit. The Hungarians were superb in both matches, but we made it easy for them.' The result left Winterbottom depressed. 'I felt helpless to do anything about it,' he said. 'On that performance, Hungary would have overrun any team in the world, but sitting there, watching goal after goal go in, I could only bury my head in my hands.' Typically, Broadis could see the funny side of it. 'It's the first time I've come off the pitch with a sunburned tongue,' he joked. Hoby struck a more serious note: 'I left that gigantic stadium with the strident song of the crowd ringing in my ears. I left it subdued by the travesty of soccer I had seen served up by my countrymen. And as I glanced up at the Magyar banners and rows of red flags waving side by side I saw, forlorn and faded, a lonely Union Jack flying above the radio stand. It seems ridiculous now, but the sight of that bleached Union Jack re-emphasised for me the difference in the football techniques of the two nations – one bright and shining, the other feeble and faltering.'

The day after Hoby returned from Budapest he received a telephone call from the Arsenal captain Joe Mercer, who was in a London hospital making a slow recovery from the injury that ended his playing career. Incensed by the mauling England had taken, Mercer said, 'We've got to start right at the bottom – in the schools, as the Hungarians are doing. We've got to get everyone interested right throughout the country – the schoolmasters, youth leaders and so on. We've got to teach boys to master the basics: trapping, turning with the ball, dribbling, passing, shooting. We've got to make it interesting. It's got to be put over with *enthusiasm* and *personality*. What we need is a national scheme. It will take six years to put English football back where it belongs, but it will be worth it. Rope everyone in – Stanley Matthews, Roger Bannister [who had recently broken the four-minute-mile barrier], Jimmy Hogan [whose methods were much admired abroad but who had no voice in his own country]. We've got to teach them how to play, how to get fit – really fit. But let's get on with it. Don't let's sit around talking.'

Incorporating Mercer's remarks, Hoby produced an abrasive column for the *Sunday Express*, many of his complaints still relevant today. 'We need a revolution in ideas, training and tactics,' he wrote. 'Most of all, we need a revolution in the attitude of the younger professionals. Many of them have come to regard football as a game of bone, brawn and no brains. They have become lazy and apathetic. They have no pride in performance. They do as little work in training as possible. Mentally, they are half asleep on the field. They seem to look on football as a part-time occupation. English football is over-commercialised. Money is the great god. Until our rulers make up their minds which comes first, club or country, we will go on losing to the foreigners.'

At a meeting of the International Committee it was decided to take only seventeen players to the finals in Switzerland and hold five in reserve. Averaging almost 29 years, it was the oldest squad England would ever send to a World Cup. Showing that little, if anything, had been learnt from 1950, it was again lopsided, containing eight forwards; three of the travelling party, Sheffield United goalkeeper Ted Burgin, Birmingham full-back Ken Green and Bill McGarry of Huddersfield, were uncapped. Public pressure had forced the return of Matthews in his 40th year. In six international matches, Merrick had conceded 21 goals. Sound at club level, he lacked the nerve for international football, but having failed to blood a replacement Winterbottom and the selectors were stuck with the shell-shocked Birmingham goalkeeper.

At least the shattering defeat in Budapest had served to quell the misplaced optimism of 1950, although a favourable draw grouping England with Belgium (beaten 5–2, 4–1 and 5–0 by England since the war) and Switzerland encouraged Winterbottom to believe that some sort of recovery was possible. 'We were used to the style of those teams, and because we were much closer to home adapting to the conditions wasn't the problem it had been in Brazil. The players were low after Budapest, but we had a lot of experience in the squad, and I felt that if we got off to a good start we might surprise the critics, few of whom gave us a chance.' Tom Finney wasn't so sure. 'I just couldn't see how we could get over that miserable experience in Budapest in time to put up a show in the World Cup,' he said. 'Hungary had ripped us to pieces and were understandably the overwhelming favourites, followed by Uruguay and Brazil, the finalists from 1950.'

The Preston winger was in a troubled phase of his career. Shortly after being voted Footballer of the Year by the Football Writers Association in May, he had flopped in the 1954 FA Cup final against West Bromwich Albion and had contributed little in Budapest. After just two games in the 1954 World Cup, one of England's greatest ever forwards would consider himself lucky to retain a place in the national team.

The 1954 World Cup, the first to be televised, was contested by sixteen teams competing in four groups of four, with two seeded teams in each. Because FIFA decided that the 'seeds' would not meet one another, only two rather than three games were played in each group. England began against Belgium in Basle on 17 June, less than a month after the trauma of Budapest. Astonishingly, all the changes were in attack, Matthews, Lofthouse and Tommy Taylor replacing Peter Harris, Jackie Sewell and Bedford Jezzard. Matthews rolled back the years to 1947, when he made all five England goals in Brussels, but the defence crumbled, Owen again struggling at centre-half. Taken to extra-time, England led 4–3 until an own goal by Jimmy Dickinson left them having to beat Switzerland to qualify.

In his autobiography *The Way It Was*, published posthumously in 2000, Matthews wrote, 'We played well enough in attack [in 1953–54], but were woefully weak in defence and midfield. Our defensive shortcomings were exposed to the full, and a few players who were favourites with the selectors, I believe primarily because they said the right things before games and at the post-match banquets, were seen not to possess sufficient quality to play at this level ... the performance of some players against Hungary [at Wembley] did not prevent them going on to win future England caps, one player in particular going on to amass a bountiful supply.' Matthews did not have to identify Wright and Dickinson. Going into the 1954 finals, Wright had 58 caps, Dickinson 35; for three years they had automatically filled the wing-half positions, making a total of 23 appearances together, and during that period England had tried six centre-halves, all of whom failed partly through lack of adequate cover. Wright and Dickinson did not create much either. In fairness, Wright was a defensive wing-half; his main assets were a quick pounce, speed in recovery, a sharp eye for interception and a spring that enabled him to more than hold his own in the air. While accepting that Wright's leadership on the field was important, critics had begun to question his and Dickinson's continuing presence in the team when half-backs with more imagination were available.

Leaving out Wright was unthinkable, however, and a decision taken after the 4–4 draw with Belgium would extend his international career beyond a century of caps. Rather than send for Allenby Chilton of Manchester United, one of five players standing by at home, the selectors went along with Winterbottom's suggestion of moving Wright to centre-half in place of Owen, who had been as ineffective against the Belgian centre-forward Coppens as he had been against Hidegkuti. Winterbottom had not forgotten how well Wright had adapted to the position when Jack Froggart was injured during a match against Wales at Wembley in November 1952. 'Wales had Trevor Ford at centre-forward, a tough, physical player, but Billy didn't give him an inch,' he said. 'I knew that he could cope in the air and wasn't against switching positions. It turned out to be one of the best moves we ever made, and hugely beneficial to Billy's career.'

With Matthews and Lofthouse both unfit, the selectors brought back the Wolves left-wing pair Wilshaw and Mullen, both of whom scored in a 2–0 victory over Switzerland that qualified England for a quarter-final against Uruguay, the reigning world champions and one of the four best teams in the tournament.

Television, of course, had begun to offer the public unprecedented access to the game. People accustomed to reading newspaper reports and hearing radio commentary could now catch glimpses of World Cup action. Sketchy as it was, this coverage brought the England team under closer scrutiny, and by the summer of 1954 the modern age of football celebrity was dawning. England's players entered it in a state of some confusion. The heavy losses to Hungary had brought home the truths of tactical naivety and blinkered assumption. Against foreign players of the highest class they had, as a team, been made to look prosaic. 'We were always being told that our League was the best in the world when it was merely the hardest,' Wright said. 'In 1954 we [England] were still playing as individuals rather than as a unit, because at club level chances were created by individual ability rather than by teamwork.'

Added to England's problems, as if somehow conspiring to further embarrass them, the daily temperatures in Switzerland consistently soared above 100°F, and the day of the match against Uruguay was no exception. Gathering his players together, Winterbottom stressed the importance of possession. 'In this heat, if we give the ball away we are going to run out of legs trying to get it back,' he said. The old guard were back, Matthews and Finney on the wings, Broadis and Lofthouse also in attack. Bill McGarry filled Wright's old position at right-half. Unwilling to risk the untried Burgin, the selectors kept Merrick in goal.

Into this edgy scene strode some of the world's best footballers. In their 7–0 annihilation of Scotland, who went out of their first World Cup without a point or a goal, Uruguay had looked even stronger than in 1950, five of the goals shared by their explosive wingers Abbadie and Borges. Santamaria would become the kingpin of Real Madrid's defence, going on to represent Spain in the 1962 finals; Schiaffino, soon to make his mark in Italy, looked the complete inside-forward, a player of exquisite touch, a creator and a scorer. Defiant in the face of such brilliance, inspired by the ageless Matthews and with Wright indomitable at centre-half, England gave their best performance of the tournament, but it wasn't good enough to beat a team cut to eight fit men for the last fifteen minutes. On top for a long spell in the second half, England's challenge petered out after Merrick's third mistake of the match gave Uruguay a 4–2 lead. Merrick had conceded 30 goals in ten matches; beneath Winterbottom's barely concealed disgust lay the realisation that he had failed to address a problem that had been evident for almost two years. 'I should have done more to persuade the selectors that our defence simply wasn't good enough to cope without a reliable goalkeeper,' he admitted. 'On his day, Merrick was as good as any, but he was prone to errors we could not afford. He was one of my big mistakes.' In his memoirs, Matthews wrote, 'For all the chopping and changing and poor performances against Hungary, I felt we had a team to go all the way to the final . . . but there is no legislating for goalkeeping errors. I felt sorry for Gil, he was a decent goalkeeper, but on the day I am sure he would agree, three of the Uruguayan goals could be put down to him. But that's football.'

Seen as proof that there was still plenty of life in English football, if not in some of the selectors, the overall performance against Uruguay brought Winterbottom some respite even if, as he suspected, it would have the paradoxical effect of hindering progress. How easy it was to dismiss the humiliation by Hungary at Wembley as merely a blip, to overlook the slaughter in Budapest.

Meanwhile, the 1954 World Cup exploded. The day following England's elimination, Brazil and Hungary, who went through 4–2, literally fought for a place in the semi-finals. Hoby wrote: 'The theatre, the entertainment and the wonderful virtuosity of the players degenerated into bloodshed and outrage as partisan passions got out of hand. Then what we saw was no longer football but a bad-smelling mixture of the circus and back-street gutter brawling. In the second half, referee Arthur Ellis of England, one of the best in the world [some felt that Ellis lost control of the game], was forced to send off Bozsik, the Hungarian right-half, and Nilton Santos, Brazil's six-foot left-back. Towards the end, Humberto, the Brazilian inside-right, hurled himself, hacking and kicking, at a Hungarian and again Mr Ellis [note the quaint adherence to title] issued marching orders. In vain Humberto's colleagues stormed and raved. Mr Ellis, quite rightly, refused to alter his decision and the dark Brazilian, tears streaming down his face, walked slowly from the field. Finally the game – if you could call it that – ended. This was the signal for another wild clash, this time on the touchline where one of the Brazilian reserves lashed out with both feet at a policeman who had tried to restrain him.

'Then an extraordinary thing happened. I was inching my way down to the exits when police whistles blasted through the stadium. At once, from every corner of the ground, grey uniformed police began to converge at the double on the passageway leading to the dressing rooms. But they were too late . . . Exactly what took place in that savage fight beneath the stands at Berne has been buried under a weight of conflicting testimony. But from the evidence, it seems that the Hungarians had hardly locked the door of their dressing room when it was broken open by the infuriated South Americans, some of whom had removed their boots. A window was smashed while one well-aimed boot struck the light and plunged the place into darkness. Then all hell broke loose. Boots and fists were used indiscriminately, and in the ensuing brawl Gustav Sebes had his cheek gashed while Joo Baptista Pinheiro, the gigantic Brazilian centre-half, was hit violently over the forehead. Puskas was also reported to be in the thick of the battle [according to one source Puskas went for Pinheiro with a bottle].

'It was hooliganism, brutal and unashamed. The British, whatever they may lack in technique, can still teach some of the others lessons in sportsmanship and self-control. The Brazilians, with their Negro stars such as Djalma Santos and Brandozinho, are the fastest things in football boots I have seen. In Julinho they have one of the world's great players, an outside-right who combines the wizardry of Matthews with a cannon-ball shot that swerves like a googly. But they must learn restraint . . .'

Hungary went on to defeat Uruguay 4–2 (so much for Matthews's theory about England's potential), and met West Germany in the final. Against all the odds, and after being two goals in arrears after just eight minutes' play, the Germans pulled off a remarkable victory. Injured when Hungary overwhelmed West Germany 8–3 in a group game, Puskas was back – a risky decision, since he'd missed the last two games and clearly wasn't fit. Most importantly, however, the Germans were not intimidated by Hungary's reputation. Well schooled by Sepp Herberger, they put down a marker that would eventually cause much gnashing of teeth in English football circles.

4. 1954 TO SWEDEN 1958

Following the 1954 World Cup finals, some English football writers became persistent howlers after antiquity. All agreed that things used to be better. Maurice Smith of the *People* wondered if England would ever again have a team to match that of the immediate post-war years. Matthews (remarkably) and Finney survived, but where were the replacements for such notable figures as Swift, Hardwick, Mercer, Carter and Lawton? 'We have become second-rate,' Smith wrote. 'Reaching the quarter-finals was only the equivalent of a Third Division team having a good run in the FA Cup.'

Winterbottom returned from Switzerland determined to press for more time to work with the team before international matches, and for better co-operation from the clubs (perennial issues). At a meeting of the Technical Sub-Committee held on 9 August 1954, he also argued that arbitrary selection hindered the proper process of team building. The result was a memorandum which began 'Within the framework of the present League system, it is thought that a great deal more can be done towards bringing England players and teams to a higher standard of performance in the next four years . . .' Only a small concession, however, was made to the contentious notion of an autonomous team manager. In future, the chairman of selectors, one other member and Winterbottom would make an initial selection before submitting the team for discussion and approval by the entire International Committee.

Eight months earlier, in January 1954, the first match played by the England under-23 team had taken place in Bologna. A 3–1 loss to Italy was of less significance than the concept. 'At last we had an opportunity to give our best young players experience of international football,' Winterbottom said. Soon, players from that area of development were breaking into the senior team, Johnny Haynes of Fulham and Manchester United prodigy Duncan Edwards among them. Haynes made his international debut in October 1954. One of seven changes from the team that had lost to Uruguay, he scored in a 2–0 victory over Northern Ireland in Belfast but immediately lost his place to Sunderland's Len Shackleton, who hadn't appeared in the national team since 1950.

Upon his death in October 2001, obituaries identified Shackleton as the footballer who refused to conform, and that is more or less accurate. He was, in the narrowest, best and most exacting sense of the term, a star whose independence exasperated the establishment as much as his showmanship illuminated the post-war football boom. Shackleton collected only five caps while gaining a reputation that became the title of a controversial autobiography, *The Clown Prince of Soccer*, one page of which was mischievously left blank under the chapter heading 'The Average Director's Knowledge of Football'. Sent home from Arsenal's nursery club in 1939 because he was thought too frail for professional football, Shackleton spent the latter war years working as a miner and playing for Bradford Park Avenue. At his best, Shackleton could make any footballer wonder what was the use; he could dribble, pass, shoot and perform astonishing feats of trickery. The legend needs no embellishment. It's true that Shackleton was able to spin the ball back to his feet, that he succeeded in beating opponents by getting rebounds from the corner flag – all of it done with a heavy leather ball and toe-capped boots (he and Matthews were the first in English football to experiment with lightweight footwear, in Shackleton's case field hockey boots) and on pitches that were often ankle deep in mud by mid-December. Shackleton's concrete achievements, however, were few. Sold to Newcastle United for a near record fee of £13,000, he celebrated the move by scoring six goals against Newport County on his debut and helped the Tyneside club to promotion from the Second Division, but he soon moved on to Sunderland where he became a huge favourite.

One of Shackleton's team-mates at Bradford was the future West Ham and England manager Ron Greenwood. In his autobiography, Greenwood wrote: 'Len had lovely, unbelievable skills and tremendous self-confidence. He was a showman, a crowd-pleaser, larger than life. Some of the things he did had nothing to do with the winning and losing of a game, but the crowds loved him. I used to play right-half behind him in the early days and he always liked to have me there for support; but when I was defending and under the whip I never got much help from Len.' Winterbottom's dilemma with Shackleton was precisely that identified by Greenwood. 'If only Len had been prepared to meet us halfway there wouldn't have been many better inside-forwards in the game,' he told me. 'With his touch, his brain, his marvellous anticipation, he should have been one of the greats. Trouble was that Len only wanted to play the game his way, purely for fun.'

Shackleton's selection against Wales in November 1954 was influenced by the north-eastern lobby. It made no practical sense. By the next World Cup he would be thirty-six years old. History. In the manner of Raich Carter, his great predecessor at Roker Park, he was also diametrically opposed to Winterbottom's coaching initiative. As for the England selectors, they were a form of life he was not inclined to acknowledge. When word reached Shackleton that he had been chosen to play it struck him that the visit of West Germany to Wembley in early December coincided with his launch of a business venture in Sunderland. If playing against Wales meant getting into the game against the world champions, perhaps conformity for once made sense. People who knew Shackleton well were surprised by the workmanlike effort he put in against Wales, parting quickly with the ball, something he had rarely done before. 'Wait until the Germany match,' he said. 'If selected, I might show you something to explain all about my performance in Cardiff.' 'That "shadow of Shack" was created for one game only,' he would say.

West Germany came with a team being rebuilt by Sepp Herberger and containing only three survivors from the World Cup-winning eleven, but still one strong enough to require a flat-out effort from the home players. Giving Matthews centre stage, Shackleton took up where he had left off against Wales. 'I played ball by not playing ball,' he said. 'But after half an hour I decided that the pretence had gone on long enough. From that moment I played my normal game.'

Although England dominated proceedings, taking the lead through Bentley from one of the many attacks Matthews inspired, they were repeatedly frustrated by the agility and daring of the German goalkeeper Fritz Herkenrath. 'Every time we looked like scoring, which was often, Herkenrath dashed out to narrow the angle,' Shackleton recalled. 'His anticipation was uncanny, and I decided he could only be beaten by a dribble or, more difficult, a chip.' After waltzing past three men, then past the goalkeeper, Shackleton was thwarted when he lost control of the ball. When a similar opportunity came a few minutes later, Shackleton went for the second option; as Herkenrath flew at Shackleton's feet the ball was sent neatly over his head. 'The best goal I ever scored,' Shackleton said.

At inside-left for the Germans that day was Jupp Derwall, who would be brought into the coaching structure, first serving as chief assistant to Herberger's successor Helmut Schoen then becoming, twenty years later, national team manager. 'It was amazing that Matthews could play so well at his age, a tribute to his fitness,' Derwall recalled from his home in Switzerland, close to the German border. 'He gave our full-back Kohlmeyer a match like he'd never had before, one he'd never forget. But we knew all about Matthews. He was famous from before the war. Shackleton came as a surprise. He did things with the ball we did not associate with English footballers. His goal came from exceptional skill and confidence. When we discovered that Shackleton was past thirty years old it made us wonder why he had not made a much bigger impact as an international player. From what Herberger told us, it was because Shackleton normally played to suit himself. Later on in Germany, we had a similar problem with Gunther Netzer. Netzer was a very talented midfield player who was at his very best in 1972 when we defeated England 3–1 at Wembley before going on to win the European Championship, which was the springboard for our success in the World Cup two years afterwards. Netzer lost out in the World Cup because Helmut always felt that Overath was more reliable.'

Praise for England's 3–1 victory in 1954, particularly the performances of Matthews and Shackleton, was lavish, in some cases typically unrestrained. Myopic in their conclusions, some leading football writers conveniently ignored the fact that England had come up against an experimental team. Less than six months after the World Cup disappointment, it didn't take much to recharge the batteries of English complacency, one correspondent writing that England's success 'bore further evidence of the gradual restoration of our national football standards'.

Support for this flimsy analysis came in the same month when Wolverhampton Wanderers defeated Hungary's leading club Honved, the club of Puskas and Kocsis, in a dramatically concluded friendly at Molineux. Building on the excitement caused three weeks earlier when they overcame Moscow Spartak with four goals in the last ten minutes, Wolves charged through a stormy night to record another famous victory. Floodlit football had come of age, capturing the imagination of a nationwide television audience as Stan Cullis's team, the reigning League champions, fought back from a 2–0 deficit to beat the Hungarians 3–2 in a thrilling finale.

A renewal of national pride was manifest in unrestrained praise for a success that many saw as a vindication of the traditional English style. The *Daily Mail* hailed Wolves as 'champions of the world'. Charles Buchan, the arch opponent of modernisation, felt joyous. 'Wolves struck another decisive blow for British football with as wonderful a second-half rally as I have seen in forty years,' he wrote. 'Wolves have made English football once again a power in the world game,' Bob Ferrier wrote in the *Mirror*. One narrow home victory in a friendly match against a tired touring team hardly marked a renaissance in English football, but after the national team's withering losses to Hungary, and another disappointing World Cup, it provided reassurance for English chauvinists. Admirable as the Wolves effort was, few critics bothered to point out that the match had been played on a heavy pitch (even after almost a week of rain it was watered by the groundstaff) more suited to the home team's muscular directness than the subtle movements of the visitors. And world champions? A few days earlier Honved had lost 3–2 away to Red Star Belgrade, a team placed only seventh in the Yugoslav league. Nobody had been moved to bestow a world title on the Yugoslavs.

Alongside the *Mirror*'s ringing reports – its star columnist Peter Wilson, who had no great love for football and normally attended only the FA Cup final and the annual fixture between England and Scotland, wrote, 'I may never live to see a greater thriller than this, and if I see many more as thrilling I may not live much longer anyway' – was a paragraph announcing the arrival in London of Milan for a friendly at West Ham. 'It doesn't matter if we lose,' Milan's manager Vittore Puricelli said. 'What is important is that the football should be good.' Putting the state of English football into clearer perspective, the Italians won 6–0 at Upton Park. 'It was another lesson in passing, movement and cunning,' Malcolm Allison recalled. 'Unlike Wolves, we didn't have the men for a power game, but in truth it hadn't been all that effective against Honved until they [the Hungarians] got bogged down in the conditions. In fact, before the ground cut up Honved were much the better team, well worth their two-goal lead. I don't want to take anything away from Cullis and the Wolves players of that time, but a lot of people read too much into those victories under floodlights, exciting as they were. How easy it was to forget that the England team had twice been humiliated by Hungary.'

Although proud of the part he played in bringing Wolves international attention, Bill Slater accepted that the claim to world supremacy was taking things too far. 'I don't remember how that started,' he said. 'I'd never seen Stan as excited as he was after the game against Honved, so maybe he allowed words to be put into his mouth. If so, it was understandable. It was less than six months since the big defeat by Hungary in Budapest and another disappointment in the World Cup. Not for one moment did I think Wolves were the best team in the world, but we'd restored some pride.'

By the money-driven values of modern football, Slater's career seems astonishing. In the spring of 1951 he was a 24-year-old amateur playing for Blackpool's reserves while studying for a degree in physical education at Carnegie College in Leeds. A week before the FA Cup final against Newcastle United he was selected to deputise for Blackpool's regular inside-left, the Scottish international Allan Brown, who had broken a leg. 'Trouble was that we were only allowed two free weekends in a term and I'd used them up,' Slater said. 'Eventually, I was given permission to play, but on the understanding that I returned to college immediately after the game. The train I took back to Leeds was crammed with Newcastle supporters celebrating their victory.' Slater sat in the corner of a third-class compartment, unrecognised.

Later, Blackpool agreed to cancel Slater's amateur registration when he took up a teaching post in London to be near his future wife. Armed with a reference from Blackpool, and holding out no great hopes for himself, Slater approached Brentford, the nearest League club to where he lived in Ealing. 'The Brentford manager, Jack Gibbons, gave me a trial and I got into the first team, making up a half-back line with Ron Greenwood and Jimmy Hill,' he said. When Slater's work as a lecturer took him to the Midlands, he pocketed another letter of recommendation, this time from Gibbons to the Wolves manager Stan Cullis. 'I told Stan that I was simply looking for a game, no matter which of the Wolves teams I played for,' Slater explained. 'Stan said bluntly that he wasn't interested in players who weren't set on making the first team.'

Having proved his worth in yet another trial – by then he had also represented Great Britain in the 1952 Helsinki Olympics – Slater decided to turn professional. 'I cleared it with my employers and put the idea of playing as a part-timer to Stan. In those days there was a signing-on fee of ten pounds, and typically he replied that he couldn't be sure that I was worth it.' Slater went on to captain Wolves to victory over Blackburn Rovers in the FA Cup final of 1960, when he was voted Footballer of the Year, and to turn out for England in the 1958 World Cup. But it was the emergence of a younger half-back that encouraged Winterbottom to believe that English football was moving forward.

No young English footballer excited Winterbottom so much as Duncan Edwards. A triumphant product of the youth scheme put in place by Matt Busby at Manchester United, he leapt from boyhood to manhood with ease. Powerfully built, Edwards had exceptional ball control with both feet, his passing and tackling were of the highest order, his shooting was awesome, and his reading of the game was startling in its maturity. Edwards was only fifteen years and 285 days old when he made his first-team debut on Easter Monday 1953. Less than two years later, he became the youngest footballer ever to be capped by England when at the age of seventeen years and eight months he played against Scotland at Wembley (England won 7–2). Busby's assistant, the tough former Welsh international Jimmy Murphy who had the vital role of custodian to a wealth of burgeoning talent at Old Trafford, said of Edwards, 'From the moment I first saw Duncan as a boy of fourteen, he had the assurance of a man, with legs like tree trunks, a deep and powerful chest and a matchless zest for the game. I must have seen thousands of players, but there was only one Duncan Edwards. Wing-half, centre-half, inside-forward – he could fill all these positions with the composure of a great natural footballer. He never bothered about where he played. All that concerned him was whether his name was on the team sheet.'

In May 1955, England undertook a tour to France, Spain and Portugal with Don Revie installed as the team's playmaker, the midfield director of attacking pace and direction. At the start of the 1954–55 season, Revie had been at a critical stage of his career. By then 27 years old, he was being shuttled from wing-half to inside-forward and back again, and could never be sure for any length of time what his position in the Manchester City team would be. 'I was seriously thinking about a move when our manager Les McDowall asked me how I felt about playing centre-forward,' Revie said. 'Before I could reply, Les said, "Not an orthodox centre-forward.

I don't see you knocking over defenders and barging into goal-keepers. I want you to play deep. I want someone as a midfield schemer who is prepared to wander all over the field – and I think you're the man for the job." I didn't know what to say. The name of Hidegkuti wasn't mentioned, but from the way Les spoke I knew that it was the Hungarian's role he wanted me to perform.' Almost abandoned after a 5–0 loss to Preston on the opening day of the season, the 'R-plan', as it became known, proved to be a big success, allowing Revie to fully develop his creative instincts. Finney found the style fascinating. 'City have done English football a service by introducing an imaginative way of playing,' he said at the time.

However, as with Tottenham's push-and-run, it was not a method that could easily be transferred to the England set-up. 'In other countries, club teams played more or less in the same way, defensively and offensively,' Winterbottom said. 'There was no set pattern in England. I admired what City had put in place but it required the full co-operation of every player for Revie to be given the freedom of the field. If lacking the pace that helped to make Hidegkuti so effective as a deep-lying centre-forward, Revie was a clever and intelligent footballer, but we simply couldn't adapt his role to the England team. We used him to orchestrate attacks from midfield, but unfortunately he picked up an injury against France in the summer of 1955 and was never afterwards quite as effective.'

By the autumn of 1955 England had at last got around to a proper process of team building. On 2 November, against Northern Ireland at Wembley, opportunities were given to the Fulham inside-forward Johnny Haynes and the Blackburn half-back Ronnie Clayton, both graduates from the under-23 team. From that day on, England played sixteen matches without defeat. Edwards, Clayton and Haynes played every match when fit. The full-backs, Jeff Hall (soon to die from polio) of Birmingham and Roger Byrne, had also benefited from international experience at a lower level.

Three of the eleven victories qualified England for her third World Cup thirteen months before the 1958 finals in Sweden. Growing resentment over the separate status enjoyed by the British teams had forced FIFA to abandon its policy of allowing two to qualify from the home internationals. England got off lightly, coming out of the hat in a group with Denmark and the Republic of Ireland – hardly a recipe for insomnia. Denmark had yet to embrace professional football, and had not even dared to compete in the 1956 Melbourne Olympics. The Republic, victors at Goodison Park eight years earlier, was decades away from the momentum subsequently created by Jack Charlton.

England, however, did not impress. A 5–2 victory over Denmark at Molineux in December 1956 looked better than it was, secured only in the last 25 minutes when Edwards, playing at inside-left, scored twice. England's remaining three games were completed over twelve days in May 1957. Tommy Taylor followed up his hat-trick against Denmark with another against the Republic in England's first World Cup encounter at Wembley, but only he, Finney and Haynes could look back on the 5–1 success with any personal satisfaction. Haynes and Matthews simply didn't go together. Throughout his career Matthews had demanded the ball to feet; now, at 42, he was being asked to connect with Haynes's trademark through-pass. Matthews' remark, 'I didn't find it easy to establish a playing relationship with Johnny Haynes', was an understatement. Taylor brought his tally of World Cup goals to eight in Copenhagen where England won 4–1, although again not as easily as the score suggested. Injured during the game, Matthews would never again be seen in England's colours.

With only four days between matches, England travelled to Dublin knowing that a draw would be enough to book their passage to Sweden, but aware that an Irish victory followed by a win against Denmark would result in a play-off. 'It was a dodgy situation,' Haynes recalled. 'We'd won all three games, scored plenty of goals [fourteen against four] but still we weren't through. The Irish had some pretty good players and they gave us a fright.' Ahead after only three minutes, the Irish were only seconds away from a famous victory when Bristol City's John Ateyo headed England into the World Cup finals. More than 40 years later, the Republic's left-back Noel Cantwell remembered an acute sense of injustice. 'On paper, England looked much the stronger team,' he said, 'but it wasn't a case of us hanging on to that early goal. We could have been two up by half-time. Bill Whelan was terrific, Charlie Hurley magnificent. We deserved better.'

Following a tour by the under-23 team (managed by Bill Nicholson, who had ended his playing career to become Tottenham's coach) in 1957, three players were added to an increasingly impressive pool of English talent: West Bromwich Albion full-back Don Howe, the tricky Blackburn winger Bryan Douglas and the powerful but technically limited West Bromwich Albion forward Derek Kevan, who was to become a controversial choice for the 1958 World Championship. 'At that stage I felt we had a good chance,' Winterbottom said. 'We had a number of outstanding young players and experienced men like Wright and Finney to guide them.'

Less than six months later, however, tragedy, real and grimly defining, plunged the football world into mourning and shattered England's hopes. On 1 February 1958 a Manchester United team still in the throes of development, the reigning League champions and excitingly on course to become one of the best sides English football had ever seen, defeated Arsenal 5–4 at Highbury. Paying alliterative tribute to the vision of Matt Busby, sportswriters had christened them the Busby Babes. It was the last time they would be seen on British soil. Within a week five of the young men who had fashioned that thrilling victory were among those who perished in the snow and ice when an aircraft bringing Manchester United home from a European Cup tie against Red Star in Belgrade crashed on take-off from Munich. Roger Byrne, David Pegg, Tommy Taylor, Eddie Colman, Bill Whelan and Geoff Bent were killed outright; Duncan Edwards sustained internal injuries, a fractured leg, fractured ribs and severe shock. It was too much even for such a giant. Edwards lingered for fifteen days, raising hopes that he would pull through, then he succumbed.

In his 82nd year, Nicholson reflected on what might have been but for that tragedy. 'Of course when the awful news came you felt first for the families of those poor lads and for Matt Busby, who wasn't expected to survive, but you couldn't help thinking what effect such a terrible event would have on the England team,' he said. Edwards was a player to gladden Nicholson's heart, displaying all the marvellous qualities he would soon find in the Scottish international Dave Mackay. 'Duncan had it all,' he said. 'The range of his ability was exceptional and, like Mackay, he had tremendous enthusiasm for the game. I think if Edwards had lived, Byrne and Taylor too, because they were both outstanding in their positions, England would have gone close in Sweden.' With Edwards, Byrne and Taylor gone, Winterbottom had to revise his thinking. 'It was a hell of a job,' Nicholson added, 'because there were not that many international-class players around, and one or two who looked up to it weren't quite ready.'

Bobby Charlton, who had miraculously survived the Munich disaster with only minor injuries, was however thought to have sufficiently recovered from the trauma and to be of sound enough temperament to be launched as an international against Scotland at Hampden Park that April. Charlton's fluent running with the ball, his acceleration and the violence of his shooting had earned him a rating by Busby's assistant Jimmy Murphy in the Edwards category. What he did not yet have was a thorough appreciation of team play. 'It took Bobby time to grasp the idea of playing short passes and going for the return. I drooled over his talent, but he kept spoiling it by hitting long balls to the wings and then standing still,' Murphy said. 'Beautiful as they were to watch, so many of those long passes were made when it would have been more productive to pass short. For a while the message was always the same: "Play it short, son, play it short. Leave the long ball until it's on." To his credit, Bobby never shirked the work we gave him, and when the message got through he was on his way to becoming a truly great player.' If impending greatness was not yet evident in Charlton's general play, his shooting alone was worth the price of admission. Poor as Scotland were, Charlton's international debut was made memorable by a ferociously struck goal, a 25-yard volley off Finney's centre that strengthened the argument for his inclusion in the World Cup party.

The following month, four days after the Manchester United team cobbled together by Murphy lost to Bolton Wanderers in the FA Cup final, Charlton scored both the goals that brought England a 2–1 victory over Portugal at Wembley. Bob Ferrier wrote: 'Even against Portugal . . . little was seen of him as a footballer helping the team and being part of the team effort. He did not feature well in progressive, linked movements, and his defensive play was non-existent. So it seemed England would have to "carry" Bobby Charlton solely for his scoring potential, or discard him in favour of a better all-round and more workmanlike performer. Considering carefully that he had consolidated his place in the Manchester United team only six months previously, considering Munich and his recovery from it, and remembering his performance for his club against Arsenal – the last League game it played before the disaster – it was decided to "carry" him and perhaps build up his capacity for work.

Charlton was a player of the highest potential, but he was not a comprehensive, adaptable footballer, and people who watched him closely concluded that he was immature and by no means of international standard, apart from his shooting, which was quite phenomenal. All these factors were exposed in the match against Portugal.'

Whether or not to persist with Charlton when the cause might be better served by a less dramatic but more reliable player was only one of the problems facing Winterbottom in the summer of 1958. Edwards was irreplaceable, but someone had to play in his position, the choice eventually falling on Bill Slater. Jimmy Langley of Fulham was tried at left-back before the job was given to the Bolton hard man Tommy Banks, who boasted that every winger who visited Burnden Park left with gravel rash. It seemed logical to bring back Lofthouse at centre-forward, but instead the selectors controversially retained Kevan.

Not once during this period of reassessment did Winterbottom refer to the shattering effect of the Munich disaster. 'Other than to express sympathy for the families of those who'd died, I never heard Walter speak about it,' Don Howe said. 'He'd lost some terrific players, not only Duncan Edwards, Roger Byrne and Tommy Taylor, but also David Pegg and Eddie Colman, who would have had a very good chance of being included in the squad. From being in a position to win the World Cup, he had to think again. But it wasn't in Walter's nature to complain. He kept his thoughts to himself and got on with the job.'

Among the players passed over at this time was Brian Clough, who had just completed a 40-goal season for Middlesbrough in the Second Division. Three things went against Clough, the least among them being his club's status. Through the force of his personality Clough insisted on being the main beneficiary of Middlesbrough's attacking play. His style was to hang back and pounce on centres put in by fast wingers, so to accommodate Clough in the England team would have meant re-casting the entire forward line. Selected for the under-23 tour in the summer of 1957, he was left out after the first match by Bill Nicholson. 'There is no disputing that Clough was a very good goalscorer,' Nicholson recalled, 'but on that tour I felt he was a lazy player.'

When the first of two World Cup warm-up games brought a 5–0 drubbing by Yugoslavia in Belgrade, serious doubts were cast on England's ability to recover from the decimation of Munich. Playing in dreadful heat, England were torn apart by the skills of Sekularac, whose brilliance blighted Ronnie Clayton's chances of a regular playing berth in the World Championship. Charlton was ineffective, Haynes unusually diffident, and Kevan was left isolated. Slater had never experienced heat like it. 'I did a lot of work on my fitness, but after fifteen minutes I was exhausted,' he recalled, 'my legs rubbery, my head swimming. We were never in the game. It seemed as though the Yugoslavs always had seven men in attack and eleven in defence.' Though allowances were made for the conditions in Belgrade, changes were inevitable when England moved on to play the Soviet Union in Moscow. Colin McDonald of Burnley replaced Bolton's Eddie Hopkinson in goal, Charlton gave way to Bobby Robson, and Eddie Clamp completed an entire Wolves half-back line with Wright and Slater.

In order to play in the World Cup finals, Slater had taken a month's unpaid leave from Birmingham University. 'The fifty-pounds match fee meant that I just about broke even,' he told me. 'Imagine that today, although it would be impossible to play in the Premiership as a part-time professional.' Slater did well in Moscow, securing the left-half berth with a solid performance that would lead to a key role for him in Sweden. 'We played much better as a team against the Russians,' he said. 'A bumpy pitch made good combination play difficult, but we moved the ball much quicker than we had in Belgrade. A 1–1 draw was less than we deserved against the country we were going to face first in the finals.'

The general feeling was that a post-Munich England could put out a middle-of-the-road team, hard to beat but not blessed with an abundance of individual skill. Critically, the team lacked speed, the ability to launch rapid counter-attacks from promising positions. Tom Finney and Bryan Douglas had the skill to get past defenders on the flanks, but they were clever, not explosive. In consultation with the selectors, Winterbottom pressed for the full permitted complement of 22 players but had to settle for two fewer, the choice of ten forwards leaving the defence seriously short of cover. Again, the England squad looked unbalanced. Only four of its members – Wright, Finney, Haynes and Clayton – had made more than seven appearances for the national team; Bobby Smith and Maurice Norman of Tottenham, Peter Brabrook of Chelsea and the Wolves inside-forward Peter Broadbent were uncapped; and with an average

age of 25 years and two months, England had too many novices for comfort.

Winterbottom found it difficult to maintain his natural civility when newspaper articles implied that the decision to make camp at the centrally located Park Hotel in Gothenburg instead of in the Swedish countryside had been taken against his wishes, mainly to suit officials of the Football Association. In fact, Winterbottom had inspected seven possible locations. Brazil had claimed the hotel at Hindas, an hour from the city by road, so the choice came down to living in Gothenburg or going to Lisekil, on the coast some 150 kilometres away. Lisekil was ideal in every detail except distance: it entailed a round trip of more than six hours for each of the three matches England had to play in a week. Advice had been sought from the Swedish team manager George Raynor, who was of the opinion that if Hindas was not available it would be better to settle for comfortable quarters in Gothenburg. To Winterbottom's astonishment and dismay, Raynor would later condemn the choice in an interview with one of the England manager's most persistent critics.

As Howe recalled, the England players found nothing to complain about. 'It was an extremely comfortable hotel, one of the best in Sweden. The food was excellent and nobody bothered us. One or two of the press lads made a fuss about us being stuck in the centre of a seaport, but it was never a problem. The World Cup was nowhere as big as it would become; sponsorship, agents, television cameras, big press conferences, all that stuff was in the future. Foreign travel was still a novelty, so very few supporters followed the England team abroad. Most of the time we moved around unnoticed and there was no security. The training ground was less than a quarter of a mile from the hotel and we walked there, boots under our arms. I don't recall any stuffiness on the part of the officials, we got on well with most of the journalists, and Walter trusted us to go out and not break an eleven p.m. curfew. There was an amusement park not far from the hotel, similar to the Tivoli Gardens in Copenhagen, and we spent quite a bit of time in there, wandering around, watching people enjoy themselves. It was a very relaxed atmosphere. Though that World Cup was shown on television, we didn't see any of the other games, and of course there were no videos to study. What we got to know about our opponents came from Bill Nicholson, who had been made Walter's assistant.'

On the brink of beginning an outstanding career in football management, Nicholson had expressed concern over England's fitness levels following the heavy defeat in Belgrade. 'The Yugoslavs were no more used to the heat than our players, but they lasted the pace much better,' he argued. 'It was clear to me that the England team wasn't in good physical shape.' Before leaving for Sweden the England players were put through a concentrated training programme at the Bank of England sports ground in south-west London. After the first session, a number were unwell. 'You expect that at the start of a season, but not when players have been training for nine months and are about to take part in such an important tournament,' Nicholson added. 'It was then that I realised how much English football had to learn about training methods and proper preparation. We were still following the old ways. We had to change. Tottenham were praised for the football we played when winning the Double in 1961, but importantly our team was the fittest in the First Division. I worked the players tremendously hard in pre-season. I brought in a weight-training expert to develop power. The approach was more scientific.'

When he discovered one day that some of the England players had got up late and eaten a heavy breakfast, Winterbottom cancelled the rest of the day's work, replacing it with a team meeting at which he emphasised responsibility. 'The breakfast thing was interesting, because at the time hardly any attention was given to diet,' Slater said. 'Ridiculous as it now sounds, steak was still being served for a pre-match meal. That apart, Walter was obviously disappointed with the way things had gone at the first training session. Some of us had come through a demanding season [Slater had been a pillar of Wolves' success in the League Championship] but we knew we had to get with the pace of Bill's fitness routines to have any chance in Sweden.'

Though two past two-time champions, Uruguay and Italy, had been eliminated, by Paraguay and Northern Ireland respectively, the sixteen qualifiers from 53 entrants constituted, certainly in Winterbottom's mind, the strongest collective assembly. For the first and only time to date, all four British teams reached the finals, Wales by the back door which had opened when lots were drawn to find a play-off opponent for Israel. The Irish, cleverly managed by Peter Docherty, had knocked out Italy, who had never previously failed to get through, and Scotland had qualified at the expense of Spain. The tournament was again divided into four eliminating groups, but geography had replaced merit in the seeding process. It hadn't worked out well for England. From South America they'd drawn Brazil, from eastern Europe they'd got the Soviet Union, and from western Europe came Austria, who had been placed third in 1954.

Ignoring a press campaign for Charlton's restoration, Winterbottom persuaded the five-man selection committee to stick with the team that had held the Soviet Union in Moscow three weeks earlier. Little by little, Winterbottom had grown in authority; if it was nonsense to suggest, as some did, that England's manager had the selectors in his pocket, he could at least be pretty sure of getting the team he wanted.

Gold medallists at the 1956 Olympic Games in Melbourne, where Igor Netto emerged as a half-back of outstanding quality, the Soviet Union had prepared for their first World Cup with typical centralised thoroughness. Club teams were permitted to play friendly matches in western Europe, and study groups were sent to monitor developments in South America. Shaken by their failure to defeat England at home, even more so by the loss of Netto through injury, the Russians introduced four new players, three in attack, none of whom had figured in Winterbottom's briefing. Caught unawares, England quickly lost control of the midfield to Tsarev and Voinov and went behind after only thirteen minutes when the ball fell kindly for Simonian after Colin McDonald had parried Ivanov's cross-shot. 'The Russians were different again from the team we'd played in Moscow,' Howe said. 'They fouled a lot [giving away 33 free-kicks to six against England], something we hadn't expected. Tom Finney and Bryan Douglas took the brunt of it [by then 36, Finney's legs were so bruised that he played no further part in the tournament]. At half-time, Walter told us to keep our heads together as a team, to try to provide Derek Kevan with more support because we weren't making chances. We were still using the old system of two wingers and a centre-forward. Both wingers preferred the ball to feet and we didn't have any real pace through the middle. Long passes weren't much good because the Russian goalkeeper, Lev Yashin, one of the greatest ever, was brilliant at cutting out through balls.'

The hard slog got harder when Ivanov put the Russians further ahead in the 56th minute. Immediately, Wright called for more effort. 'Billy was a terrific leader,' Howe recalled. 'He was well into his thirties but hadn't lost any of his enthusiasm for the game.' Neither were the other two Wolves players, Bill Slater and Eddie Clamp, about to give up. 'Stan [Cullis] had always instilled in us that no cause was ever completely lost,' Slater said. 'I remembered that Wolves had come back to win after going two down against Honved. I'm sure Billy and Eddie felt the same.'

The break England needed came when Kevan out-muscled the Soviet defence to wrongfoot Yashin with an untidy but effective header. Written off in the press box as the clumsiest attacker ever to wear England's colours, a symbol of the team's ineptitude, Kevan had got the team back on track. From then on, ignoring the pain of a rapidly swelling ankle, Finney was England's inspiration. Smothered until then, he began to take the Soviet left flank apart. From one of the Preston man's centres Robson, now more prominent in attack, shot wide; from another he smashed the ball home only to realise that the referee had penalised Kevan for impeding Yashin. 'We'd taken over the game,' Slater said. 'The Russians were on their heels, but time was running out.'

With only five minutes left, Winterbottom looked up from an anxious glance at his watch in time to see Haynes upended in the Soviet penalty area. Unmoved by Yashin's theatrical protests, the Hungarian referee Istvan Zsolt pointed to the spot. All now rested on Finney's nerve. As he carefully placed the ball, most of the England players, Wright among them, couldn't watch. Tommy Banks's eyes were on the kicker. 'It were never in doubt,' he said after Finney coolly sent the ball inside Yashin's right-hand post. England were still alive. In the stand, Italy's pre-war hero Vittorio Pozzo remarked that England would be extremely difficult to beat. 'They lack class,' he said, 'but, as always, they have the hearts of lions.'

Simultaneously, a plan was forming in Bill Nicholson's mind. He'd been sent by Winterbottom to watch Brazil play Austria and had identified Didi as the key figure in a revolutionary tactical formation, the first since Herbert Chapman's introduction of the stopper centre-half. Brazil's rotund coach Vicente Feola had withdrawn a midfielder to provide cover for the central defender, a duty normally performed by the full-backs, who were now able to close down quickly on wing play. One of the inside-forwards joined the central attacker as a twin striking force, leaving two men to forage in the centre of the field.

With less than three days to find an answer, Winterbottom held a team meeting. 'As Walter explained it, our biggest problem was that Billy [Wright] could be left with the impossible task of trying to hold two centre-forwards,' Howe said. 'Then he turned the meeting over to Bill Nicholson. Bill looked straight at me. "Brazil's outside-left [Mario Zagallo] plays deep so I think you can afford to drop back and cover the middle," he said. I was startled, but no more than Eddie Clamp who was told to position himself wider on my side of the field, becoming, you might say, the first wing-back.'

Between them, Winterbottom and Nicholson decided that Slater was the best man to put on Didi, whose cerebral play had reminded Nicholson of Danny Blanchflower. 'In a poor team, Danny was a liability,' Nicholson said, 'but in a good team he was brilliant. Didi was playing in a good team, so we needed to put an intelligent player on him.' It was an entirely new task for the thoughtful Slater. 'I wasn't sure that it would work,' he said. 'I was used to a freer role, getting up and down the field. My instructions were to hamper Didi, not to rough him up. That would never have crossed Walter's mind. Just stay tight so that he didn't get much time and room.'

The move worked well, as did Howe's unusual deployment in defence. Despite the loss of Finney, who barely recovered in time for the next League season, England took Brazil to the wire, often looking the better team. 'The further the game went the more anxious Brazil became,' Slater said. 'What we lacked in flair we made up for with superior teamwork. Colin McDonald made some outstanding saves, and Brazil hit our crossbar, then a post. But in the second half we came more into the game. The idea that we just about got away with it wasn't entirely fair. A goalless draw was the least we deserved. And it could have been better. It pleased Walter that we had held our own tactically.'

Fretting over Brazil's first failure to score in a World Cup game as much as the loss of a point, and aware that his formation was under close scrutiny, Feola reached a decision that would illuminate the finals and the game for many years to come. No more would he accept that the seventeen-year-old prodigy Pele was too young for the rigours of a World Cup, or that the barely literate Garrincha was psychologically suspect. Their time had come.

Provided that Brazil took care of the Soviet Union, victory over Austria, whose position was irretrievable, would take England through to the quarter-finals. A team in decline, Austria had lost both their matches, conceding five goals without reply. England drew further encouragement from history: only one of eight previous meetings had been lost. Before asking the selectors to approve an unchanged team, Winterbottom consulted with his two most senior players, Wright and Finney (a fitness test had confirmed the severity of Finney's injury). Douglas was off form, and Kevan, whose ability to browbeat defences was offset by obvious technical shortcomings, was again getting a bad press, adding to the clamour for Charlton's inclusion.

A close watch had been kept on Charlton. He appeared to have recovered remarkably well from the awful experience of Munich, but Winterbottom felt that the World Cup had come to soon for a player of limited international experience. In his book *Finney on Football* published later that year, Finney wrote: 'In view of the tremendous interest aroused by the non-selection of Manchester United's Bobby Charlton, I should try to correct the many wrong impressions concerning young Bobby in Gothenburg. What is the real Bobby Charlton story? I must have been asked that question a hundred times since I returned from Sweden . . . There is no "real" Bobby Charlton story, no hidden mystery behind his rejection, no backroom squabbles, clashes or misbehaviour calling for disciplinary treatment . . . the only reason for Bobby missing the World Cup lay in the decision that he was too inexperienced for the series. My assessment of Bobby is that he shows great potential. I like him a lot, and given normal progress, I have no doubts about his talent proving good enough for a regular berth in the England team.'

When Nicholson was informed of an unchanged team, he winced. He shared the general misgivings about Kevan and felt that Douglas threatened to achieve more than he accomplished. 'I would have replaced Kevan with Bobby Smith, who was a much better all-round centre-forward, but since I wasn't asked I kept my opinions to myself,' he said.

Still, it was a confident England team that made the 60-mile trip to face Austria in the small town of Boras. 'Walter was delighted with the performance against Brazil, and we were in good spirits,' Howe said. 'After two defeats, Austria had only their pride to play for. They hadn't scored a goal, and defensively we'd looked solid.' Not solid enough to prevent Austria taking the lead after sixteen minutes when

Koller strode on to a carelessly cleared corner to beat McDonald from 25 yards. 'The goal threw us completely out of our stride,' Howe added. 'Where we'd kept the ball pretty well against Brazil we were giving it away, using too many long passes.' Eleven minutes into the second half, Haynes brought England level, pouncing to score from close range after Austria's goalkeeper Zsanwald spilt a simple shot from Alan A'Court. Again, however, McDonald was beaten from long range, Korner's low drive going in off the foot of a post. With less than fifteen minutes left, England were looking at elimination when Haynes and Robson combined to create an opportunity for Kevan. The much-maligned West Bromwich Albion forward brushed aside Austria's veteran stopper Hapel before scoring with a powerful shot. 'I was thrilled to bits for him,' Howe said.

With the game almost over, Robson was the victim of an atrocious decision, his second in the tournament. Having had a goal disallowed against the Soviet Union, he was denied another for a questionable handball offence called by one of the linesmen, Istvan Zsolt, who had refereed against the Russians. Robson threw his head back in frustration. Haynes was furious. 'It was diabolical,' he recalled. 'I was following up, just a few yards away, when Bobby put the ball into the net after his shot struck the goalkeeper. His hands were nowhere near the ball.'

Brazil's 2–0 victory in Gothenburg left England and the Soviet Union level on points with identical goal counts. Forced to play each other for a place in the last eight, their third meeting in a month, they had only 48 hours to prepare. One sure thing was that Zsolt would not be referee. Following a petition by Rous he was withdrawn from the shortlist. At last, Winterbottom made changes. Clamp, reckless against Austria, made way for Clayton's return at right-half; the England manager's contention that inexperience weighed against Charlton was then contradicted by the inclusion of Chelsea's 20-year-old outside-right Peter Brabrook and the Wolves inside-forward Peter Broadbent, both new caps.

Two chances fell to Brabrook: he turned the first into Yashin's shovel-like hands; the second bobbled against an upright. In the manner of England's luck throughout the tournament, when the Russians hit a post the ball went in, Ilyin scoring with a low cross-shot. It was enough to put England out. 'We were bitterly disappointed, 'Howe said. 'We played our best football in that game and deserved to win. Walter came in for a lot of unfair criticism. The Munich crash had ripped the heart out of his team. How would Brazil have fared in Sweden if they'd lost three of their key players? To this day people don't appreciate how much Walter did for English football. He was always encouraging the England players to think about the game, to take back to our clubs what we'd learnt from playing international football. It was because of Walter's inspiration that many of us went into coaching.'

The Russians soon followed England out of the finals, defeated two days later by Sweden in the quarter-finals. 'That didn't surprise me because the schedule was ridiculous,' Slater said. 'As we would have had to do, the Russians played three World Cup ties in five days. They were shattered.' Similar physical demands did for Northern Ireland and Wales, the surprise packages of the tournament. In defeating Hungary for the right to meet Brazil in the last eight, Wales lost John Charles, who had recently been voted the most valuable player in Europe. 'Had John been fit, who knows what might have happened,' the Wales and Arsenal captain Dave Bowen said. Without their titanic centre-forward, Wales lost out to Pele's first World Cup goal. Northern Ireland had Danny Blanchflower, Jimmy McIlroy, Billy Bingham and Peter McParland against the France of Kopa, Fontaine and Piantoni; on his way to an unbroken record of thirteen goals in one World Championship, Fontaine scored two of the four that put paid to Peter Docherty's team. If more competitive than in the 1954 finals, Scotland had long gone, holding the dismal record of just one point from a total of five World Cup matches.

Brazil went on to take the trophy, overwhelming Sweden 5–2 in the final to become the first country to win the World Championship outside its own continent. The best team had won, and the best of Brazil had yet to be seen. England were the only one of Brazil's opponents to avoid defeat in Sweden, but Winterbottom's record in three World Cups was now just two wins in ten matches. There were, as always, questions for the England manager, one of them from his young son at the airport: 'Dad, why didn't you pick Bobby Charlton?'

5. 1959 TO CHILE 1962

On 28 May 1959, ironically in a country almost oblivious to association football, Billy Wright made the last of his 105 appearances for England. The curtain came down in Los Angeles, where fewer than 13,000 spectators saw England beat the United States 8–2 at the end of a fractious summer tour that had seen them suffer debilitating losses to Brazil, Peru and Mexico.

By the time England arrived in California they were breathless, and not just because of the exhausting altitude in Lima and Mexico City: adapting to Brazil's 4–2–4 had proved difficult; Charlton had not made the transition from club to international football; Wright was heading for the exit, following quickly in Finney's footsteps; nineteen-year-old Jimmy Greaves had marked his international debut with a goal against Peru but the defence had collapsed under the weight of Seminario's hat-trick; and wherever Winterbottom looked he seemed to find a problem. Always subject to emotional disturbance, relations between the Football Association and the travelling press reached breaking point when a number of correspondents suggested calling off the game against the USA to avoid a repeat of the 1950 embarrassment. Claiming that this had seriously affected the attendance, the FA pathetically reported them to the Press Council.

The following season brought no improvement. Emulating the Hungarians of 1953, Sweden came to Wembley and won 3–2, and Yugoslavia managed a 3–3 draw there in May 1960. With Peter Swan of Sheffield Wednesday now at centre-half and Charlton and John Connelly on the wings, the month before England had held Scotland to a 1–1 draw at Hampden Park, but not with sufficient authority to silence the critics. That May, two months before the Soviet Union won the inaugural European Nations Cup (later the European Championship), a competition the four British associations had declined to enter, England set off for matches against Spain and Hungary, and lost both. Simultaneously, a strong under-23 squad was sent to East Germany, Poland and Israel. It would yield a rich dividend: eight of the players who travelled under Ron Greenwood's management graduated to the national team. Three of them – George Cohen of Fulham, Terry Paine of Southampton and the

Newcastle inside-forward George Eastham – were selected for the 1966 World Cup squad, Cohen to fill the right-back position. Eastham was the unluckiest. Also selected for the 1962 finals in Chile, he didn't kick a ball in either tournament.

Eastham, however, was destined to dominate the sports headlines. When the under-23 squad flew to East Berlin on the first leg of a two-week journey, Eastham was harbouring a secret that was dramatically to improve working conditions in English football and influence the development of a successful World Cup team.

Eastham was born in Blackpool but began his playing career in Northern Ireland where he turned out for a season alongside his player-manager father, also George, a pre-war England international, in the Ards forward line. In 1956, Eastham senior sold his son to Newcastle for £8,000. Four years later, after serving the club well, Eastham asked for a transfer. It was immediately refused.

We were sitting beside a hotel swimming pool in Tel Aviv when Eastham confided his intention to stand out against the iniquitous system under which footballers employed in England were held.

'I want to ask you something,' he said to me. 'What would you think if I told you that I'm going to tell Charlie Mitten [Newcastle's manager, and ironically one of the defectors to Bogotá in 1950] to get stuffed?'

'I'd say you're mad,' I replied. 'Others have tried it and failed. Wilf Mannion held out against Middlesbrough for almost four months, but in the end they broke him. After that he was never the same.'

'I know that,' Eastham said, 'but I've made up my mind. I'm supposed to go from here to meet up with Newcastle in Spain. No chance. I'm going home.'

'That's not the best idea you've ever had,' I persisted. Signed annually, playing agreements ran until 30 June. 'If you don't show up in Spain you'll be in breach of contract,' I added. 'No sense in being left without a leg to stand on.'

This is a guy, I was thinking to myself, who is determined to get his own way. This is a stubborn guy who is going to cause a great deal of trouble. But eventually he agreed with me that there was nothing to be gained from not showing up in Spain.

'Go there, say no more to Mitten, and call me when you get home,' I said.

He nodded.

The call came three weeks later.

'I'm in Reigate,' Eastham said.

'What the hell are you doing there?' I asked.

'Come over and I'll explain it all.'

Reigate was about an hour by road from where I then lived in south London, so I made the journey and we met in the offices of a refrigeration company owned by Ernie Clay, who had served in the army with Eastham's father. A blunt though affable Yorkshireman, boisterous in manner, Clay had no great interest in football; nevertheless he was in a position to become one of the key figures in an unfolding drama that sent shudders through England's football establishment.

Eastham had taken up Clay's offer of £20 per week (exactly the Football League's wage ceiling) plus commission to work as a salesman. Clay had also arranged for him to train at Reigate Football Club.

'What do you think?' Eastham asked.

'Fine for the moment, but is it going to get you anywhere?'

'There's something else,' Clay said. 'The Players Union [the Professional Footballers Association] are involved.'

'Does that suit you?' I asked, looking directly at Eastham.

'Suppose so.'

I looked back at Clay. 'This is a hell of a story,' I said. 'But George has got be sure that he's strong enough to go all the way because I can see how the PFA will want to play it. At last they've got someone who can afford to oppose the system. It won't end with George getting away from Newcastle.'

'I realise that,' Eastham said.

But I wasn't sure how much he realised. He was no standard bearer, just a guy trying to sort out his career. Frail-looking on the field, where his exquisite touch, exceptional dribbling ability and judgement of a pass put him in the highest class of contemporary inside-forwards, he was unobtrusive off it. Always soberly dressed, he could have passed for a bank clerk. I liked him, and I feared for him.

Shortly afterwards, less than a week before the start of the 1960–61 season, Eastham called to say that he'd heard from Mitten.

'Charlie's made me an offer,' he said. 'If I re-sign, Newcastle will allow me to live and train down here, and carry on working for Ernie.'

'And?'

'Not interested,' Eastham said. 'I want to get away from the place, put Newcastle behind me.'

To relieve the boredom of living in Surrey without his family, Eastham took to spending weekends at my home. He was there one Monday morning when a telephone call came through from Tottenham's assistant manager Harry Evans. Evans wanted to know if he had the time to meet with him and Bill Nicholson at White Hart Lane.

'For what?' I asked.

'I'd rather not speak about it on the phone,' he replied.

'Expect me in two hours,' I said.

Alerting Eastham to Tottenham's interest, I set off for north London, promising to call him later.

It was soon clear to me that Nicholson was uncomfortable with this way of doing business. He was eager for information about Eastham – character, habits, family ties – but couldn't bring himself to make personal contact.

'If you like, I'll get him on the phone,' I said.

Nicholson declined. 'I can't expect you to keep this conversation from the player,' he said, 'but I don't want it to go any further.'

'You have my word.'

With Tottenham launched on a brilliant campaign that would bring them both the League Championship and the FA Cup, the first modern 'Double', we heard no more. Eastham's frustration grew, eased only by the PFA's encouragement. Solicitors appointed to act for him had served a writ on Newcastle seeking a declaration that his agreement with them was not binding, and asking for an injunction to let him go and a declaration from the Football Association that the retain-and-transfer system was an unreasonable restraint of trade.

If not yet to Eastham's personal satisfaction, a battle plan drawn up by the PFA's solicitor George Davis and its secretary Cliff Lloyd was beginning to take effect under Jimmy Hill's shrewd direction. Appointed PFA chairman in 1956, the flamboyant Fulham forward had organised the players into a mood of self-assertion that would lead to the threat of strike action when the clubs stupidly refused to increase by five pounds the £20 maximum wage.

Growing increasingly nervous, the Football League wanted the Eastham case resolved. The news Eastham had waited so long for came in November 1960: Newcastle had agreed a £45,000 deal with Arsenal; Eastham's share was a £20 signing-on fee. The following year the PFA, led daringly by Hill, won the wages battle hands down, and from 1961 onwards players were able to negotiate their own contracts. The League had recognised that not to concede this point would bring a lawsuit they had no chance of winning.

The final battle was not fought until June 1963, when Eastham v. Newcastle appeared in the High Court before Mr Justice Wilberforce. Wilf Taylor, a Newcastle director who sat on the League Management Committee, said in evidence: 'Eastham was the key man, the schemer, and we wanted to retain him. We had no intention of injuring him. Without the retain-and-transfer system the situation would be hopeless. Regulated football would be finished.' The League's splenetic secretary Alan Hardaker warned of complete anarchy in football if the retain-and-transfer system were to go. Gerald Gardiner QC, who appeared for Eastham, spoke of a system from the Middle Ages. The judge agreed. On 4 July, almost exactly two months after Eastham won the first of his nineteen England caps, Mr Justice Wilberforce delivered a 16,000-word judgement which included the one paragraph that really mattered: 'The rules of the Football Association and the regulations of the Football League relating to the retain and transfer of players of professional football, including the plaintiff, are not binding on the plaintiff and are An Unreasonable Restraint of Trade.' Though the League had taken the precaution of putting in place a system of legally binding agreements, footballers now had the freedom to negotiate terms once their contracts had ended or a transfer had been agreed. This had a profound effect in the sixties, contributing to England's first World Cup success. 'There has never been any doubt in my mind that the huge improvement in working conditions helped enormously in producing that England team,' Jimmy Hill said. 'Players grew in self-confidence, worked harder at the game. They felt better about themselves. And it showed.'

Even before the wage ceiling was lifted in 1961, the England team began to show fresh purpose. Attendances at League games were worryingly in decline, reaching a post-war low of 28.6 million by the end of the 1960–61 season, but no blame could be attached to the national team's performances. Beginning with a 5–2 victory over Northern Ireland in October 1960, England racked up six straight victories and scored 40 goals, including nine against Luxembourg in a World Cup qualifier, nine against Scotland and eight against Mexico. Jimmy Greaves helped himself to eleven of them; Charlton and Bobby Smith, unused in the 1958 finals, shared a further sixteen, Smith, like Greaves, scoring in five consecutive matches and strengthening Nicholson's contention that the burly leader of Totten-ham's vaunted attack was a much better bet than the technically flawed Derek Kevan. 'We were on a roll,' Smith said. 'I'd been disappointed not to get a game in Sweden, but playing in a terrific Tottenham team with Danny Blanchflower, Dave Mackay, Cliff Jones and John White was doing wonders for my confidence. I thought I had a real chance of going to Chile for the 1962 World Cup.'

Unfortunately for Smith, things didn't work out as he had been entitled to imagine. Troubled by knee injuries, he soon had to give way to Gerry Hitchens of Aston Villa. Two other centre-forwards, Ray Pointer of Burnley and Ray Crawford of Ipswich, were tried before Winterbottom recalled Smith against Scotland at Hampden Park in April 1962. It was Smith's last chance of getting to Chile. England lost 2–0, and Winterbottom took Hitchens, Roger Hunt of Liverpool and the uncapped Middlesbrough striker Alan Peacock. 'I thought Bobby was extremely unlucky not to be selected,' Cliff Jones said. 'He was big and powerful, and had more skill than he was given credit for. None of the teams we came up against in European competitions fancied trying to deal with him. When we [Spurs] met Slovan Bratislava in the Cup Winners Cup their goalkeeper was Schroif, who had played for Czechoslovakia against Brazil in the 1962 World Cup final. We lost the first leg 2–0, but the return at White Hart Lane was a massacre. Most of it was down to Bobby. He terrified Schroif. People who put him down as just a bruiser were surprised when Bobby scored with a clever chip against Spain at Wembley [in October 1960]. But I knew he had that skill.'

Qualification for those 1962 finals was achieved more easily than seemed likely when England were grouped with Luxembourg and Portugal. Luxembourg looked like cannon fodder, but Portugal constituted a real threat, a team vastly improved from that which had given up twenty goals to England in three matches between 1947 and 1951. Among the first European countries to identify Africa as a potentially rich source of football talent, Portugal could now call on a number of outstanding players who had joined its leading club

Benfica from the old colony of Mozambique: Germano was a strong centre-half, Coluna a shrewd and inventive midfielder, and, most excitingly of all, the teenaged Eusebio had exceptional pace and phenomenal shooting power. In 1961 Benfica's name was inscribed on the European Cup, the only other club alongside Real Madrid, whose five-year domination of the competition had ended in a first-round defeat by Barcelona, whom Benfica beat in the final in Berne.

Winterbottom was therefore wary, but due in part to the growing influence in management of men who had come through the coaching system, he could now count on better co-operation from the clubs. Ironically, however, some of his most ardent disciples were reluctant to take on the 4–2–4 formation he had in place. 'Whenever Walter had a group of England players together he implored us to push for it at our clubs,' Howe said. 'He argued that it was no longer possible to defend with fewer than four players and difficult to mount attacks with fewer than four forwards. But, of course, the switch could not be made overnight. Players, especially defenders, had to familiarise themselves with new disciplines. It wasn't simply a case of arranging a line of four defenders across the field with one of the centre-backs acting as cover. The back line had to operate as a unit, passing defenders on from one defensive position to another. While maintaining close contact with the opposing wingers, the full-backs had to be ready for tucking in when attacks were launched from the other side. Good understanding between the two men in midfield was vital. Unless players were doing these things week in and week out they could find it difficult to take them on board. That was one of Walter's problems.'

Another, of course, was the presence in Portugal's team of no fewer than eight men from that European Cup-winning Benfica side. 'To have so many players from one club gives Portugal a big advantage,' Winterbottom stated before England left for Lisbon in May 1961. Since goal average had been ruled out as a determining factor, both teams wanted to avoid the play-off that would result if they completed their group games level on points. The imperative of victory dawned on Portugal, and England could not afford to lose. Defeat was avoided when they came back strongly after Aguas put Portugal in front on the hour. With only eight minutes left Johnny Haynes took a short free-kick, Ron Flowers sent in a powerful drive, and England had their point.

England immediately left for games against Italy and Austria that were played amid speculation over the future of Jimmy Greaves. In November 1960, at the age of twenty years and nine months, Greaves had become the youngest ever player to score a hundred League goals. A week before this trip, he had asked Chelsea for a transfer. 'Chelsea had a lot of potential that seemed to be coming to nothing,' Greaves explained later. 'I was enjoying my football with them but knew there was little chance of winning anything. Ambition pushed me into asking for a move.' After scoring one of the three goals that brought England their second post-war victory on Italian soil, Greaves revealed that he had signed an option tying him to AC Milan. Before it could take effect, the PFA won its fight for the abolition of the maximum wage. Greaves tried but failed to wriggle out of the transfer to which Chelsea were now fully committed. A signing-on fee of £15,000 made pleasant reading for Greaves, but scheduled earnings of £5,000 a year were pitched at the level to which Johnny Haynes had been instantly elevated by Fulham's chairman, Tommy Trinder. Greaves had turned his life upside down for a salary that now would probably have been within his reach in England. 'I got tied up with Milan only for the money,' he admitted. 'Had I thought for one moment that the wage ceiling was going to be lifted I would never have put pen to paper. It was like a joke – only I couldn't see the funny side.'

By early autumn, when England got around to playing Luxembourg at home, Greaves's career was in turmoil. Successful on the field, having scored ten goals in nine appearances, he quickly fell out with Milan's coach Nereo Rocco, the stern promoter of defensive tactics that dominated Italian football for two decades. And unlike John Charles, who serenely adapted to a different culture on his transfer from Leeds to Juventus in 1957, Greaves was desperately homesick. Before the year ended, Tottenham came to his rescue.

Fearing that Greaves, and Hitchens, who had joined Internazionale, would not be released for every international match (Charles missed many for Wales during his time in Italy), Winterbottom cast around for replacements, and for a deputy for the injured Haynes. One of the Munich survivors, Dennis Violett, was brought in together with two recruits from Greenwood's under-23 squad, the Burnley centre-forward Ray Pointer and John Fantham of Sheffield Wednesday.

Expecting an avalanche of goals against a Luxembourg team that could field only one professional player, the 30,000 England supporters at Highbury on 28 September soon felt entitled to ask coarse questions of the national team. One unforced error followed another, the passing was abysmal, the shooting erratic. It took England half an hour to break through, and not before Ron Springett had saved, luckily, with his legs. Though three up at the interval, England did nothing to win over the crowd. The biggest cheer came when Dimmer's free-kick reduced England's lead. Charlton completed the scoring, but it was a chastened England team that left the field with jeers ringing in their ears. 'This simply won't do,' Frank McGhee wrote in the *Mirror*. For a while, Winterbottom had been chilled by memories of the débâcle in Belo Horizonte eleven years earlier. 'It showed again that you can't take anything for granted in football,' he said.

That thought hit Portugal right between the eyes when they lost 4–2 in Luxembourg. To qualify for Chile they would have to beat England twice, first at Wembley, then in a play-off. A draw would be enough for England. After just ten minutes' play at Wembley on 25 October, England were two up. Ray Wilson, a real find at left-back despite playing in the Second Division with Huddersfield, remembered supplying the first with a long free-kick. 'It wasn't anything we'd planned,' he said. 'John Connelly got on the end of it and prodded the ball in. Quite a simple goal really.' Pointer got the second, winning a race for the ball with Connelly. Eusebio was destined to suffer worse disappointments at Wembley, but never as much misfortune. Twice the prodigy struck violent shots against the woodwork; on each occasion Springett was hopelessly beaten. When Aguas muffed two chances and then headed against the bar, Portugal's players knew their luck was out.

Winterbottom could start preparing for Chile, but this was also a time when he was seriously considering his future in the game. When Stanley Rous took over the leadership of FIFA, the third Englishman out of six presidents elected since 1904, Winterbottom was encouraged to believe that he would be invited to succeed his mentor as secretary of the FA, a job for which he was eminently suitable. Shamefully, Winterbottom was passed over. Fearing an extension of Rous's influence by proxy, the FA appointed Denis Follows, a council member and secretary of the Airline Pilots

Association. Winterbottom took the insult with dignity. He'd managed England for sixteen years, through three World Cups, built up a sound coaching structure, done more than anyone to move English football forward, and was under no direct pressure. But it had been a long and often lonely road. With his background in physical education, with the knowledge and experience he'd accumulated and with the respect he'd earned at home and abroad, Winterbottom would not have to look far for a major post in sports administration. Winterbottom's fourth World Cup would be his last. Shortly after returning from Chile, he tendered his resignation to the FA to become, early in 1963, general secretary of the Central Council of Physical Recreation.

From having all four home countries through in 1958, in 1962 Britain was back to one. Unable to emulate their heroics in Sweden and disgracefully weakened by Juventus's refusal to release John Charles for important matches, Wales were put out by Spain. Although at last having the sense to select their best players, Scotland lost unluckily to Czechoslovakia in a play-off. Northern Ireland's hopes disappeared in two narrow defeats by West Germany. But England were destined for no great achievement themselves in a tournament Johnny Haynes remembers with one word – 'crap'. By then England's captain was finding international football less enjoyable. Taking Brazil's example from 1958 of 4–2–4 (often made 4–3–3 by the scurrying industry of their outside-left Zagallo, the 'little ant'), many coaches had gone to the flat defence that made it more difficult for Haynes and others of his type to switch play and create openings with long through-passes. Not that Haynes's blunt description relates only to personal frustration. If the 1990 finals are generally considered to be the worst on record, devoid of an outstanding team or one great player, those of 1962, marred by cynicism and violent play, were instantly forgettable.

One of the competition's few pluses, so far as England were concerned, was the emergence of young Bobby Moore of West Ham. Uncapped, pedestrian, not up to much in the air, suspect stamina – how could England select the 21-year-old Moore for the 1962 World Cup finals? But they did, and in so doing launched a celebrated international career: Moore won 108 caps and the accolade 'the best defender I ever faced' from the best forward of them all, Pele. Added to the squad only as an afterthought, Moore could scarcely have expected to be in the frame, but he never looked back after selection for England's final warm-up game against Peru in Lima in May 1962, his first international steps taken as an all-purpose wing-half, not as the uncannily perceptive central defender he would soon become.

Again, Winterbottom chose not to take to South America the permitted 22 players, leaving Kevan and the young Leicester City goalkeeper Gordon Banks at home on standby. And again, England paid dearly for not including an official doctor in the party. Suffering from a throat infection throughout the flight from London, the Sheffield Wednesday centre-half Peter Swan fell seriously ill after being given the wrong treatment. After nineteen consecutive appearances, and soon to be embroiled in a match-fixing scandal that ruined his career, Swan took no part in the tournament.

The appointment of Burnley's captain Jimmy Adamson as Winterbottom's assistant met with general approval. Recently elected Footballer of the Year after leading Burnley into the 1962 FA Cup final against Tottenham, and a deep thinker about the game, Adamson replaced Billy Wright who had been appointed manager of Arsenal. Although Adamson was registered as a potential World Cup player, it was made clear by the FA that he would function principally as a coach.

When it came to the choice of quarters, it seemed that Winterbottom just couldn't win. In 1958 he had come under heavy fire in the press for setting up camp in a centrally located Gothenburg hotel. In Chile, much to Adamson's annoyance, it was the players who found fault. After visiting the area around Rancagua where England's group games against Hungary, Argentina and Bulgaria were to be played, Winterbottom had accepted an invitation from the American-owned Braden Copper Company to use its facility at Coya, a small settlement perched 2,500 feet up in the Andes and about an hour's drive from the stadium. It had a golf course carved out of the mountainside, a cinema, a bowling alley and tennis courts. Paired off in bungalows, the players took meals in a communal dining area, cooked for by an Englishwoman. Howe, who had lost his place in the team to Jimmy Armfield, had no serious complaints about the accommodation. 'Some of the players didn't settle down there, but once I got used to it I thought it was fine. It depended a great deal on how you were made. If you were easily bored, I suppose being so isolated had to be a problem,' he told me. 'In any group of footballers you are bound to get moaners, and we had our share.'

Chile had contentiously been given the World Cup even though the country was still recovering from a dreadful series of earthquakes. It was precisely because they had nothing, insisted Carlos Dittborn of the Chilean FA, that they should have the tournament. The argument prevailed, though it can hardly be said that they made a success of it. Apart from a new national stadium in Santiago, facilities were primitive. Ticket prices, insanely high for a depressed population, meant that many matches were played in near empty stadiums. And with only four centres available – Santiago, Arica, Vin del Mar and Rancagua – the distances involved left no time for play-offs and replays. Consequently, the organising committee decided that goal average should count in the first phase, and if teams were still level their fate would be settled by drawing lots. 'It meant that nobody took risks,' Haynes recalled, 'and it led to a lot of nastiness.'

Soon, from all four centres came reports of violent play and serious injuries. Less than a week after the opening matches it was announced that there had already been more than 40 casualties among the sixteen finalists. The Soviet Union full-back Dubinski, Colombia's captain Zuluaga and the Swiss inside-left Eschmann were in hospital with broken legs; Bulgaria had lost their centre-forward Hrstov and outside-right Diev for the duration of the tournament. Four players had been sent off, two of them, David and Ferrini of Italy, by the Ilford schoolmaster Ken Aston, later described as a man among boys and a boy among men. A headline in the Santiago newspaper *Claron* read WORLD WAR. Summoned to appear before the World Cup organising committee, the sixteen managers were warned that further rough play could lead to expulsion from the finals. 'We weren't involved, but I'd never known anything like it,' Haynes said. 'I've never been more glad to get out of a place.'

England opened against their old tormentors, Hungary, on 31 May. Twenty-four hours earlier, in the same stadium, Argentina had played brutally to defeat Bulgaria 1–0. Coached by Juan Carlos Lorenzo – who would be in charge of Atlético Madrid when three of their players were sent off against Celtic, and the Lazio team that attacked Arsenal outside a restaurant in Rome – Argentina, giving a hint of things to come, had revealed the darker side of their nature. Again England lost to Hungary, not by the crushing scores of 1953 and 1954, just 2–1 this time, against a team bearing little resemblance to the past thrilling assembly but enough to leave a large dent in England's confidence. 'We didn't get together,' Haynes said, 'and it didn't help that only about 3,000 people showed. I'd played in front of bigger crowds as a boy in Fulham's reserves.'

Donald Saunders of the *Daily Telegraph* wrote that he did not envy Winterbottom the job of persuading a beaten team that they were equal to the task of retrieving the position in a hard game against Argentina. Other critics were caustic in assessment, citing slowness and predictability as the main reasons for defeat. 'Yet again, England has been found wanting at this level,' McGhee reported in the *Mirror*. Howe dismissed the idea that England felt inferior, that they were deeply concerned about facing Argentina. 'There was plenty of experience in the squad and we had players who were more than capable of looking after themselves without being drawn into feuds. It didn't surprise me when the team played well.'

Indeed, England, showing just one change, the untried Peacock for Hitchens, gave a vastly improved performance. Argentina, too, were transformed, their generally good behaviour probably resulting from the respect Lorenzo held for Winterbottom. 'I never worked Lorenzo out,' Winterbottom told me many years afterwards. 'I first met him when he came on one of our coaching courses at Lilleshall. He struck me as a pleasant sort of chap who was eager for information. I certainly didn't associate him with the militant way Argentina went about things in the 1966 World Cup, or with Atlético Madrid's alarming behaviour in that match against Celtic. I do remember, though, something he said to me in Chile after Argentina failed to qualify from our group. He said he was frightened to go home.'

A 3–1 victory over the Argentinians was followed by a goalless draw against Bulgaria that secured a place for England in the quarter-finals. Not until the players of Austria and West Germany engineered a result in Spain twenty years later would a World Cup tie be as lifeless as that final group game. 'The worst match I ever turned out in,' Haynes said. 'It was between England and Argentina for second place; all we needed was a point. People said afterwards that Bulgaria wanted us to go through because they were upset with Argentina for roughing them up. I don't know, but I do know that the game was dreadful. The further it went the worse it got. We'd play the ball around in our half of the field, and when the Bulgarians got hold of the ball they'd knock it around at their end. We had a bit of a scare when one of the Bulgarian forwards was left with a free header right in front of goal, but he sent the ball yards wide. It was all very strange; eerie, too, because there wasn't any atmosphere. There could not have been more than 5,000 people in the ground.'

In Group 3, as well, did Czechoslovakia deliberately lose to Mexico, thus avoiding Brazil in the last eight? Whatever the truth of the matter, the upshot was that England had to face the world champions in Vin del Mar. 'It was a relief to know that Pele was still injured [out of the finals with a groin injury],' Haynes said. 'On the other hand we were up against Garrincha, who could win a match on his own.' Crippled from birth, his legs bowed in parallel, Garrincha would die prematurely, a poverty-stricken alcoholic, but 1962 saw the glorious flowering of his outrageous gifts. 'Walter talked a lot about possible ways of dealing with Garrincha, and warned us especially about his free-kicks, which were as threatening as David Beckham's are now,' Haynes recalled. 'But how do you set about stopping the unstoppable? Garrincha walked like a cripple, which I suppose he was, but he was even quicker off the mark than Stan Matthews in his heyday. No matter how the ball came to him it was under control in an instant. Then he was gone, like a startled hare. He was deceptively strong, beautifully balanced and his shooting was explosive. Brazil emptied the space in front of him. From halfway line to corner flag, the right wing was his exclusive property.'

Winterbottom's warnings were to no avail. Garrincha scored twice, in the 31st and 59th minutes – England had drawn level in the 39th when a shot from Greaves rebounded from the bar to Hitchens – and finished the match off shortly after half-time with a wickedly spinning, ferociously struck free-kick that rebounded from Spring-ett's chest to Vava. Brazil went on to retain the World Cup, defeating a muscular but unimaginative Czechoslovakia in the final, but, disfigured by cynicism and generally defensive, it was not a World Cup from which many people took fond memories, least of all the England captain.

Critics singled out Haynes for blame, arguing that his style of play had become obsolete. The debate was soon of no consequence: on the eve of an away match for Fulham against Blackpool two months later, Haynes was pulled from a car crash, his right knee so badly damaged that he did not play for almost a year and was told by doctors that he may never play again. Haynes recovered sufficiently to play a further 236 games for Fulham, but his international career ended with England's elimination from the 1962 finals. Interestingly, however, he was not completely written off until Alf Ramsey's second year as manager of the national team. George Cohen recalled Ramsey asking him about Haynes. 'Alf was still experimenting with his midfield, and he asked me about John, how well he was doing week in and week out. Considering the severity of his injury, I thought John was playing exceptionally well. Alf had been to one of our games. "I don't think he'll ever be properly fit again," he said. After all the work John had put in I thought he would be upset to hear what Alf said, but he agreed. "Alf's a good judge," he said. Contrary to what some people have written, Alf never held anything against John Haynes.'

One of Winterbottom's last official acts as an employee of the Football Association was to conduct a coaching course for professional players at the Lilleshall training centre. The course had been going for three or four days when he invited me into the staff room. There was a tacit understanding that nothing from the conversation that followed would appear in print. Winterbottom appeared to be in good spirits, conveying the air of a man from whom a great weight had been lifted. He talked at length about England's efforts in Chile. 'We could have done a lot better, you know,' he said. 'If we'd met Czechoslovakia not Brazil in the quarter-finals I'm pretty sure we would have got through. Even against Brazil we missed chances before they put the game beyond our reach. And look how naively we defended the Garrincha free-kick.' Winterbottom's eyes went up to the ceiling. He could again see England hurriedly trying to form a wall, failing to notice that Didi had moved the ball wide from where a free-kick against Flowers was given eight minutes into the second half. 'I was sitting there thinking, "Come on you lot, wake up, complain to the referee!" We had highly experienced players out there but they couldn't see that Brazil had worked a trick on them. It seemed to sum up everything, all the World Cups we'd been in.'

Having agreed to remain in charge of the England team until his successor was appointed, Winterbottom stressed, as he would to Denis Follows, that the new man must be given absolute power of selection. 'It's something the International Committee will have to concede,' he said. 'He will have problems enough without having to put up with interference. Many of the most influential players in the

League, Scots, Welsh, Irish, are not available to us. There is still resistance to change. If, at all levels, from schoolboy upwards, we played a hundred matches against any other country, I feel sure we'd win the majority, maybe as many as 80; most of the defeats would come at the top. Whether that's because our League system is strong or because the game here is traditionally physical, I'm not sure. But if England are ever to win the World Cup we've got to take a new direction.'

6. 1962 TO ENGLAND 1966

The Charity Shield match in August 1962 between Ipswich, the League champions, and the FA Cup holders Tottenham Hotspur would impact greatly on the future of English football. Before a League meeting between the two the previous season, Bill Nicholson had produced a plan to counter the strategy that continued to flummox team after team as Ipswich maintained their remarkable progress under Alf Ramsey. Many of the players Ramsey continued to use after bringing Ipswich up through two divisions probably would have struggled to hold down a first-team place at more fashionable clubs, but within the framework of his tactics they formed a formidable unit. Operating from deep positions, the Ipswich wingers Jimmy Leadbetter and Roy Stephenson served up opportunities for two hard-running attackers, Ray Crawford and Ted Phillips, who in turn were supported by an advanced midfielder. It was the shape of things to come. With refinements, most obviously in defence, it would be England's shape in the 1966 World Cup.

Nicholson's proposal the previous season had been to curb the natural flourish of his great wing-half backs Danny Blanchflower and Dave Mackay and sit them on the Ipswich wingers, at the same time pulling his full-backs in to help protect the middle. 'Mackay and Blanchflower didn't fancy it, didn't do the job properly, so we reverted to our normal system. We lost 3–2, and when Ipswich played us at White Hart Lane later in the season we were beaten 3–1 playing the same way.' Before the Charity Shield match, Nicholson pointed out to the Tottenham players that two points from the games lost to Ipswich could possibly have brought a second successive Double (in third place, Tottenham finished four points worse off than Ramsey's team but with a superior goal average). This time, things would be done his way. 'It could hardly have gone better,' Maurice Norman said. 'Very little came from the Ipswich flanks, and there were three of us to deal with their two centre-forwards. We won 5–1. It was almost a doddle.' Ramsey's tactics had been rumbled; the majority of his players, average at best, had been rung dry. Before September was out, Ipswich, with only eight points from eleven games, had the look of a team heading for relegation.

Ramsey's energy had been concentrated on producing a competitive first team; seven years after his arrival, Ipswich had no youth scheme, no properly organised scouting structure. 'I didn't realise what I was walking into,' Ramsey's successor Jackie Milburn told me before his premature death in 1988. 'Alf had done a magnificent job in bringing Ipswich from nowhere to win the championship, but there was nothing underneath the first team, not a player coming through who could possibly have been sold to fund replacements. I discovered that there wasn't a scout on the books. The Ipswich chairman John Cobbold, a lovely man, had never questioned Alf's running of the club. He had no cause to, but I've often wondered about what Alf intended to do before the England job came up for him.'

In a caretaker role, Winterbottom first recommended Jimmy Adamson, his assistant in Chile, but put off by the griping he'd heard at England's base camp there and thinking it symptomatic of changing attitudes, Adamson declined. Winterbottom's second recommendation, the former Wolves and England inside-forward Denis Wilshaw, preferred his teaching career. Nicholson was Tottenham through and through. 'I'd enjoyed working with the under-23 team and helping Walter out in Sweden, but the England job wasn't for me,' he said. Ron Greenwood's reputation was spreading, but he had only recently entered management at West Ham after coaching Arsenal. In his autobiography *Yours Sincerely* published in 1984, Greenwood wrote: 'I sometimes wonder how I would have coped if I had been given the job seventeen years earlier when it was first mentioned. I was manager of England's under-23 team at the time, during my days as coach with Arsenal, and the subject cropped up on the way to a match at Norwich . . . Walter asked me, quietly, how I'd feel about becoming England manager if he succeeded Sir Stanley Rous as secretary of the Football Association. "I'd be delighted," I replied, and no more was said. Walter did not get the job and Alf Ramsey eventually took over as manager. That was, with hindsight, a blessing in disguise because it is a job that demands experience. I was not ready for it then while Alf Ramsey certainly was. He had done a first-class job at Ipswich . . . with methods that were original and efficient, and he was a stable, positive, deep-thinking person. He knew where he was going and how he was going to get there. He was the right man, and he proved it in the best way possible.'

In the first week of October 1962, the Football Association approached the Ipswich chairman for permission to speak with Ramsey. 'It didn't come as a surprise,' Cobbold said. 'We'd got word that the FA had decided to approach Alf, so the call from Follows was no more than courtesy. In fact, I'd already discussed with my brother Patrick the possibility that we might be able to keep Alf at Ipswich. Alf had become more than our manager. I thought of him as a friend. We'd learnt from him, and he'd learnt from us. Losing Alf was an enormous blow, but how could we stand between him and the most important post in English football? If it wasn't much of a consolation, we were proud that a small club like ours was providing the next England manager.'

Shortly after the initial approach, Ramsey took a train from Ipswich to Liverpool Street station in London, then the underground to Lancaster Gate, a journey he would make hundreds of times in the future. The interview was not a long one. Conducted by the FA chairman Graham Doggart, its main point of discussion was Ramsey's insistence on total control over playing affairs – his policy, his team. Fearful of being held responsible should England fail to benefit from home advantage in the 1966 World Cup finals, and realising that no manager of substance would tolerate the interference Winterbottom had fought against, the five members of the International Committee agreed to Ramsey becoming the sole selector. 'The selection committee, as such, is finished,' Doggart announced.

Ironically, the selection committee was still in place when Ramsey was released by Ipswich to take charge of England for a Nations Cup tie against France in Paris in February 1963, three months before his appointment was due to take effect. Held by the French to a 1–1 draw at home four months before, England lost 5–2 and went out of the competition. 'It wasn't as though France had a good team,' Ramsey recalled, 'just that England were awful. Our goalkeeper [Springett] did well to carry on after being kicked in the ribs, but it didn't explain why we gave up five goals. I would have expected the Ipswich reserve team to defend better.'

Already, Ramsey had formed opinions about the men who had given up power to him: Doggart, Chelsea chairman Joe Mears, Sunderland chairman Sid Collings, Joe Richards of Barnsley, who was also president of the Football League, and Follows. 'I could see right away how difficult things had been for Walter Winterbottom,' he later told me. 'In their way they were enthusiasts, but they had no judgement I could respect. I'd been told that Mears was embarrassed to discover that each member of the selection committee was expected to put forward his version of the team, and had as much say as the manager. I thought well of him for that. Doggart struck me as a nice man. But none of them could offer a worthwhile opinion. From my first meeting with them, I knew I'd been absolutely right to seek the authority I'd been given at Ipswich.'

Ramsey's official introduction to the press coincided with the FA's announcement that he would have charge of the England team in Paris. Afterwards, he accepted my offer of a lift to Liverpool Street. Together with a *Daily Express* reporter, Norman Giller, we set off through heavy late-afternoon traffic. Ramsey was amiable; he spoke freely in a precise way, careful with his diction, a change that would puzzle former playing colleagues when they heard him interviewed on television and radio, people who remembered more of a cockney accent.

It was almost ten years since Ramsey's last appearance for England. He'd seen little on television of the three World Cups played between then and his appointment to succeed Winterbottom. 'I have a great deal to learn about international football,' he admitted. 'I will have to look closely at the players and settle on a system that suits the best of them.' For the time being he intended to stick with the 4–2–4 system favoured by Winterbottom while monitoring the available talent. Ramsey had, more or less, made up his mind about the team for Paris. It made sense, he reckoned, to go with Tottenham's successful strike force, Greaves and Smith; Charlton and Connelly would fill the wing positions. The ease with which Ramsey communicated these thoughts struck a chord in the future when he became more withdrawn, keeping reporters as much at arm's length as he would the FA officials. The impression I shared with Giller was that Ramsey did not regard advancement in the Nations Cup to be of any great importance. If anything, he saw qualification for the 1964 European Championship finals in Spain as a trap, one into which he would stumble if England got through and failed to give a good account of themselves.

I was listening to Ramsey. I was listening to him speak about various things, and I thought I had it all figured out for myself. This is a guy, I was thinking to myself, who has only one objective, who knows that he will stand or fall by England's efforts in the 1966 World Cup. As at Ipswich, his thoughts were entirely concentrated on the production of a winning team. The wider aspects of English football, so dear to Winterbottom, held no interest for him. Ramsey had made this abundantly clear when first approached by the Football Association, informing Follows that he had no desire to take on Winterbottom's duties as director of coaching. He saw that as a separate responsibility from which he was happily divorced. 'I'm not a coach,' he told me some time afterwards. 'I'm the manager of the England team.'

Allen Wade was appointed director of coaching in January 1962. A lecturer at Loughborough University who had played professionally for Notts County, he had very little contact with Ramsey. 'I don't think many people got to know Alf, and I certainly didn't,' he said. 'He was always courteous, but I was never made to feel that he was keen to share his thoughts. Alf could surprise you, though. On one of the rare occasions we got together I had lunch with him in a restaurant close to the FA offices. I can't remember how long he'd been England manager, but right out of the blue, in that clipped way of his, he said how disappointed he was in many of the players who were generally considered to be good enough for the England team. He complained that the press were always building up players who in many cases were not remotely good enough. It bothered him that some of those who were up to standard had a poor attitude. It was beyond Alf's comprehension that a footballer could not be relied on to give every last drop of sweat for his country.

'Alf never once asked me about the work I was doing. He never showed any inclination to speak at our courses. He wasn't interested in coaching as such, just playing ideas. He was keen to find out how the game was developing in other countries, and he had this trick of putting provocative questions so that he could count on an objective response. And if Alf had his teeth into something he could be brusque, almost to the point of rudeness, if anybody intruded upon the conversation.

'People have written that Alf put industry above flair. But that was never the case. His ideal was both. If you think about it, there wasn't a player of promise in the country who didn't get a chance to impress him. I don't think England were the best team in the 1966 World Cup. Technically, Argentina were. Nevertheless Alf selected players who in some cases were above any others in their position: there was no better goalkeeper than Gordon Banks; Bobby Moore was out on his own as a covering central defender; nobody had a full-back of Ray Wilson's quality; and Alf's patience with Bobby Charlton paid off when he finally broke through as a truly great player.'

That match against France merely confirmed some of Ramsey's suspicions. The defenders were operating individually, not as a unit. Too much of the defending was unnervingly heroic. There was no reliable link between defence and attack. There was nothing in the general behaviour of the players to disturb Ramsey, but some members of the team were too casual in their application. Ramsey was already forming opinions. Only two from the team defeated in Paris would play in the 1966 World Cup final; only seven would make the squad of 22.

For the match against Scotland at Wembley in April 1963, Ramsey made his first important move, replacing Springett with the Leicester City goalkeeper Gordon Banks and thus beginning a long and illustrious international career. Banks would share in Ramsey's greatest triumph, make the most spectacular save in World Cup history, and inadvertently bring about the England manager's biggest disappointment. But he could do nothing to prevent Jim Baxter scoring both goals, one of them a penalty, in a 2–1 Scottish victory. The goal from open play had resulted from a careless pass by Jimmy Armfield. Baxter stepped in, rifled the ball past Banks with his left foot and then stood with arms aloft, declaring, 'That's the greatest goal in Wembley's history.' Ramsey looked on bleakly. 'I don't want to see you do that again,' he said to Armfield after the game. Armfield had planted doubt in Ramsey's mind. As a result of that one mistake his days as England's first-choice right-back were numbered. When Armfield returned to the squad following an injury, it was only as cover for George Cohen.

Leaving Ipswich safe in seventeenth place in the First Division (they were relegated the following season), Ramsey took full control of the England team in May for a match against Brazil to celebrate the Football Association's 75th anniversary. Two months before the successful conclusion of his case against the Football League gave players a much greater say in negotiations with their employers, George Eastham gained his first cap. 'It was a relief to know all that was coming to an end,' Eastham said. 'Some of the players wanted to know how I thought things would turn out, and what it would mean to them if I won. Even though I'd been involved from the start I wasn't sure myself what difference it would make if the courts ruled in my favour. Cliff [Lloyd] and Jimmy [Hill] were very confident, but I just wanted to get it over and done with and get on with playing football.' Ramsey did not mention the court case. 'He just asked me how I was, told me to operate pretty much as I did for Arsenal and wished me luck,' Eastham confirmed. 'In fact, I never heard Alf tell anyone exactly how he wanted them to play. It was always "I've chosen you to do what you do for your club". In team talks he seldom mentioned the names of players we were coming up against. It was always number this or number that – "the number 10 is good in the air, the number 4 wanders out of position". Alf only dealt in specifics when it came to free-kicks and corners. He hated giving away goals in those situations because he always went through them in detail. Before the match against Brazil he warned Gordon Banks to watch out for Pepe's swerving free-kicks. When Pepe scored with precisely the sort of shot Gordon had been told about, Alf was angry. He didn't raise his voice, never did; it was more the look in his eyes, the way he spoke. "Gordon, perhaps the next time you'll listen." '

Even against a weakened Brazil team – at the end of a marvellous playing career, one of Pele's few regrets was that he never played at Wembley – a 1–1 draw was thought to be creditable, enough to send England off in good heart for a tour to Czechoslovakia, East Germany and Switzerland. First, Follows had to deal with an extraordinary request from the Brazil delegation. Like Ramsey, the FA secretary was new to the ways of international football. 'I'd prepared a money draft to cover Brazil's guarantee, but their people showed up at Lancaster Gate saying they wanted cash, not sterling but US dollars,' Follows said. 'I tried to explain that we'd never done business that way, and could see no way of getting the equivalent of about £20,000 in dollars. They wanted cash, and said they needed it in a hurry because they had a flight to catch. I had to contact the Treasury who in turn contacted the Bank of England. It took a few hours, but eventually the money was delivered to my office. The Brazilians stuffed the banknotes into a couple of kitbags and left for the airport.'

Meanwhile, Ramsey finalised plans for the summer tour, adding to his squad the Chelsea full-back Ken Shellito and Tony Kay, a talented, combative midfielder who had been transferred from

Sheffield Wednesday to Everton. For different reasons, one sad, the other scandalous, their international careers would be limited to just one cap. Shellito, clearly the closest challenger to Armfield, did well in the opening game of the tour, a 4–2 victory over the 1962 World Cup finalists Czechoslovakia, but later suffered a serious injury from which he never fully recovered. 'If Ken had stayed fit I don't think I would have broken through into the World Cup squad,' George Cohen said. 'When I was too old to play any more under-23 matches I felt that was it as far as international football was concerned. Ken was such a good full-back that it didn't seem likely that I would have a chance once he got into the team. A lot of people reckoned Jimmy Armfield was unlucky not to play in the 1966 World Cup, but they forgot about Shellito. That's how cruel football can be.'

Kay was given his chance when England notched up a third successive tour win by defeating Switzerland 8–1 in Basle, with three goals from Charlton and two from Johnny Byrne. Kay made a big impression on Ramsey. He was exactly the sort of mobile midfielder he needed to make a success of 4–2–4, and was immediately marked down as one to be watched in the months ahead. With three more victories under his belt, including an 8–3 thumping of Northern Ireland in Wembley's first floodlit match, Ramsey had Kay under consideration for a tournament in Brazil when, on 12 April 1964, the Everton player was alleged to have been involved in an attempt to rig the result of a match between Ipswich and Sheffield Wednesday. The *People* newspaper revealed that Kay, Peter Swan, who was still a challenger for the England centre-half position, and David 'Bronco' Layne had each taken a bribe of £100 in a betting coup organised by a former Swindon Town player, Jimmy Gauld. A number of other players were named. Armed with tape-recorded statements and affidavits, the *People* spared none of the suspects.

They had Gauld on their side. Having approached and corrupted players in a wide area of England and Scotland, he had sold his story to the *People* for £7,500. Gauld claimed that he made thousands of pounds from bets during a period from April 1960 to April 1963; the men he used had generally made very little – some only £60. He said that he had involved 30 players, promising them big winnings from fixed-odds betting. Gauld added, 'I went bent because of the easy money there was to be made.' Kay threatened libel, saying, 'If someone offered me £10,000 to play badly I would tell him what to do with his money.' But soon afterwards summonses were issued against fourteen players, ten of whom were subsequently jailed. Gauld got four years; Kay, Swan and Layne four months apiece. Inevitably, the Football Association banned them for life.

When the scandal was at its height, I attended a press conference at Lancaster Gate, suspecting that there was more to it than the *People* had been able to establish. Sitting alone at one end of a large oval table in the council chamber after the conference broke up, I casually turned over a crested tablemat to discover a sheet of FA notepaper carelessly left by a member of the committee that had met to discuss the most sensational revelations British football had ever known. Written on it were the names of players equal in prominence to Kay, Swan and Layne. Startled, I folded the notepaper, slipped it into a pocket of my coat, left the room and took a cab back to the *Daily Mirror* offices in Holborn, where I was employed as a football writer. I showed the names to nobody but my friend Bill Holden, a man of wide experience. 'Some of them I can believe, some of them I can't,' he said. 'But in any case, there isn't anything we can do with this stuff. We have no proof. The names could have been written down by anyone, anywhere. Apart from that, you are in possession of stolen property, a document you took from the FA offices without permission. Burn it. Now.' I put a match to it, waited for the flame to burn out, and let the crushed embers fall into a bin.

Ramsey had not led a sheltered life. As a young man in Dagenham he had regularly visited dog tracks in Essex, and where betting was involved little surprised him. However, he could not entertain the idea that English football might not be entirely above board. It astonished him that the charges against Kay, Swan and Layne concerned a match at Ipswich in December 1962 when he was still in charge at Portman Road. 'We had to fight hard to win that match 2–1,' he said. 'I remember feeling relieved to get the two points because we were at the wrong end of the table.'

The story broke on the morning after England were beaten 1–0 by Scotland at Hampden Park. On his arrival in Glasgow two days before the game, Ramsey was jovially greeted.

'Welcome back to Scotland,' one Scottish reporter said.

'You must be joking,' Ramsey said.

Defeat did not improve his humour, particularly when one critic wrote of it as failure of football by numbers. 'Alf hated losing to the

Jocks and we didn't play well, that's for sure,' Roger Hunt said. 'He didn't say much after the game but you could tell from the look on his face that he wasn't best pleased.' Ramsey had also passed a remark that would fuel a conspiracy against him within the Football Association. 'I suppose I'd better inform those people,' he'd said, making off towards a group of now powerless senior officials with belated word of the team he had just announced to the press. 'Who does this man think he is?' one of the officials muttered. Ramsey would not be forgiven.

During the summer of 1964, Ramsey extended his knowledge of international football with an ambitious programme of matches. Eager to test his players in competitive action, he persuaded the FA to enter a tournament with Brazil, Argentina and Portugal. Hosted by Brazil, it followed on from matches in Lisbon, Dublin and New York. On the eve of departure, the squad assembled at the Hendon Hall hotel in north London which, on the basis of its proximity to Wembley and good local training facilities, had already been chosen as the 1966 base camp. Ramsey allowed the players a free evening. 'There was no team dinner, no briefing,' Bobby Charlton said. 'Within reason, we could please ourselves. Bobby Moore mentioned that we were invited to a restaurant one of his friends had just opened. There didn't seem any harm in it, not like we were going to a club or something, so six of us went along: Bob Moore, me, Ray Wilson, George Eastham, Gordon Banks and Johnny Byrne. It wasn't all that late when we got back to the hotel, and we hadn't done anything to embarrass Alf. Other than wine with the meal, we hadn't been drinking. But when we got to our rooms, our passports were on our beds. Obviously, Alf knew that we'd been out. None of us slept well that night.'

Ramsey was furious. He would have refused the players permission to leave the hotel, and they had not shown him the courtesy of seeking it. Ramsey's problem was how to address what he saw as a serious breach of discipline without giving rise to scandal. He said nothing to the six players until he reached Lisbon. After breakfast on the second day there, he said, 'There are some people who I need to see.' They looked at one another and followed him out of the room. 'We knew we were for it,' Charlton said. 'And it wasn't just a case of sitting us down to say how disappointed he was with our behaviour. He said that had there been time to organise replacements we would have been left at home. I don't know whether Alf would have taken things that far. But he had made his point.'

Soon, however, Ramsey would be given another reason to wonder whether Moore was the right choice as captain. England had gone on from confident victories in Lisbon and Dublin to a 10–0 thrashing of the USA in New York that went some way towards erasing the humiliation of 1950. The following day, Ramsey was watching the players check in for the long flight to Rio de Janeiro when Bernard Joy of the London *Evening Standard*, who had turned out for Arsenal and England as an amateur, told him that Moore, Greaves and Byrne had been at a party thrown by the press. When word of this reached the *Mirror* columnist Frank McGhee, who got on well with Ramsey, he immediately intervened on their behalf. 'The party was in my room,' he told Ramsey. 'Bernard could only have learnt about it, because he wasn't there. The players stayed for about half an hour, had a beer and then went to bed. There was nothing in it.' Resenting Joy's interference, and identifying him as an establishment figure, Ramsey took no action. It troubled him, though, that Moore and Greaves (he felt Byrne was easily led) had put themselves in a potentially embarrassing situation so soon after the incident in London.

From the beginning, Ramsey had sensed that his fellow east Londoners were mocking his correctness and diction. Following an under-23 match at Norwich, he'd heard them sniggering behind his back. 'If needs be, I'll win the World Cup without those two,' he'd said darkly to the trainer, Harold Shepherdson. With or without Moore and Greaves, however, victory in the World Cup seemed a long way off on 30 May 1964 when England were thrashed 5–1 by Brazil, the circumstances recalling for Ramsey his experience there fourteen years before. Although the Arsenal doctor, Alan Bass, had been recruited to serve the squad's medical needs, general organisation remained primitive. The loss to Brazil came just 36 hours after an exhausting journey from New York that involved a further time zone complication. In New York there had been a disagreement between Ramsey and Moore over training schedules, Moore complaining on behalf of the players that they were being overworked after a long season. There was no fitter member of the squad than George Cohen, and after 30 minutes against Brazil he was clearly distressed, only just able to carry on. 'In the second half I was absolutely knackered,' Cohen recalled. 'The next day, Alan Bass took me for a walk, let me describe my symptoms, and then told me I could forget about playing in the rest of the tournament. It worried me because I thought that if Alf felt I couldn't handle a tough schedule that would be it. But Alan was firm. I could forget about turning out for the remaining two matches.'

Ramsey's reaction to defeat was positive. 'Don't let it get you down,' he told the players. 'You did well in the first half [England were level 1–1 at the interval] and from what I saw Brazil will not be a big threat in England. Some of their best players are growing old, and unless others come through it will be left to Pele to carry the team. No one player is that good.'

Argentina made a much bigger impression on England's manager. They had skills to equal those of Brazil, good organisation, and they were hard. 'Unfortunately, they have no respect for the game,' Ramsey said. 'We saw that when they played Brazil. If they weren't kicking the Brazilians they were moaning at the referee, putting him under constant pressure.' Seated along one of the touchlines, Ramsey and his players saw the match between Brazil and Argentina develop into a series of violent exchanges. The principal target for Argentina's hostility, Pele became so incensed that he head-butted one of their defenders. 'It was one of the roughest games I've ever seen,' Cohen said. 'Before long, practically every player on the field was putting the boot in. Our next match was against Argentina, and in a way it was a relief to know that I wouldn't be playing. Johnny Byrne was sitting a few seats away and I remember him shouting, "George, always knew you were a shrewd bastard." When riot cops went into the crowd with batons, Alf announced that it was time to go. "Gentlemen, I'm ready," he said, and off we went at the double, ducking stuff that was being thrown on to the pitch.'

Needing just one point to win the tournament, Argentina settled for a no-risk policy against England, who didn't have the wit to break them down. 'They pulled eight players back behind the ball, and if you got past the first line of defence, down you went,' Eastham said. 'Alf had told us not to get involved if Argentina cut up rough, just to look after ourselves. He didn't have to tell me twice. I remember looking up from the floor to see Rattin standing over me. He made as if to stamp on my leg, and then stepped over me. Goodness knows to what lengths Argentina would have gone if they'd needed to win the game. It was amazing, really, because they were a terrific team. They let us have most of the ball and won 1–0. In the end, I think Alf was just glad to get out of there. He detested them.'

In his first seventeen matches Ramsey had used 31 players, the number of changes consistent with that of the old selection committee over a similar period. The difference was that Ramsey paid little account to vagaries of club form. Unlike Winterbottom, he had the power to try to build a team. By 1966 he would have worked with every candidate, if not in the national team then in the under-23s and Football League representative matches. Nobody of potential would be able to complain about being overlooked.

Throughout that first phase of Ramsey's stewardship, Bobby Charlton remained an enigma. Most of his more than 50 appearances for England had been made at outside-left, the position he was given at Manchester United to avoid close marking. On the wing, Charlton's natural speed, swerve and firepower could excite the crowds, but too often he was lost in brooding anonymity. It was said of him that he thought the game began and ended 30 yards from goal. For a match against Northern Ireland in October 1964, Ramsey brought Charlton in from the left flank to form a midfield partnership with Gordon Milne of Liverpool. 'He looked up and at last became a great player,' Ramsey would say. To Ramsey's relief, Charlton conquered the failing of being so occupied with his piece of the action that he rarely saw the big picture of the team or the game. Another year passed before Charlton was deployed as the pivotal figure in England's midfield, but the breakthrough had been made.

Jimmy Murphy, however, refuted the idea that Ramsey was the man behind Charlton's conversion to a deep centre-forward. 'Over the years we did a lot of hard thinking at Old Trafford about how to make the best of Bobby's exceptional ability,' the Manchester United assistant manager said. 'Pre-Munich his great shooting ability was an asset when he played alongside Tommy Taylor. After Munich he was so closely marked that I switched him to the wing to give him more room. Later on, another change was necessary. With ball players and match winners like Denis Law, George Best and Charlton in attack there was always the possibility that they would get in one another's way. It was Matt Busby, not Alf Ramsey, who decided to use Bobby Charlton as a midfield general.'

Busby himself said, 'There are few players in the world with Bobby's ability to bring the ball under control. There are few players who can strike a ball so accurately. And it was because of his touch, his passing accuracy; and the way he can quickly get forward to send in tremendous shots that he was switched to the centre of midfield. His game now [in 1966] is very reminiscent of Alfredo di Stefano [Busby's favourite player].'

If Bobby Charlton had seen the light, so had his brother Jack. Older by two years, Jack Charlton had rediscovered himself at Leeds after agreeing to make peace with Don Revie and the coaching staff at Elland Road, where he was known as a one-man awkward squad. When Revie was promoted from player to manager in 1962, the year Charlton returned from Lilleshall with a full coaching qualification, he and Charlton quickly fell out over playing policy. 'Don had to make a choice between myself and Freddie Goodwin, because we had different ideas about defensive play. Don chose Freddie at centre-half and moved me to centre-forward – and then dropped me,' Charlton said.

Revie sent for Charlton and told him, 'I'm putting you on the transfer list because you're not my type of centre-half.'

'Centre-half?' Charlton exploded. 'I've been playing centre-for-ward.'

'Yes, but you're not the type of centre-half I want, so I'm putting you on the list.'

Had Bill Shankly not jibbed at the fee, Charlton would have joined Liverpool; instead, he was recalled to the first team in time to help prevent Leeds from slipping into the Third Division. As the threat of relegation faded, Charlton found himself back in Revie's office.

'I want you to come off the list,' Revie said. 'The way you've been playing, if you get the attitude right, there is no reason why you shouldn't play for England. You know you've got the ability, it's only a case of putting your mind to it and doing the job.'

Promoted in 1964, Leeds were on their way to becoming one of Europe's most successful clubs when Charlton learnt that he did indeed still have a chance of playing international football. Left to find a centre-half when Maurice Norman was injured – worse followed for the Tottenham centre-half when he broke a leg against a Hungarian Select XI in December 1965 – Ramsey selected Charlton for the Football League versus the Scottish League at Hampden Park in February 1965. Coming up against the Celtic centre-forward John Hughes, a strong and skilful runner with the ball who liked to drop off into midfield, Charlton was in a dilemma as to whether to follow him or stay put. 'I think he wanted to see if I could sort things out for myself because he didn't mention the problem at half-time,' Charlton recalled. 'But I was in the mood for a row. Why were our full-backs stuck out so wide? It didn't make any sense for me to follow Hughes, so I wanted him picked up whenever he went deep. Guessing that it might be my one and only chance of getting into the England team, I wasn't going to be pissed about.' Ramsey was as much impressed with Charlton's tactical response as he was with his overall performance. Two months later, Charlton was selected at centre-half against Scotland at Wembley. At 30, he was the oldest member of the team.

The line in front of Banks now read Cohen, Jack Charlton, Moore and Wilson. Ramsey had his defence. Another piece of the puzzle fell into place with the introduction of Manchester United's combative half-back Nobby Stiles. An England schoolboy international, Stiles was a product of the Old Trafford youth system. Although a more skilful footballer than he was given credit for, his passing sharp and perceptive, Stiles's principal assets were tenacity and awareness; he saw danger early and dealt with it quickly. Short, slightly built and so shortsighted that he had to play in contact lenses, Stiles's spirit was infectious. 'When I saw Nobby coming away with the ball from players twice his size, I thought, well, if he can do it so can the rest of us,' Bobby Moore said after the match against Scotland in April 1965 ended in a 2–2 draw. 'There and then, it was a pretty safe bet that barring an injury Nobby would be in the World Cup team, never mind the squad.'

The arrival of Charlton and Stiles, probably the most significant steps forward in Ramsey's planning, emphasised the importance he attached to creating a solid team base. At Ipswich he had first built a reliable defence and then gambled on the unlikely figure of Leadbetter as the team's fulcrum. Under much wider scrutiny as England's manager, he was not about to be influenced by the inconsistency of press criticism. Ramsey's public assertion that England would win the World Cup in 1966 astonished the press and players alike. 'It was so unlike Alf that I couldn't believe he'd said it,' George Cohen recalled. 'The expectations were already high enough without him going that far. We thought it was strange, but I don't recall that he ever mentioned it to us. Of course, the press made a big thing of it, and after that whenever the team fell short they were on his back.'

There was little cause for criticism in May 1965 when England returned with two victories and a draw from their tour of Yugoslavia, West Germany and Sweden. The launch of 4–3–3 against the Germans in Nuremberg went unnoticed. Unable to call on Bobby Charlton and Stiles because of Manchester United's involvement in a Fairs Cup semi-final (two days after returning from tour, Bobby Moore turned out for West Ham against Munich 1860 in the European Cup Winners Cup final), Ramsey had brought in the 20-year-old Blackpool inside-forward Alan Ball.

From an early age, Ball had been schooled in dedication by his father Alan, himself a former professional player who would die in a crash when coaching in Cyprus. 'Everything I achieved in the game I owe to him,' Ball said. 'Whenever I got to one step, he drove me on to the next. He was always at me to improve my skills and fitness. When people said I was too small to make it in football, he told me to think of it as a challenge. When I got into the Blackpool first team he told me to go on and play for England; first the under-23s, then a full cap. When I called him to say that Alf had picked me to play against West Germany, all he said was, "Make it permanent." When I was included in the World Cup squad, he said, "Now get into the team." ' With his highly developed close-quarter skills, energy and drive, Ball was Ramsey's type of player, ideally suited to the formation he had in mind.

Closer to the World Cup finals, Ramsey took Ball and Stiles aside for analogous instruction. 'Alf had odd ways of putting things across, so when he asked if either of us owned a dog we guessed there was something coming,' Ball said. 'Nobby didn't have a dog, but I did. Alf then asked if I threw a stick for the dog when I took it for walks. I replied that I threw a ball. He then wanted to know if my dog brought the ball back. I nodded. "Well," he said, "that's what I want the pair of you to do for Bobby Charlton. Run for the ball and give it to him." ' By that stage Ramsey had convinced himself that Ball's dismissal for dissent in an under-23 game against Austria in Vienna shortly after the senior tour in 1965 was due to inexperience against foreign opposition, not a flawed temperament. The first player to be ordered off in England's colours since Stan Anderson failed to complete an under-23 match in Bulgaria eight years earlier, Ball remembered his tearful exit. 'I was convinced that I'd blown my chance of playing in the World Cup,' he said. 'It was Alf's team, but I imagined the FA telling him not to select me. I could tell from the way the officials looked at me that they were very upset. Alf was brilliant. I don't know what went on between Alf and the officials, but the next day he put my mind at rest, saying that everything would be all right as long as I learnt not to react when decisions went against me. "There isn't anything to be gained from losing your temper," he said, adding, "And Alan, I can't win World Cups with only ten men. Please remember that." '

If pleased that his gradual adoption of 4–3–3 had not registered with the main body of football correspondents, Ramsey was again at odds with them after Austria became, in October 1965, only the third foreign team to win at Wembley. 'We did not play well,' Ramsey admitted after England were jeered from the field. 'Unfortunately, you people [the press] see everything in black and white. I stand by my belief that England will win the World Cup, but I didn't say that I expect to win every match in the meantime.'

Before the year was out, Ramsey's 4–3–3 made headlines. On 6 December England won 2–0 in Madrid, their first victory on Spanish soil. Delighted with the outcome, Ramsey took the unusual step of introducing startled reporters to the fundamental details of a system into which Brazil had fallen during the 1958 finals in Sweden when their outside-left Zagallo dropped back to assist the midfield. The match, played on a bitterly cold night, remains clear in Jack Charlton's memory. 'I don't think many of the press lads fully understood what Alf was going on about,' he said. 'They'd grown up with the idea that players functioned according to the numbers on the backs of their shirts; the centre-forward wore number nine, the centre-half number five, and so on. Numbers no longer meant anything. Alf had told us that he wanted a secure balance between defence and attack, so that we were never outnumbered. At first we weren't sure, but the match in Madrid changed everything. The Spaniards were baffled, didn't know whom to mark, where to go. We could have scored six.

'If Alf had been able to call on the terrific wingers of the time, George Best and Cliff Jones, say, who got behind defences, scored goals and tackled back, I'm fairly sure he would have settled for two men in midfield. Alf was blamed for forcing wingers out of the game, but he included three in the 1966 squad, John Connelly, Terry Paine and Ian Callaghan, giving each a game. They were good players, hard workers, but Alf wanted more than they could give him.'

Lost in the general enthusiasm for Ramsey's tactics in Madrid was the reason behind his decision to send on the uncapped Leeds defender Norman Hunter in place of the Arsenal centre-forward Joe Baker. In the latter stages, Bobby Charlton twice gave the ball away in positions close to England's goal, fresh proof of his inherent carelessness. Upfield it was an irritation, further back it courted disaster. Hunter galloped on to assist in midfield, carrying an instruction for Charlton to move forward into Baker's position. 'I don't want him [Charlton] messing about around our penalty area,' Ramsey snapped.

The enthusiastic response to England's efforts in Madrid did not last, Ramsey coming under fresh criticism when an England team playing under the Football League banner was defeated 3–1 by the Scottish League at St James's Park, Newcastle, in February 1966. Reflecting on a setback that came shortly after a disjointed, derided 1–0 victory over West Germany at Wembley, where Stiles contributed a rare goal (although Stiles was given the number nine shirt merely as a convenience, an already confused press referred to him as England's centre-forward), Ramsey told me, 'We were so poor that it's a wonder we didn't get a worse hiding. But I see no reason to change the system of play. It still offers us our best chance of success in July. My main concern is for players who have heavy club commitments. Some are beginning to show the strain of games played under great tension, so I must see to it that they are given as much rest as possible once this season is over.'

Faced by growing demands for a return to a more orthodox strategy, Ramsey argued that the generally inadequate standard of English-born wingers and the absence of a consistently effective centre-forward made this impossible. 'I resent the suggestion that my main concern is effort,' he said. 'England are playing to a system that offers the best players we have the greatest opportunity of doing well. The performances against Wales, Northern Ireland and Austria last year were unacceptable. Since then there has been an improvement.'

Ramsey's last flirtation with expansive football came at Hampden Park in April when England defeated a moderate Scotland team 4–3. Typically, his most persistent critics went from one extreme to another. While acknowledging fluent application in attack, they came down heavily on Ramsey's defensive structure. 'It was an odd sort of game,' Cohen said. 'We made so many chances that it probably affected our concentration. Normally, Alf would have been delighted to beat the Jocks, but giving up three goals to any team, never mind a poor one, wasn't on his agenda. He didn't say too much after the game, but he would have plenty to say later.'

When at the beginning of May England defeated Yugoslavia 2–0 in their last match before going into World Cup preparation, Cohen was in Majorca recovering from an injury that kept him in hospital for more than a week. 'I was playing for Fulham at Stoke, where we badly needed a point to be safe from relegation,' he said. 'I lunged in to block a shot from Harry Burrows and felt his studs slice into my knee. It was those damned plastic studs that wore down like razors if they weren't properly attended to. The blood spurted out and I thought, "Christ, I could be out of the World Cup." I had goodness knows how many stitches, inside and out, but fortunately there was no infection. Vic Buckingham [Fulham's manager] came to the hospital and said, "Once you get out of that bed, piss off on holiday. Alf has been on the phone, and I told him you are going to be OK." '

Before dispersing for a three-week break, the England players were warned to expect a tough time at Lilleshall. 'Get some rest,' Ramsey told them, 'because I intend to work you extremely hard.' Recalling the complaints carried to him by Bobby Moore in New York two years earlier, Ramsey was aiming for the highest possible level of fitness before the squad left in late June for warm-up matches against Finland, Norway, Denmark and Poland. As long as England finished top of their qualifying group they would not have to leave Wembley, and the Wembley turf was tiring. 'If we can last, then yes, I think we can win,' Ramsey said prophetically.

Allowing only limited access to the press and broadcasting companies, Ramsey assembled his provisional squad of 27 players at Lilleshall on 6 June. The Leeds and under-23 team trainer Les Cocker joined the back-up team, along with the former Manchester United half-back Wilf McGuinness, who was on the coaching staff at Old Trafford. After dental checks and medicals (Dr Bass discovered that many of the players needed treatment for athlete's foot), the squad was put through an intensive fitness programme while being held under the tightest discipline.

In a book we did together in 1984, Bobby Charlton recalled: 'It wasn't quite like being back in the army, but almost! We slept in dormitories, stood in line for our meals and took turns at helping with the dishes. We queued to make telephone calls from a coin box at the foot of an elegant staircase, and there were no weekend passes. As for nights out, well, we got one during the entire time when Alf *ordered* us to join him for a beer at the local golf club.

'Lilleshall was the main centre for FA coaching courses and I'd heard some tales from players who had been there. One or two pubs in the area were reckoned to be lively, but Alf made it absolutely clear that any of us who wanted to sample them might as well forget about playing in the World Cup. After about a week some of the players spoke about forming an escape committee, just as a joke really, but Alf took it seriously. "Don't even think about it," he said one morning. "It's my way, or not at all." We all thought we were in good shape after a full League season even if some of our fitness had fallen off in the time Alf gave us to rest. But that wasn't good enough for Alf.

'The work we were put through by Harold [Shepherdson] and Les [Cocker] was so strenuous that when the press were allowed in for a day they were convinced that a punishing session had been put on for their benefit. That was definitely not the case. What the press saw was what we did every day. Not being able to have a change of scenery got to a few of the players, but frankly I was so worn out after the evening meal that I'd fall asleep during the films they'd brought in for us.'

Once it was established that George Cohen's knee wound had completely healed, he too was worked to exhaustion. 'I was a good trainer,' Cohen said, 'loved it. I'd done some light running and a lot of upper body work in Majorca, and anyway, as long as you look after yourself, you don't lose much fitness in a couple of weeks. However, I soon found out that Alf had me down for special treatment. I had never been pushed so far. I finished every session utterly exhausted. Alf had no sympathy. He came by one morning just after Les had told me to take a breather. He looked across and said, "George, I don't want to see you slacking." At least it suggested that I didn't need to worry about not getting into the squad.'

There is an undercurrent of tribalism on every team, based on position, salary, geography, lifestyle and so on. It is rarely harmful, it seldom comes to the surface, and winning usually keeps it submerged. There was little evidence of it in the England squad, but

Ramsey guarded against the formation of cliques by moving players around so that they didn't always share the same hotel room. 'As far as he could, Alf kept everything in the open,' Cohen recalled. 'If anyone had something to say it had to be said to him. Not that he ever changed his mind once it had been made up. Not long after Jack Charlton came into the team he was given the responsibility of attacking the ball when we defended corners. If Gordon had a weakness it was in those situations, which is why Jack was told to position himself so that he could make the best use of his height. Jack was used to marking a player, but Alf said, "That is the way we are going to do it." End of story.'

On 17 June, the day Ramsey announced his squad, together with my friend Brian James of the *Daily Mail* I drove from London to Lilleshall, a journey of about three hours. Expecting no great surprises, our thoughts settled on Johnny Byrne. The first player to be capped by England from a Third Division club, Byrne had picked up a further ten caps since moving from Crystal Palace to West Ham, where he had formed an illuminating partnership with Geoff Hurst under Ron Greenwood's advanced management. Short, alert and technically superior to most of his contemporaries in English football, Byrne's chance of making the World Cup seemed to depend on whether a risk could be taken with his happy-go-lucky nature. He didn't make it, discarded along with Peter Thompson – the most expressive but least reliable of Ramsey's wingers – Gordon Milne, Keith Newton and Bobby Tambling.

Privately, Ramsey had reached another decision, one that would startle the squad as much as the press corps. Bobby Moore's development as one of the game's leading central defenders had brought with it an irritating complacency that his big-game instinct wasn't sure to stifle. With perfect timing, Ramsey brought Moore up sharp, replacing him with Norman Hunter for the warm-up opener against Finland in Helsinki on 26 June. Speculation that the Leeds pairing of Hunter and Charlton might be Ramsey's preferred option had the desired effect. Later, Moore wrote, 'From that day on I never took my place in the England squad for granted. Alf was driving it home to me that nobody is indispensable.'

Whether wingers were dispensable remained to be seen. Callaghan was used against the Finns in a comfortable 3–0 victory, and both Connelly and Paine against Norway three days later when Greaves went on the rampage, scoring four of England's six goals to suggest that he was at last free from the debilitating effects of hepatitis. Ironically, the third match of England's tour brought Geoff Hurst to the conclusion that he was unlikely to play a big part in the finals. Struggling to master the difficulties imposed by a dry, bumpy pitch in Copenhagen, unable to achieve any understanding with Greaves, and making very little impression on Denmark's defence, Hurst played so poorly in an unimpressive 2–0 victory that Shepherdson was of a mind to write him off. 'A big disappointment,' he confided as we made our way through the airport the following day. 'Geoff didn't look anything like an international player.'

The official numbering of Ramsey's squad had indicated to Roger Hunt that Hurst was the preferred choice as a partner for Greaves. 'Geoff was number 10, I had 21, so it seemed that I was in the second string,' he said. 'Geoff didn't have much international experience but he was better than me in the air which was important because it gave our defenders the option of hitting him with long, high passes.' Soon, however, it became clear that the choice of second striker was between Hurst and Greaves. Hunt had become permanent.

The last match in England's build-up, against Poland, was always going to be the toughest, a defining test of the team's potential. First, the shock caused by the inclusion of Martin Peters. Announcing his line-up on the eve of the match, Ramsey mischievously paused before reading out the last name.

'At number eleven – Martin Peters,' he said.

Frank McGhee of the *Daily Mirror*, who got on well with Ramsey, was the first to speak. 'Can you tell us what role Martin will be expected to perform?' he asked.

Ramsey replied, 'No, Frank,' got up and left the room with a smile on his face. England's manager was not about to fall into the trap of pre-match tactical discussions with the press.

A gifted, versatile footballer, Peters had been selected to organise the left side of England's midfield. Ramsey's later remark in relation to him, 'a player ten years ahead of his time', wasn't far-fetched. A modern player in every sense of the word, Peters could operate in defence and attack and knew how to look after himself on the field. Wingers were not entirely out of the reckoning, but in selecting Peters and Ball for the flank positions Ramsey had gone beyond 4–3–3 to 4–4–2 with Stiles in the role of a frontal sweeper.

Shortly before England left for the game, Alan Ball came to my hotel room. He looked tense.

'Got any scotch?' he asked.

I took a bottle from a drawer and handed it to him. 'Help yourself,' I said. 'You'll find a glass in the bathroom.'

Ball poured himself a stiff shot and took it in two gulps. 'Thanks,' he said, turning to leave.

'Reckon it will be a tough match,' I said.

'Reckon you're right,' he replied. Then he was gone.

Ramsey's team talk was brief. 'Alf told us that he'd chosen to play Poland because it would get us as close as possible to what the World Cup would be like,' Cohen said. 'That because the Poles had failed to reach the finals they would have plenty to prove.' Hunt's twelfth goal from thirteen caps brought England a 1–0 victory that established them as genuine contenders. 'I don't think many of us went into the game entirely sure about the system, but it worked really well,' Cohen added. 'For the first time I believed that we were good enough to win the World Cup.'

Nobody made a bigger impression that day than Moore. His decision-making was flawless, one of his tackles delivered with such force that gasps were heard in the press box. 'I sent two people to watch the game, and they came back full of praise for England's performance,' West Germany's coach Helmut Schoen told me some years afterwards. 'Their impression was that England had made big strides tactically and would be enormously difficult to beat in their own country.'

Defence was one thing, attack another. Drawn with Uruguay, Mexico and France in the first round of matches, England's initial effort was a let-down. Dictated by the importance of avoiding defeat, Uruguay's negative tactics had practically everyone in withdrawn positions, including their two most creative players, Rocha and Cortes; whenever England threatened to break through they were fouled, often brutally, one of the worst offences committed against Stiles, who stowed it away for future reference. For the many thousands at Wembley, and the millions who were being introduced to blanket television coverage of the finals, it was a crashing bore. No sooner had the final whistle blown than boos swept around the stadium.

Answering my press-box telephone, I heard a *Mirror* executive say, 'You can hear what people think about this man's team and his bloody tactics, so take him apart.'

'Hold on,' I argued. 'It's Uruguay they're booing, not England.'

Nevertheless, England had come up well short of expectations. Nothing had come from Connelly's return to the left wing; Greaves was unable to extricate himself from Uruguay's web; and Cohen and Wilson found only blind alleys when attempting to carry out flank attacks. Cohen said, 'We had most of the ball, most of the play, but Uruguay just sat there. One thing not many people realised about Wembley was that it was a good pitch on which to defend. The texture of the turf made it difficult to keep long shots down, and the more we attacked the more energy we gave up. I remember Jimmy Greaves saying that we'd outlasted one of the fittest teams in the tournament, which was pretty remarkable because I reckoned we'd done twice their running. We could understand the frustration of the crowd, but a lot of the criticism in newspapers was unfair, showing hardly any understanding of the problem we'd come up against.'

The next day, on a visit to Pinewood Studios, the England squad were introduced to a number of film actors, including Sean Connery. A keen football fan, and a promising player in his youth, Connery was incensed by the press criticism and said to the players, 'Take no notice. Typically, they've already written you off. Bloody hell, it isn't as though you lost. Forget it.' If only it had been as easy as Connery made it sound. Analysis of Ramsey's policy focused on a perceived rejection of flair. In his dealings with the press, Ramsey became increasingly terse, challenging the right of football correspondents to question his decisions. 'I don't want you upset by what some of these people write,' he told the players. 'They like to think they know everything when they don't know anything.'

Charged with not knowing his best team, Ramsey's head was again on the block when he made two changes for the game against Mexico on 16 July, replacing one winger with another, Paine for Connelly. Peters came back to the left side of midfield, and Ball was left out. Mexico quickly made their intentions clear. To the crowd's astonishment and despair, they whacked the ball upfield and retreated deep into their own half. 'I'd never seen anything like it,' Bobby Charlton said. 'I thought, "Here we go again." I could imagine Gordon only getting a touch of the ball if it was passed back to him.'

Charlton himself broke the deadlock. In the 37th minute, he latched on to a short pass from Peters and found Mexico's defence opening up. 'Roger had drawn a couple of players out of position, and when nobody plugged the gap I kept going. It's an odd thing, but I had Jimmy Murphy's voice in my head. When I first started at Manchester United, he used to say, "If you're in range, just bloody shoot. Don't try and place them. Just get on target." I let fly from about 25 yards and I knew right away that it was a goal. All the frustration of the Uruguay match flooded away. Roger got a second, and that was it.'

It was not the prospect of exciting football that drew a near capacity crowd to Wembley four days later to see England complete the fixtures of their qualifying group by playing France. As long as England avoided a defeat by two clear goals they would go through to the quarter-finals. Yet again, Ramsey called on a winger, although one closer to his concept of the position: Callaghan, a grafter, for Paine. With nothing to gain from defence, France played with enough verve to worry England's supporters until a goal in each half from Hunt saw them off. But the last had not been heard of an incident involving Stiles. With fifteen minutes remaining of a match that had already seen him cautioned, Stiles strayed beyond the bounds of acceptable aggression with a ferocious tackle that flattened France's key midfielder, Jacques Simon.

Watching Ramsey walk towards him the day before England met Argentina for a place in the semi-finals, Stiles feared the worst. 'That's it, I'm out,' he thought. It was no secret that FIFA, angered by the foul on Simon, were bringing pressure on the FA, seeking his withdrawal from the tournament. 'There was plenty about it in the newspapers and on television,' Stiles recalled, 'rumours of a row between Alf and the FA, but he hadn't hinted that he was having a battle to keep me in the team.' Ramsey, his late arrival on the training ground puzzling the England players, repeated the question he had asked Stiles immediately after the game against France.

'I want to know,' he said, 'whether you intended to kick the French player.'

Stiles, a devout Catholic, answered in the negative. 'I swear I didn't mean it. My timing was bloody awful. It must have looked bad, but it was just bad timing. I didn't deliberately kick the lad.'

That was good enough for Ramsey. 'I believe you,' he said. 'I take your word as an Englishman.' Then he went off to tell waiting members of the FA's Senior International Committee that they could have his resignation unless Stiles was permitted to play.

Later that day, in the company of a Danish journalist, Sven Nielsen, I came across Ramsey at the Hendon Hall hotel.

'What's the verdict on Stiles?' I asked.

'I think you know me well enough to have the answer,' he replied.

As we drove away, Nielsen grew agitated. 'But we don't yet know about Stiles,' he grumbled.

'We do,' I said, 'we do. Nobby plays.'

Would Ramsey have carried out his threat to resign over Stiles? 'He was on pretty safe ground because most of the officials were nervous of him,' Stiles said. 'From things that were said afterwards I'm convinced that I would have been taken out of the team by most managers but Alf. Alf always went with what he believed was right for the team.' Years later, many players from the 1966 finals, Simon among them, took part in a five-a-side tournament at Wembley Arena. The itinerary included a boat trip on the Thames. Looking across the deck, Stiles saw Simon. 'I'd never had the chance to apologise, so I went over to him. "Look," I said. "I didn't mean it, you know. It really was an accident – clumsy, but an accident." Jimmy Greaves spoilt it all. Creeping past Simon, he whispered, "Don't listen to the dirty little bastard!" '

There is no doubt in Stiles's mind that Argentina were the biggest threat to England's aspirations. 'They had some terrific players, some of the best we came up against, and if they'd concentrated on playing football they might have been too good for us.' Instead, believing that the dice was loaded in favour of the European nations – Pele was among those convinced that FIFA president Sir Stanley Rous had instructed the referees to go easy on the more forceful European style – they resorted to cynical fouling whenever anything displeased them or it looked as though they were losing technical control of a game. One of Argentina's defenders, Albrecht, had been ordered off in the group game against West Germany, and FIFA had censured the entire team for 'unethical tackling'. Nobody was more startled by Argentina's militancy than Ramsey's predecessor. 'I knew from 1962 that they were liable to turn nasty at the slightest provocation, but I'd never come across a team with so little respect for the spirit of the game,' Walter Winterbottom said.

FIFA's ill-advised appointment of a German referee, Rudolf Kreitlein, may have fuelled Argentina's suspicion of European bias, but their anarchic behaviour in the quarter-finals prompted suggestions that future World Cups would be better off without them. Having watched Argentina play West Germany on television, at least the England players knew what to expect. 'There was no doubt in my mind that they were the most serious threat to our chances,' Bobby Charlton said. 'Onega was outstanding in midfield. They had outstanding full-backs – Marzolini was brilliant. Mas looked dangerous on the left wing, and, of course, there was Rattin. They seemed to do everything slowly, but they were so physically strong that it was impossible to brush them off. They were always together and, one way or another, they always got the job done. No fair races were allowed. Anyone who attempted to run past them was upended. At that time, they were the roughest, meanest team I played against.'

Argentina's tall, Grenadier-backed captain Antonio Rattin was easily identified as their key player and chief troublemaker. 'Like all terrific footballers, he appeared to have all the time in the world, and everything revolved around him,' Stiles added. 'But he could have started a row in an empty house. In the game we watched he never left the referee alone, questioning every decision. Alf told us not to get involved, to walk away from trouble, which in my case was easier said than done.' Independently, Shepherdson and Cocker took Stiles to one side. 'It was funny in a way,' he reflected, 'because both said very seriously that Alf had put his reputation on the line and that I must not let him down. I was always inclined to be excitable on the field, getting worked up over bad decisions, that sort of thing, so I understood exactly what Harold and Les meant. If I did just one stupid thing, got my name taken or, worse, got myself sent off, it would embarrass Alf and weaken his position.'

Although England actually conceded more free-kicks than Argentina, and Kreitlein's fussy interference didn't help matters, there was no excuse for the persistent abuse of authority that led to Rattin's dismissal in the 36th minute. After fouling Bobby Charlton and Hunt in quick succession, Rattin, whose name had already been added to Kreitlein's growing list of offenders, remonstrated with the referee over a caution issued to Artime and was told to leave the field. As Ramsey frantically waved his players away from the chaos that followed – play was held up for eight minutes while Rattin attempted to argue his way back into the game – he realised that Stiles and Ball were not responding to the signal. When Ramsey then saw that Stiles had been spat at – 'six or seven times in the match' – he buried his head in his hands. He looked up to see Stiles being ushered away by Ray Wilson. 'There was more to it than just relief,' Ramsey would admit. 'Regardless of Nobby's will to win, the tremendous job he did for England, those people [his pejorative term for members of the Senior International Committee] would happily have kicked him out.'

The growing importance of Stiles soon became evident when Argentina reorganised to such good effect that it was all England could do to keep them out. Twice Stiles intervened to rescue England's faltering defence, angrily waving his arms, first at Jack Charlton, then at Wilson. After further alarms, particularly when Mas outpaced Cohen to shoot low into the side-netting, England finally broke Argentina's resistance with a goal that would have serious repercussions for Greaves, whose injury against France had given Hurst an opportunity to make his mark. Timing his run to the near post perfectly, Hurst leapt to head a floated pass from Peters into the far side of Argentina's net. A classic West Ham goal, it brought Hurst into serious contention for a permanent place in the side.

For the first time since 1934, the World Cup had two all-European semi-finals, causing the South American countries to mutter darkly about Rous's influence, although the suggestion that they would withdraw from FIFA to form their own championship was more rumour than threat. Portugal's free-wheeling approach to their semi-final against England remains something of a mystery. Maybe believing that their best chance lay in tempting England into an open game, or perhaps to avoid castigation in the home of football, they left out their hard men Morais and Vicente – a significant move, since both had brutally targeted Pele during the group stages. The result was a match that reminded Moore, Hurst and Peters of many League games they had played for West Ham. 'Teams enjoyed playing against us because we opened so much space,' Moore said. 'It was a bit like that against Portugal. They didn't try to close things up, which meant there was plenty of room in midfield. Bobby Charlton loved it, really came on to top form.'

The tone was set in the opening twenty minutes when not one foul was committed. Considering that Stiles had been designated to police Eusebio, the odds against that would have been enormous. 'Do you mean for life?' Stiles replied, smiling, when Ramsey handed him the task of marking the tournament's leading scorer. Stiles, in fact, simply shepherded Eusebio down blind alleys, and on to his weaker left

e unthinkable: USA 1 England 0. Alf Ramsey watches a header from Joe Gaetjens
ieeze past goalkeeper Bert Williams in the 1950 finals. The Americans then survived a
mbardment by England's famous forwards to register the biggest shock in World Cup
tory. (© Popperfoto)

England sprang a
prise by selecting 21-
r old Bobby Moore for
1962 finals in Chile.
e of England's few
cesses, Moore stands
 at the heart of
land's defence as Brazil
k towards a 3–1 victory
he quarter finals.
Popperfoto)

ht 'Of all the players to
 it had to be him,' Alf
nsey said of Gordon
ks after England lost
 to West Germany in
n at the quarter final
e of the 1970 Mexico
ld Cup. When Banks
ill, Peter Bonetti took
r. Here he fails to
vent Gerd Muller
tching the winner in
a time. (© Popperfoto)

With Pele injured for
st of the 1962 finals,
zil drew inspiration
n Garrincha who ran
 against England,
ring two and making
other for Vava. Bobby
rlton gets a close look
arrincha's sorcery.
Popperfoto)

ht The look on the faces
Bobby Moore and Alf
nsey tell it all as they
e the field following
land's defeat by West
many in Leon.
land's most successful
nager and their greatest
tain would not again be
 in the World Cup
ls. (© Popperfoto)

Right The 1986 quarter final between Argentina and England seemed to rest on the outcome of a duel between the world's greatest player, Diego Maradona, and the world's best goalkeeper, Peter Shilton. Maradona claimed divine assistance, the 'Hand of God', when scoring the first of his two goals. (© Popperfoto)

Below Every point covered, everybody marked. Then Brehme's free kick took a deflection and looped over Peter Shilton to put West Germany ahead 1–0 in the semi finals of Italia 90. (© Popperfoto)

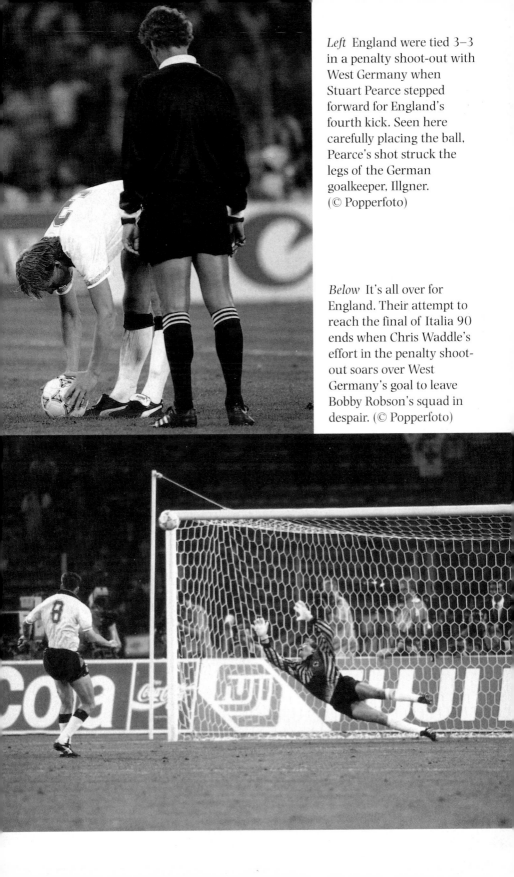

Left England were tied 3–3 in a penalty shoot-out with West Germany when Stuart Pearce stepped forward for England's fourth kick. Seen here carefully placing the ball, Pearce's shot struck the legs of the German goalkeeper, Illgner. (© Popperfoto)

Below It's all over for England. Their attempt to reach the final of Italia 90 ends when Chris Waddle's effort in the penalty shoot-out soars over West Germany's goal to leave Bobby Robson's squad in despair. (© Popperfoto)

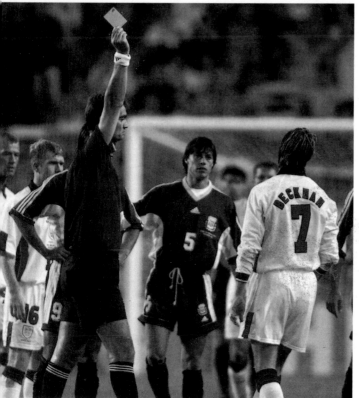

Above England were a goal behind against Romania in Toulouse when Michael Owen made his mark in the 1998 finals, coming on as a substitute to level the scores at 1–1 with seven minutes left. To the despair of England's supporters, Dan Petrescu won the game for Romania in the final minute.
(© Popperfoto)

Left One petulant act and England are reduced to ten men against Argentina in the quarter finals of France 98. In the moment that changed his life, David Beckham is red carded by the Danish referee Kim Neilsen. (© Popperfoto)

Above Glenn Hoddle shows his frustration when Sol Campbell's header hits Argentina's net only to be disallowed for Alan Shearer's push on the goalkeeper. 'Even with a man short we could have gone through,' he said. (© Popperfoto)

Left Normally, David Batty would not have figured in England's front rank of penalty takers, but with David Beckham sent off and Paul Scholes and Darren Anderton substituted he was pressed into service against Argentina in St Etienne. Batty had never before taken a penalty, not even as a junior. Carlos Roa celebrates the save that sent Argentina through. (© Popperfoto)

Above Surely Ronaldinho wouldn't attempt to score from 40 yards out. David Seaman expected a swinging centre; instead the ball curled and dipped into the top far corner of his goal. Fluke or not, Brazil were ahead 2–1 in Shizuoka. (© Popperfoto)

Right The foot injury David Beckham sustained six weeks before the 2002 finals in Japan and South Korea left him well short of match fitness. Apart from converting a high-pressure penalty against Argentina, he made little impact on the tournament. Beckham leaves the field in Shizuoka a disappointed man. (© Popperfoto)

foot. 'I would say that was the best game I ever saw Nobby play,' Cohen said. 'He did the job perfectly and against a guy who could give him four yards. Alf had worked out that Eusebio was less effective on his left side and Nobby moved him that way all the time, or made him play where there wasn't much space.' Eusebio had thus far been bursting through defences like a cyclone, unleashing shots of such alarming velocity that if he got on the ball 40 yards out goalkeepers developed a nervous twitch, but he contributed little against England other than the successful conversion of a second-half penalty, his eighth goal of the finals and the first conceded by Banks. In the England camp, Eusebio's eclipse was put down to a failure of nerve. 'A glory hunter,' Ball piped. Harsh? Not according to João Saldanha, who managed Brazil for two years until shortly before the 1970 finals in Mexico. Saldanha saw no valid comparison between Eusebio and Pele, none in fact between Eusebio and Denis Law. 'Eusebio – PR player,' he snorted. 'Law – out of this world.'

Despite Eusebio's ineffectiveness, Portugal rallied after Bobby Charlton put England two up with barely ten minutes left to play. Charlton's first goal was testimony to his growing confidence: it was simply passed into the net; his second went in like a missile. 'I thought, "That's it, we're there," ' Cohen recalled. 'But then Eusebio put away a penalty, and Portugal came right at us.' Banks saved from Coluna, and it took an alert interception by Stiles to foil Simões. Furious, Stiles waved his arms at Wilson and Moore. But it was his day, his and Bobby Charlton's.

The question of whether Ramsey would bring back Greaves was central to every debate about the final against West Germany. 'I tried to put myself in Ramsey's shoes,' the West German coach Helmut Schoen told me. 'England's performance against Portugal surprised us. They were much improved technically from the previous matches, and the combination of Hurst and Hunt, who were both strong and worked hard off the ball, seemed to suit Bobby Charlton. Hurst was also good in the air. I would have to try to do something about Charlton, but was Greaves still in the picture? He was a brilliant scorer, a quick dribbler with outstanding anticipation, but he was not a good team player. And he'd missed two games with an injury. My feeling was that Ramsey would select the team that defeated Portugal. What we didn't have at that time was the possibility of substitutes. Once you selected the team, that was it.'

For once, Muhammad Ali had to take a back seat. Shortly to defend his world heavyweight championship against Brian London at Earls Court, he was baffled by the relative indifference. 'Some sort of soccer game,' explained his trainer, Angelo Dundee. Two days before the final on 30 July an arrangement was made for a group of England players to attend one of Ali's training sessions at a gymnasium in north-west London. Disappointingly, Ali went down with a chill.

Disappointment soon gave way to tension, Ramsey delaying the announcement of his decision over Greaves until eleven a.m. on Saturday morning. The choice was not between Greaves and Hurst but between Greaves and Hunt. 'I was pretty sure about that,' Hunt said. 'There was a lot of speculation, some of the writers suggesting that if Alf preferred me to Jimmy it would simply confirm a prejudice against flair players. I thought this was ridiculous. What about Bobby Charlton, wasn't he a flair player? I never really understood the criticism of Alf because he worked along similar lines to Bill Shankly. The difference was that Bill had a much better relationship with the press.'

On the eve of the final, Hunt was still sweating on his place. 'When I spoke about it at a dinner many years afterwards, Ray [Wilson] said he didn't realise until then just how much I was going through,' Hunt said. 'In fact, I envied Ray and the others who were sure to be in the team. Alf wasn't about to mess around with the defence [the best-kept secret was that Moore had been laid up with tonsillitis and might have missed the game but for Alan Bass's diligent medical supervision], Bobby Charlton and Nobby were certainties, and I couldn't see either Alan Ball and Martin Peters being left out. Apart from his other skills, Geoff Hurst was good in the air, so that left me and Jimmy. We went to the cinema on the Friday evening, and as I climbed off the coach Alf told me I was playing. He must have told everyone in turn because when the whole squad met for a meeting the next morning there was no formal announcement of the team. Only then did I think about Jimmy, his disappointment. But what could I say to him?'

While Bobby Charlton shared Hunt's sympathy for Greaves, he wasn't startled by Ramsey's decision. 'On the one hand Alf had Roger and Geoff who could be relied on to work hard against close marking, and on the other Jimmy Greaves, a fantastic finisher but a moderate team player. It's been said that Alf showed courage when he went into the final without Jimmy, but I don't think he saw it that way. He did what he thought was best for the team. Mind you, if we'd lost, Alf would have been crucified.'

The thought of defeat didn't enter Charlton's mind until a few hours before kick-off. 'I was sharing a room with Ray Wilson, and we went for a walk around Hendon. It was a different time. There was no security. I don't think we even checked with Alf. As long as we were back in time for the team meeting, nobody bothered. Today, there would be officials everywhere, television cameras, photo-graphers, and it wouldn't be possible to wander around the streets without being mobbed. If people recognised us in 1966, they wished us good luck, but quietly, almost shyly. But it made me realise just how much the game meant to the nation. If winning the World Cup meant so much to so many people, what if we lost?'

Ramsey's team talk followed a familiar pattern. He went over the opposition, pinpointing individual strengths and weaknesses; no chances were to be taken when defending corners and free-kicks, and everyone was reminded to support the man on the ball. 'Alf never said much to the defence because we operated as a unit, marking zones, passing attackers on from one to another,' Cohen said. 'But everybody was expected to take care of the ball. People accused Alf of playing football by numbers, which was nonsense. He never bombarded us with detail. All the points he made were solid. As far as my job was concerned, and I'm sure Ray felt the same, it helped that Alf had been an international full-back. If you came across a problem on the field you could be pretty sure that Alf had experienced something similar. He told us to watch for the German wingers, Held and Emmerich, changing positions. Held was a head-down sprinter, you could run him into blind alleys; Emmerich was skilful with a great shot, but slow. As long as you closed down on them quickly you could cope.'

Reaching the World Cup final was more than Schoen had expected to accomplish. A tall, heavily built man with a lugubrious face, formerly Dresden's centre-half, he was taken on as Sepp Herberger's assistant following the World Cup triumph of 1954, succeeding him ten years later. Schoen, too, played percentages, employing a defensive sweeper, Schulz, and a solid midfield that could be lifted by the emerging brilliance of Franz Beckenbauer, much as England turned to Bobby Charlton for inspiration. Simultaneously, Schoen and

Ramsey arrived at a decision that curbed the attacking glories of both men. Given responsibility for each other, they cancelled each other out.

In accordance with one of Wilson's many superstitions, Bobby Charlton had packed his bag for him. When thinking about the task ahead, he hadn't seen Helmut Haller as much of a threat. 'I'd played against him as a youth international and thought he was going to be an outstanding player, but he'd got big around the backside.' But with only thirteen minutes played, Wilson, of all people, made an error that enabled Haller to put West Germany in front. Mishearing Banks's call "Leave it!" Wilson jumped too soon and sent a headed clearance to Haller, whose half-hit shot bobbled between Banks and Jack Charlton. It was Wilson's first mistake of the tournament, and the first goal England had given up in open play. Ramsey sat stone-faced on the touchline.

The first incident of the game had seen Hurst in a mid-air collision with Tilkowski that flattened the German goalkeeper, leaving him light-headed. 'I don't think he got over it,' Hunt said. However, even a goalkeeper in full possession of his senses would have been helpless to prevent Hurst bringing England level six minutes after Haller's opener. Fouled by Overath when coming out of defence, Moore quickly took the free-kick himself, sending it into unmarked space; with a perfectly timed diagonal run, Hurst put a flawless header past Tilkowski. Moore held one arm aloft while Hurst was smothered in congratulations. Schoen was furious. 'I'd warned them against it,' he said. 'Told them to watch for Hurst attacking "dead" space.' Seated in the stands, Ron Greenwood wore a satisfied smile. A goal made on West Ham's training pitch.

It stayed 1–1 until thirteen minutes from the end, when England scored a second goal. Alan Ball, whose tireless hustling put years on Schnellinger, forced a corner which he took himself. From it, Hottges hacked at a shot by Hurst, but there wasn't anyone to prevent Peters getting to the rebound. 'Because Geoff went on to get a hat-trick, it's often forgotten who got England's other goal,' Peters said. 'Without extra-time I might be remembered as the man who won the World Cup for England.'

But that would have deprived the World Cup of a dramatic climax. With only a minute left the Swiss referee Gottfried Dienst awarded West Germany a dubious free-kick after Jack Charlton had jumped with Held for a high ball. Immediately, Stiles took over, dragging the England players into a defensive wall. 'Normally we would have got ourselves together, but coming so late in the game, so close to winning, we didn't get it right,' said Cohen. 'Our "wall" wasn't properly organised. Emmerich drove the ball in, it hit my knee, flew across goal to Weber, and suddenly, instead of celebrating, we were going into extra-time.' Jack Charlton held his head in his hands. 'I thought, "Oh God, I'm going to be the one who cost England the World Cup," even though I knew I'd done nothing wrong. It still haunts me, that moment.'

It was at that moment, as the whistle went and both teams fell to the turf, that Ramsey made what was possibly his most decisive contribution to England's ultimate victory. 'Alf came on to the pitch in his usual businesslike way, and he was pretty angry that we'd wasted so many opportunities,' Cohen recalled. 'He struck exactly the right mood. He wasn't the least bit sympathetic that the Germans were still in with a chance because of a dodgy free-kick. He was firm. His remark that we'd won the World Cup once so go out and win it again is famous, but it was the way he said it that counted. It was his way of kicking our arses. Some of our players, including Bobby Moore, had flopped down on the pitch. Alf told them to get up. Most of the Germans were lying down getting massaged. Alf pointed to them. "Look, they're knackered," he said. "Nothing left." ' Schoen feared as much. 'I thought that getting another chance when it looked as though we were beaten would give us a big psychological advantage,' he later told me. 'But it is very tiring to play at Wembley. In a number of positions the team was exhausted. We could only hold on and hope that something would happen for us. Substitutes still weren't permitted, so it wasn't possible to introduce fresh legs, which might have made a difference.' Had substitutes been allowed, would Ramsey have resisted the temptation to bring on Greaves? 'No point in discussing that,' Ramsey would say later. 'Even if I'd been able to make a change it is unlikely to have involved the attackers. Perhaps if things had gone against us in extra-time . . . but I've never given that much thought.'

Extra-time saw the vindication of Ramsey's policy: a team at the peak of contemporary fitness levels, well organised, too functional for some tastes, but relentless in the pursuit of victory. It was more than twenty years before Jack Charlton watched the entire match on video.

'The thing that struck me most was how well we passed the ball,' he said. 'When we won the World Cup I didn't give a monkey about what people thought, whether they reckoned we were a good team or not. But make no mistake: we *were* a good team. I've got only one word for anyone who says otherwise. Bollocks!'

It was nearly halfway through extra-time, in the 100th minute, when England got in front again. Ball, who ran Schnellinger ragged, was sent clear by Stiles. Hurst controlled Ball's centre, pivoted and struck a shot that rebounded down from the crossbar right in front of Hunt, who raised an arm in celebration of what became the most controversial goal in World Cup history. Pursued by German players, Dienst consulted with the silver-haired Russian linesman Tofik Bakhramov. Bakhramov raised his flag to indicate a goal, prompting the suggestion that he had answered Dienst with one word: Stalingrad! Although all subsequent attempts to prove or disprove the legitimacy of Hurst's strike have been inconclusive, Hunt admits that his celebration meant nothing. 'I wouldn't have beaten Weber to the rebound, but show me a footballer who wouldn't claim a goal in those circumstances? It could have gone either way. The decision went for us, as it went against England twenty years later when Maradona punched the ball past Peter Shilton.' Cohen admitted to being 'too far away to judge, and I don't think the linesman was best placed either. Beckenbauer always annoys me about that, saying to me, "Co-hen, it was not a goal." It always needles me because he calls me "Co-hen", but I just tell him that the referee said it was a goal, and anyway we scored four.'

Hurst's completion of the only hat-trick in a World Cup final came a minute from time. Fearing another calamity, Jack Charlton looked on in horror when Moore exchanged passes with Ball – 'I was yelling at him to kick the bloody ball into the crowd' – on the left side of England's penalty area. But Moore strode forward, looked up and released Hurst with a pass that cut a hole in West Germany's defence. Hurst's first thought, his only thought, was to send the ball so far behind the German goal that there would only be enough time left for a goal kick; instead, his powerful left-foot drive tore between Tilkowski and the near post. It was the last kick of the 1966 World Cup.

After a brief celebration with the players, Ramsey left the lap of honour to them, saying, 'It's your day.' When Bobby Charlton finally got back to the dressing room he was rebuked for shooting when it would have made more sense to retain possession of the ball. 'What the hell do you think you were doing out there?' Ramsey said, harshly. 'We should never have been dragged into extra-time.' Suitably chastened, Charlton muttered an apology. 'It was not what you expect after winning the World Cup,' he said. 'But that was Alf. He always chose his moments.'

As hosts, England had completed their World Cup with a performance that obliterated memories of past failures. They had won on merit. 'England played to their strengths,' Schoen said, 'and you had to admire that. They had the ideal blend of great players and workers.'

At the Royal Garden Hotel, where both teams attended a banquet, there was a visit from Harold Wilson, who joined England on a balcony to join in the singing with the crowds outside. Bobby Charlton remembered gifts: a crate of port, a suit length. 'Grey, it was. I gave it to Uwe Seeler. I don't know why. Maybe I was embarrassed when he came over to congratulate me. Anyway, he took the cloth.' The day after the game, the squad, together with their partners, met for the last time at a lunch organised by ATV, one of the World Cup broadcasters. Ramsey arrived with his wife Victoria. I congratulated him and asked if he had a few minutes in which we could speak about the game. 'Sorry, but it's my day off,' he replied. 'I've been working for nine weeks.' So had I, and I told him I thought he was being unnecessarily difficult. Ramsey gave me a hard look. 'Just a few minutes, then,' he said.

The FA gave Ramsey a £5,000 bonus, allocated £22,000 to the players who agreed to split it equally throughout the squad ('a grand each, less tax'), and lost a chunk of World Cup profits in tax because of an administrative error. 'Bloody typical,' Cohen remarked. Moore, who had now lifted the FA Cup, European Cup Winners Cup and World Cup at Wembley in successive seasons, was voted best player of the tournament, and Bobby Charlton would shortly become European Footballer of the Year.

A month or so afterwards, Ramsey and Moore were the principal guests at a dinner of the Anglo-American Sporting Club in London. Before proposing a toast to them, I checked with Ramsey a remark he was said to have made when Harold Shepherdson and other members of the England party leapt up to celebrate Hurst's third goal.

'Is it true that you told Harold to sit down because you couldn't see?' I asked.

'Something like that,' Ramsey replied, smiling.

In fact, Ramsey hadn't seen Hurst's shot go in because he was watching Overath, a player he much admired, straining to get back. 'After such a game, it was a magnificent effort,' he said.

7. 1966 TO MEXICO 1970

In its report of the 1966 finals, the Technical Study Group of FIFA concluded, 'As has frequently happened before, it is expected that the winning teams will tend to dictate future style and method, and it is thought that the success of England and West Germany in this competition is likely to influence measures of team preparation for Mexico, with even more stress on the two factors of physical condition and tactics.' Faced by the forbidding prospect of defending the World Cup at altitude and in extreme heat, Ramsey immediately began to stress the importance of possession. 'We must have heard Alf say "Treat the ball like a precious jewel" a hundred times,' Ball said. 'He'd already worked out that we wouldn't have a prayer in Mexico unless our passing improved. If it didn't, then we'd just be pouring out energy trying to get the ball back.'

But the 1970 World Cup would not be contested by the 1966 World Cup-winning side which, from the quarter-final against Argentina onwards, turned out only six times, beginning to break up when Jimmy Greaves replaced Hunt for a match against Scotland at Wembley in April 1967. Greaves failed to score. Scotland won 3–2 and cheekily proclaimed themselves linear champions. Presumably, the title passed on when Scotland lost to the Soviet Union in their next match. Surprising as it was to hear Ramsey compliment the Scots – 'I always said it would take a very good team to beat us, and this was probably it' – his main concern was the loss of two points in the British Championship, which was being used over two seasons as a qualifying zone for the 1968 European Championship finals.

As the months wore on the excitement caused by the World Cup, naturally enough, began to wane, the united front of 1966 to disintegrate into doubts and second thoughts. 'I can't help thinking that there are people in English football who didn't want us to win the World Cup,' Ramsey complained, his relations with the press remaining subject to frequent emotional disturbance. Mainly, however, Ramsey had in mind the Football League management committee whose secretary Alan Hardaker asserted that the World Cup success would have no significant effect on English football. Arguing that they'd already done enough to support the national team, the clubs demanded first call on their players for tour matches in the summer of 1967, and it was announced that there would be no senior England tour. Upset by the FA's feeble agreement to this, Ramsey sent a depleted under-23 squad to play three matches in the Balkans under Bill Nicholson's management while he took a scratch squad to Montreal, Canada, where it turned out under the banner of an FA XI in a badly organised tournament against foreign club teams. 'It was hardly the thrill of a lifetime,' John Hollins recalled. 'A circus had only just moved out of the stadium, and there were holes all over the pitch. The teams stayed in a university, sleeping in dormitories, eating together in a huge mess hall. Alf said we had to make the best of it, but you could tell that he wasn't amused. Every day, Johnny Byrne sneaked off to a nearby pub for steak and chips.'

Early in 1968, there was a significant new addition to the England set-up when Dr Neil Phillips was appointed the squad's senior physician (Alan Bass had left to take up a post in Canada). Welsh born and raised, a director of Middlesbrough and their medical officer, Phillips had worked extensively with the under-23 team and alongside Bass during the 1966 campaign. He had his first brush with Ramsey during England's two-leg European Championship quarter-final with reigning champions Spain. If yet to achieve international importance, the European Championship of 1968 at least afforded England an opportunity of competitive football against foreign opposition, for they had qualified for the competition after two seasons of domestic tussling during which they earned four wins and a draw from six fixtures. When the squad flew to Madrid in early May, they were already 1–0 up in the tie and needed only a draw to progress.

Dr Andrew Stephen was the only senior FA official present in Madrid for that second leg. On the eve of the game, Stephen sought Ramsey's permission for Phillips to join him at a reception put on by the Spanish Federation. 'I didn't want to go,' Phillips said, 'but Andrew felt that it would look bad if he showed up alone, so as I was a Middlesbrough director . . . anyway, Alf agreed, which I found astonishing.' The following day, Hurst was found to have a poisoned toe. Furious, Ramsey asked Hurst why he hadn't reported the condition earlier. 'I tried to,' Hurst replied, 'but I couldn't find the doc.' When it became clear that Hurst wasn't fit to play, Phillips felt compromised. 'It was the first time I ever went against Alf, but it was his fault and I let him know that he should have told Andrew Stephen that my place was with the team, not at a reception. "Don't ever do that again," I said.' Revising his formation, Ramsey brought in Norman Hunter as Hurst's replacement – 'For what they are about to receive,' Ball cracked upon hearing of Hunter's selection – and England managed a fairly comfortable 2–1 victory. Proving that his right foot wasn't merely for standing on, Hunter swung it to score a rare goal.

A month later – after losing 1–0 to West Germany in Hanover en route, their dominance over the Germans coming to an end with Beckenbauer's goal – England were eliminated by Yugoslavia in Florence, again to a single goal. An ill-tempered affair, the match was settled by an error by Moore; it also saw Alan Mullery become the first Englishman to be sent off in a full international fixture. Moodily, England defeated the Soviet Union 2–0 for third place. The title went to Italy. 'We were never at our best,' Ramsey admitted, 'but people who complain that we are too physical should think about some of Yugoslavia's tackling. We're no angels, but we have to put up with a lot.' The complaint fell on barren ground. 'Live by the sword, die by the sword,' somebody said.

The heroic assembly of 1966 was finally broken up. A serious knee injury had sent Cohen into retirement; Wilson's international career had ended against the Russians in Rome; a cartilage injury reduced some of Stiles's effectiveness; towards the end of a long career, Jack Charlton's fitness was frequently in doubt; and Hunt was beginning to find international football too much. 'I was pushing 30, and at that age the game gets hard,' he said, 'particularly when you are constantly involved in important matches, as I was with Liverpool. And by then the game had got more defensive.' After two more caps, Hunt disappeared from the reckoning.

A new attacking partnership was formed when Ramsey brought in Francis Lee of Manchester City, blooding him against Bulgaria at Wembley in December 1968. Later to become a millionaire in the food industry, a successful racehorse trainer, and, briefly, City's chairman, Lee was ideally suited to England's formation. Explosive, direct, more than capable of looking after himself on the field, he was told to use his initiative, supporting Hurst as he saw fit. 'Getting into the England team mattered a great deal to me,' Lee said. 'I had plenty of self-confidence and knew I was good enough. You don't know quite what to expect, but the most encouraging thing I'd heard about Alf was that he didn't try to change players. People said he was a dour, defensively minded manager, but he wasn't really. He told me not to worry about making a big impression, just to play for him exactly as I played for Manchester City. "You've got a free role with us too," he said. "Go wherever you want as long as it's in support of Geoff." '

After a 5–0 thrashing of France in March 1969 and two good victories over Northern Ireland and Wales, a 4–1 defeat of Scotland at Wembley in May was so comprehensively achieved that even England's fiercest critics were obliged to agree that the team before their eyes was not only equal in cohesion with the 1966 combination, but superior in style. Three weeks after that Scotland match, England left for the most important phase of their World Cup preparation, a two-week tour of Central and South America involving matches against Mexico, Uruguay and Brazil.

England had known since 1964 that Mexico would host the 1970 finals, and since 1966 their qualification had been assured, but nothing had been done to address the physiological difficulties Mexico would pose. Neil Phillips had had to start from scratch. 'The FA had a medical committee but I never worked out its function,' he said. 'There wasn't one file on Mexico. I remember saying to Alf that I was a GP with no qualifications in sports medicine, so how was I expected to supply him with the sort of information that teams of doctors were producing in other countries? Alf replied that he didn't care how, just to make sure that we were as good if not better than everyone else in our medical preparation.'

Giving up all the time he could manage from his medical practice, unpaid and allowed expenses of just two pounds a day when abroad but nothing for home matches, Phillips immersed himself in the problems of acclimatisation. First, he obtained a list of some 400 papers that had been written about the effects of altitude on physical functions. One that caught his eye was by Griffith Pugh, who had accompanied Sir Edmund Hillary's expedition to Everest in 1953. 'At our first meeting he sat for more than an hour with his back to me, looking out of a window,' Phillips recalled. 'I think it astonished him that such a responsibility had been given to a doctor who was normally used to dealing with coughs and sneezes. Certainly it amazed him that the FA didn't have an active medical set-up. Griffith

Pugh was a tremendous help, and we became good friends.' In 1969, Phillips also got his hands on a report the Dutch Olympic Committee had prepared for the 1968 games in Mexico; subsequently passed to the Dutch FA, it fell into Phillips' hands when Holland failed to qualify for the World Cup.

Before the start of the 1969–70 season Ramsey issued a list of 48 players under consideration for the World Cup so that Phillips could arrange a programme of blood tests, dental checks and immunisation. Reports were sent to the clubs involved; one of the players had eleven decayed teeth. 'He told me that he hadn't seen a dentist since his schooldays,' Phillips said. 'It was staggering to think that while clubs were prepared to pay big transfer fees they were so lax in monitoring the health of their players. I actually put it to the Football League that they should set up a central file of medical histories. I offered to organise it for them, but the reply was that the clubs wouldn't agree to it.'

Throughout his time with the England team, Phillips received just £1,000 in *ex gratia* payments. Once, when asked by Ramsey to attend an under-23 match in the Midlands, he made the journey by road from Redcar after taking morning surgery. The FA refused to meet his charge for petrol, Denis Follows pointing out in a terse letter that only a second-class rail fare was allowed. 'Sarcastically, I pointed out that I hadn't travelled by train, but I heard no more. It was the rail fare or nothing.' The FA agreed to reimburse Phillips for the cost of a locum during his absence in Mexico, but not in time to prevent his account from falling into the red. 'As if I didn't have enough to think about, my wife called to say that we'd run up an overdraft. That was the FA for you.'

No sooner had the squad set foot in Mexico City in the summer of 1969 than Banks flew home to attend his father's funeral. When he returned, in time to play against Uruguay in Montevideo, it was with the complaint that he'd made the fifteen-hour journey in an economy seat while an FA official on the same flight had travelled first class. 'Is it any wonder that I have no respect for these people?' Ramsey muttered.

Not that Ramsey had done anything to improve his own popularity rating. Following England's 0–0 draw in Mexico City, he'd chased Mexican journalists out of the England dressing room and then launched a litany of complaints about the noise outside the hotel, the non-appearance of a motorcycle escort and a poor reception at the stadium. 'I think the England team were entitled to more respect,' he said. Ramsey had sown the dragon seeds of trouble.

For the next test, against a Mexican XI in Guadalajara, the location for England's group matches, Ramsey experimented with substitutes, ordering Alan Ball and Martin Peters to run themselves out in the first half before giving way to Bobby Charlton and Alan Mullery. But he ended up with ten men when Mullery was sent off for the second time in a year. Ramsey had been faced with the problem of how to make tactical use of substitutes ever since FIFA's announcement that two would be allowed in the 1970 tournament. He continually made statements such as 'Football has become a thirteen-a-side game and the England players have to recognise this without dispute. We must learn how to make best use of the extra men.' But behind this public front a doubt, one held by other managers of Ramsey's generation, remained. The events of Leon a year later would seem the logical conclusion of this uncertainty.

Arriving in Montevideo after a journey of more than twenty hours, Ramsey was in no mood to meet with FA officials who had flown directly to Uruguay rather than run health risks in Mexico. Nevertheless, at the request of Sid Collings, chairman of the Senior International Committee, he went over Alan Mullery's headlining dismissal in Guadalajara. Collings asked for the report in writing. Tetchily, Ramsey looked across at Denis Follows and said, 'He's the secretary, let him give you a written report.'

Reporting from Uruguay after England's 2–1 win there but ahead of their visit to Rio, a prominent Brazilian journalist, Jose Werneck, warned the world, 'They are better than in 1966, just as strong defensively and with more imagination. England can no longer be described as a team typical of English football.' And England's performance at Maracana was impressive, too, in all but the result: after taking the lead they conceded two late goals, mainly through fatigue. 'By then we were pretty much knackered,' Lee said. 'But if Brazil were going to be the World Cup favourites I was all for having a punt on our chances. I couldn't wait, although Alf told me not to get carried away. "Do that, and I'll drop you like a stone," he said. And he would have.'

Heat became a problem only relatively late in the day. 'Of course we'd taken the possible temperature into account,' Phillips explained, 'but our planning was based on the supposition that the World Cup matches would be played at a cooler time of the day.' Instead, to suit the demands of European television companies including BBC and ITV, both of whom were heavily committed to the tournament, FIFA agreed to staging many of the matches at noon. 'Alf was appalled,' Phillips said. 'He'd gone to the Mexico Olympics and found the temperature reasonable, but the Olympics had taken place in October. The World Cup was in June. On top of everything else, the players would have to contend with the full heat of the day.'

In a television interview given shortly after his return from this summer tour, Ramsey warned that heat, not altitude, could be the biggest obstacle to England retaining the World Cup. The interview was seen by Hugh de Wardener, a professor in the renal unit at Charing Cross Hospital in London. Shortly afterwards, Ramsey received a letter from de Wardener offering assistance. 'It was a lucky break,' Phillips said. 'In his work with kidney patients de Wardener had tackled the problem of replacing lost salt, which became ours once we knew the heat would probably be extreme. By itself, an oral intake of salt was not the answer. Taken in one dose, it can bring on nausea, for all the salt is released at once, not steadily over the period of a game.' De Wardener had come up with a simple but brilliant idea that met his own and England's requirements.

I had become friendly with Phillips by this time, and we were in the habit of getting together whenever he was in London. 'Try this,' he said to me one night, handing over a round tablet, in shape like most others.

Stupidly, I bit into the pill instead of allowing it to dissolve. Offended by the taste, I spat it into a handkerchief. 'Jesus,' I gasped, 'what is it?'

'Slow sodium,' Phillips replied.

It was a honeycomb of salt cells, each cell covered by a soluble membrane, allowing salt to be released into the system at regular intervals. First tested on medical students, then on players in League matches, slow sodium would prove to be an important breakthrough.

In November 1969, Brazil's manager Joo **Saldanha** arrived in Europe on a fact-finding mission. At least, that was the official explanation. The hidden purpose of Saldanha's visit was to mount a sustained campaign of propaganda with the intention of persuading FIFA to curb 'the physical excesses' of European football; in other words, to bring about in time for the World Cup an interpretation of the laws favourable to the South American challengers. A man in his fifties of above medium height and slender in appearance, Saldanha could have started a row in an empty house. In some reports of the time he was loosely described as a journalist whose vehement criticism of the CBD (the Brazil Sports Federation) and the national team had led to his appointment as coach. The CBD were not that daft, though; there was much more to Saldanha. A left-wing activist with a degree in economics from Prague University, his attacks on the state-controlled CBD were fearless sallies on the government itself. As a coach he had won the Rio Championship with Botafogo; as a player he'd turned out against Ramsey when Southampton visited Brazil in 1950. They were about to meet again.

Informed of the statements Saldanha had made, Ramsey thought them insulting and took it personally. 'I don't know this man,' he said. 'What right has he to condemn our way of playing? We do not play in an unfair manner.' Ramsey and Saldanha met for a joint interview with the broadcaster Peter Lorenzo shortly after England defeated the Netherlands 1–0 in Amsterdam. Where Saldanha was relaxed, Ramsey was tense and uncomfortable. He took the bait. 'I don't remember playing against you, and I don't know why I agreed to be here,' he said to Brazil's manager.

Saldanha would not hold that title for long. In turning Brazil around from the disaster of 1966 he'd done a remarkable job, storming through the qualifiers with 22 goals scored and only two against. But even Brazilians who publicly acknowledged the value of Saldanha's groundwork felt the need for a more straightforward, more technical and less volatile manager. A convenient opportunity to remove Saldanha from office arrived fewer than two months before the finals when Brazil lost 2–1 at home to Argentina. Swapping a philosopher for a pragmatist, the CBD appointed Mario Zagallo, the 'Little Ant' of 1958 and 1962. It had become Zagallo's destiny to be the first man to win the World Cup both as player and manager.

In January 1970, England learnt that Brazil would be one of their opponents for the preliminary group in Guadalajara, along with Czechoslovakia and Romania. It was a tough task, but hardly impossible for a team that had lost only four of 34 matches since winning the world championship. With two to qualify it would be difficult to find an excuse if England failed to reach the quarter-finals. Splenetic as ever, Alan Hardaker said on television that it would be a miracle if England won the competition after being given such a tough assignment. But Jack Charlton didn't think the draw was at all bad. 'We should have beaten Brazil in Rio the previous summer, and from what I remembered of our two matches against Romania they weren't up to much. They had some tough customers, a couple of guys who were prepared to put themselves about, but as a team I didn't think they were anything to worry about.'

Now hard-pressed to resist Brian Labone's urgent challenge for the central defensive position, Ramsey included him and Charlton in a pool of 28 players and 14 reserves from whom the final squad of 22 would be selected. Ten players survived from 1966, including Stiles, a contentious choice since he had not turned out in England's colours for more than a year and was still struggling to recover form after a knee operation. 'To think about taking Stiles when he clearly isn't fit will suggest to the football world a policy of intimidation,' one critic wrote. Ramsey's comment was typically cryptic: 'I know no reason for not including Stiles,' he said. 'He is good for the team.' Certainly good enough to book his passage on the evidence of three bitterly contested FA Cup semi-final matches between Manchester United and Leeds that spring.

Leeds eventually won through, but were beaten by Chelsea in a ferocious FA Cup final replay – a Chelsea side without Alan Hudson, who'd been injured a few weeks before. Chosen among England's reserves, Hudson had been on Ramsey's mind for months. Dave Sexton, then Chelsea's manager, said, 'Every time I saw Alf he asked about him. I could only say that Alan was doing everything for us, getting up and down the field, always running at defences, if you like an old-fashioned inside-forward. Then he got injured, which was sad because not only did he miss out on the FA Cup final but probably a place in the World Cup squad.' Sexton's reference to the World Cup was spot on. Before the injury, Ramsey had privately told me, 'Hudson may be the most exciting young English footballer I have seen. There is no limit to what he can achieve. I might take him.' Immediately after the FA Cup final, together with one other reporter I took a late train from

Manchester to London. We came across Hudson sitting by himself. He was philosophical, but it was possible to detect the depth of his disappointment. Perhaps as a result of it, his career stood still. Hudson gained just two England caps, both awarded when he was turning out for Stoke City.

In 1970, Hudson's loss was Peter Osgood's gain. A languid stylist, not Ramsey's type at all, the Chelsea centre-forward was blooded against Belgium on 25 February and included in the squad of 28 that left for South America in early May. Acting on Phillips' well-researched advice, the party spent almost a week in Mexico City, a day for each hour of jet lag, before heading onwards and upwards for warm-up games in Colombia and Ecuador, the capitals of both countries standing higher than the altitude England would have to endure on their return.

No England team had been more scientifically prepared. A careful programme of acclimatisation had been put in place to rationalise fears about playing in thin air, and the use of slow sodium strengthened the players' belief that they could cope with the heat. Why, then, did Bobby Charlton feel a sense of foreboding, even before England ran into the trouble that lay ahead? Quite simply because Ramsey had committed the extraordinary blunder of announcing that England were not only bringing their own rations, but their own bus. As Charlton put it, 'I was sure that all the other European teams made similar arrangements [not buses, though]. The difference was that they kept quiet about it.' Hardly an option for England once the players engaged George Best's agent Ken Stanley to negotiate sponsorship deals with a number of companies, including Findus Foods. Immediately, England became the subject of enraged editorials. Did the English think that Mexico had yet to discover the wheel and the internal combustion engine? If Mexico's water was good enough for the President of the United States on a recent visit, what right had the English to assume that it was teeming with bacteria? 'We were about as popular with the Mexicans as an outbreak of plague,' Charlton added.

Compounding the bad feeling he'd caused a year earlier, Ramsey made no effort at appeasement when dealing with the Mexican press, brushing past the reporters and photographers who besieged England's training sessions. 'I will not accept that I'm being rude,' he snapped when a FIFA official attempted to intervene.

Despite being warned against muggers, pickpockets, con-artists and wandering the streets at night, it was with some relief that England arrived in Bogotá for two games, to be played one after the other on the same day – competitive tests at 8,600 feet which would give an approximate indication of how well the players were adapting. But hardly had they settled into the Tequendama hotel than there was a commotion. A shop assistant accused Bobby Moore of stealing a bracelet from a tiny boutique, Fuego Verde, situated in an arcade near the hotel lobby. Moore, together with Bobby Charlton and Neil Phillips, had already left the shop to sit on a settee when he was accused to his face. Phillips said, 'Bobby denied it, and I went to find Alf who was in the basement of the hotel sorting through the kit. It was strange, really, because something similar happened the night before in Mexico City. A jeweller who came to the hotel offering cut-price watches complained that one had gone missing. I don't know whether Alf believed it or not, but to avoid a scandal he was going to pay for it himself until the players decided to chip in.'

This was how Bobby Charlton remembered the incident in *Bobby Charlton's Most Memorable Matches*: 'After wandering around the hotel we ended up in a tiny shop near the main reception desk. I asked the assistant if I could take a closer look at a necklace that was in a locked cabinet. There were no bracelets. I handed back the necklace, which was very expensive, thousands of pounds, and followed Bob Moore and Doc Phillips out of the shop. We hadn't been sitting on a settee for more than a couple of minutes when the shop assistant appeared and asked Bob to stand up. She spoke in Spanish, and began rummaging beneath the cushions. We didn't understand. Then a man appeared, making a fuss, saying that a bracelet had gone missing from the shop. When Doc Phillips realised what was happening he told us not to move, and went off looking for Alf. They showed up with an interpreter and the hotel manager, who confirmed that Bob Moore was being accused. "Look," I said, "I was in the shop with him and we weren't shown any bracelets." '

Phillips utterly rejects the theory that Moore might have been covering up for another member of the squad. 'Over the years there has been talk of a "third man", but I was the only other person in the shop with Moore and Charlton. When, after his death, the *Daily Mail* serialised a biography of Bobby Moore, the "third man" thing came up again. I wrote to the *Mail*, saying that it was nonsense. All they did was acknowledge my letter.'

Moore's willingly given statement, and the apology both he and Charlton received from the authorities, slowed the impetus of story gathering for those of us outside the England party who had been told of the incident. As Hugh McIlvanney put it in *World Cup '70*: 'Subsequent raucous assertions in some Fleet Street offices that news of the case was suppressed by chauvinistic journalists were touchingly romantic. Those reporters not excused by total ignorance of the incident, and the uninformed were the great majority, realised that there was nothing solid to be printed at that stage, that any attempt to make a story of it would involve jeopardising Moore's reputation on the strength of a complaint the police had still to decide to pursue.'

It was only the beginning of Ramsey's problems. Before England concluded their preparation with another double-header, playing at 9,300 feet in Quito, Ecuador, six players had to be cut from the squad in time for Ramsey to notify FIFA in Mexico of his final 22. Ralph Coates, Brian Kidd, Bob McNab, David Sadler, Peter Shilton and Peter Thompson (for the second time) didn't make it. Their disappointment was heightened by the extraordinary concession Ramsey made to representatives of Sunday newspapers, providing them with embargoed news of the squad so that they could meet deadlines made difficult by an eight-hour time difference. It was given on the strict understanding that the players were not to be approached until Ramsey had informed them himself, but the England manager was seriously compromised when a reporter in the Manchester office of the *Sunday Mirror* telephoned Sadler's wife. The following morning, Sadler confronted Ramsey in the hotel dining room. 'I only had to look at his face to know what had happened,' Ramsey said in retirement. 'He had every right to be angry. I'd been let down over something in which I should never have got involved. Until then I'd never let anything come between me and the players.'

The games in Quito, thankfully, went well. After England's B team beat the Ecuador club champions Liga Deportiva Universitaria 4–1, the A team beat the Ecuador national team 2–0, but they were somewhat discomforted by the severe difficulties of playing so far above sea level. 'Normally, Alan Mullery makes a lot of noise on the field,' Ball said. 'Always shouting. Well, when he tried that out there all that came out was a sort of gurgle and a mouthful of froth. Nobody had enough breath to run, let alone shout. I thought the talk about altitude were crap, me. But I found out different today.'

Ramsey was to find out that he'd made another mistake. Sharing the concern of those of us who felt that it might be asking for trouble to fly back through Bogotá, where the party would have to wait five hours for a Mexico connection, trainer Les Cocker was all for seeking an alternative route. 'I was for that too,' Phillips said, 'but Alf argued that changing our arrangements to avoid Bogotá might suggest that there was something to the bracelet business. Anyway, Bobby Moore didn't voice any concern over going back there.'

Arrangements had been made in Bogotá for the press party to visit a local salt mine – 'perfect for you lot,' Jack Charlton said, chuckling – while the England players killed time watching a film at the Tequendama hotel. In two minds, I made my way there with *Daily Mirror* photographer Monte Fresco, who had mail to collect. On our way out we fell into conversation with Nobby Stiles. 'Why don't you stay here?' he said. 'Watch the film, game of cards, cup of tea – better than the bloody salt mines.' We went to the mine. An hour later, Moore was approached quietly and escorted out of a darkened conference room to be formally charged with the theft of an emerald bracelet from the Fuego Verde boutique.

Assuming that Moore and Ramsey had simply been required to perform some official duty, the England players were not aware of their captain's plight until only Ramsey showed up at the airport. Bobby Charlton recalled, 'Sensing that something was wrong, I went to Alf and said that if Bob was in trouble I ought to stay. I'd been in the shop with him, so maybe I could help. Alf ordered me on to the plane. He had trouble enough without me getting mixed up in it.'

Oblivious to the drama, I settled down in an aisle seat next to Billy Wright, by then a television executive. We'd been airborne for about ten minutes when Neil Phillips came over and whispered the news that Moore was not on board. I turned to see Ramsey sitting stony-faced, staring straight ahead as though seeing nothing and hearing nothing. I could imagine the reaction in the *Mirror* office, in every London newspaper office, when the news of Moore's arrest came out of Bogotá. All their men were airborne, flying away from sensation.

Approaching Panama, the aircraft ran into a violent electric storm that had most of the passengers clinging nervously to their seats.

Ramsey remained impassive; it didn't seem that he'd moved a muscle. At the back, Jeff Astle, a nervous flyer, called for a drink, then another. When we reached Mexico City he had to be helped down the steps of the aircraft, legless. Protectively, Monte Fresco threw a cape over Astle's head and dumped him in a chair, but not quickly enough to thwart an alert Mexican photographer. Published the next day, his picture sat beneath a headline that denounced England as 'drunken pirates'.

Concerned about the effect of Moore's arrest on morale, Ramsey waited anxiously for news from Bogotá, where the England captain had been placed under house detention at the home of a Colombian football official, watched over by two detectives who occasionally joined him in a kick-around with a ball in a yard behind the magistrate's office. Contrary to the supposition that the relationship between Ramsey and Moore was based purely on mutual respect, the warmth of the manager's concern for his captain was unmistakable. 'You won't see a smile on my face until I see Bobby Moore,' he said. 'And I won't feel happy until I find out how he is. This feeling has nothing to do with England and the World Cup. How can I drive the players in these circumstances?'

Support came from an unexpected quarter. Saldanha, who had returned to journalism, vehemently defended Moore in newspaper columns, revealing that his Botafogo team had come under similar suspicions in Colombia. 'The jewellery had been hidden in a drawer,' he said. 'It was an attempt to embarrass us into paying up to avoid a scandal. The allegations against Bobby Moore are disgraceful. This is slander. It is against nature, against football. Moore is an honourable man.'

Denis Follows, who had remained in Bogotá with Dr Andrew Stephen, the FA chairman, reported that Moore was bearing up well, and that inconsistency in the evidence against him was encouraging. Diplomatic pressure was being brought to bear. Three days later, Moore was released pending further investigation and on the understanding that he would report to the Colombian Embassy in London if required to do so. Moore then flew to Mexico City, spending the night at the home of an embassy official, where he was tracked down by Jimmy Greaves, who was competing in the *Daily Mirror*-sponsored World Cup Rally. 'I got in over a wall,' Greaves said.

The following day, Moore rejoined the squad in Guadalajara. Arriving by private plane, he was met at the airport by Ramsey and Harold Shepherdson. Moved by the closest thing to a hug he was ever likely to get from the England manager, Moore was then driven to the Hilton hotel and a warm reception from fellow players. Moore's icy demeanour at a subsequent press conference prompted me to think that nobody in a right mind should fancy the idea of playing against him in the World Cup. Emboldened by Moore's return, Ramsey ended the press conference with this confident assertion: 'England will keep the World Cup. This squad has all the qualities to do it again. Their enthusiasm, confidence, skills and, above all, their peak physical fitness command the respect of the rest of the world. Now, perhaps we'll be allowed to get on with our preparation.'

'It was great to have Bobby Moore back,' Jack Charlton recalled, 'but I never thought for one minute that he wouldn't be with us for the start of the tournament. It didn't really affect us at all because we felt that the charge was a joke.' Bobby Charlton, unsurprisingly, since it could have happened to him, not Moore, disagreed. 'I think it did have an effect,' he said. 'It wasn't that any of us were particularly close to Bobby, but he had an air about him that gave the team confidence. And I wasn't as sure as some of the lads that Bobby would be released in time for the first game. When he walked into the Hilton I was thrilled to bits.'

England's choice of headquarters was again the subject of criticism. Curiously, in view of his unyielding firmness in every matter concerning the players, Ramsey had offered them a choice between staying at a training complex some twenty miles outside the city and the centrally placed Hilton. They chose the latter. 'We felt that to be locked away, hardly seeing any faces other than our own, would drive us round the bend,' Hurst said. 'Not many England supporters travelled in those days, and few could afford Hilton prices. Alf wasn't entirely happy with the arrangement but he went along with it.' Ramsey's instincts were right. The Hilton proved to be a bad call, making England an easy target for local hostility. First, they had to deal with Romania, a team containing enough hard men to suggest they might be prepared to risk FIFA's wrath.

A few weeks before leaving for Mexico I'd met with Dutch referee Leo Horn at his home in Amsterdam. No ally of Sir Stanley Rous, whom he blamed for the fact that he was not given the 1962 World Cup final, Horn feared a repeat of the violence he'd seen in that tournament. 'There is too much politics involved in the appointment of World Cup referees,' he said. 'Rous puts in his own people, men who may not be strong enough to deal with collisions between the European and Latin American temperaments. Unless FIFA is very careful there will be explosions like in Chile.' But Horn had overlooked three factors: altitude, heat, and the possibility that FIFA would set an example when Mexico and the Soviet Union met in the opening game. Indeed, the five cautions, extraordinary at the time, issued by the West German referee Kurt Tschenscher served as a warning to all the participants. That and the enfeebling effects of the conditions would ensure a relatively trouble-free tournament. 'It was daft even to think about playing an aggressive game out there,' Lee confirmed. 'The idea was not to give the ball away so that you didn't waste energy charging around trying to get the ball back. As Alf stressed time and time again, it was vital to keep possession. Despite everything that had gone on, the Bobby Moore business, the hostility, we all felt pretty confident, just wanted to get into that first game and make our mark.'

Doubtless sharing this sentiment, some of the Romanian players applied it literally, especially Mocanu and Dimitru, both of whom committed a series of vicious fouls that might have unnerved players of lesser experience than those Ramsey sent out at the Jalisco Stadium for England's opening match on 2 June. There were no surprises in a line-up that included six men from 1966, all encouraged by a drop in temperature and the promise of rain. With his usual aplomb – he was always a man of few words in the dressing room – Moore led England on to the field. Ball felt more nervous than ever. 'I don't know why, maybe it were the build-up and everything, knowing that the first match is always dangerous, but I just wanted to get a foot on the ball so that I could settle down,' he said.

Chances quickly fell to both sides. Hurst wasted a reasonable opportunity, mishitting a hooked shot as he spun on a low cross from Peters. That was nothing, however, to the alarm caused on England's bench after only five minutes when Dumitrache broke through on the left to fire in a centre that caught Terry Cooper unawares; Dembrowski might have beaten Banks with a header, instead he prodded the ball wide. 'I knew the boss [the Leeds manager Don Revie] was at the game, and I could imagine what he was thinking,' Cooper said. 'He was always at me about cover positions, not being drawn to the ball.'

The first clear hint that Romania were prepared to test FIFA's stern edict on foul play came just before half-time when Dimitru cut down Mullery; Keith Newton was the next victim, fouled so badly by Mocanu that he had to be replaced by Tommy Wright, who became the first substitute to appear for England in a World Cup tie. Wright was no sooner on the field than Lee became Mocanu's next victim, followed by Wright himself. Under the instructions given to referees those fouls should have brought at least a caution, but the referee, Vital Loraux of Belgium, took no action. Perhaps he'd slept through the lecture.

England took revenge where they could. After Lucescu's elbow had rattled his jaw, Mullery went in so hard that the Romanian's boot came off. 'When he stuck his face into mine, swearing, I laughed and said, "When you going home, then? June the fifteenth?" By then, England had taken the lead, Hurst scoring in the 64th minute from a centre by Ball. A quarter of an hour from the end, Osgood came on for Lee.

'Where does Alf want you to play?' Mullery shouted.

'Never mind, this is me in for seventy-five quid from Adidas,' Osgood replied.

Fortunately for Osgood, the remark didn't reach Ramsey's ears.

As the teams left the field, Ball couldn't resist taunting Dumitrache, who'd predicted that he would score two goals against England. 'I went over to him and held up two fingers,' Ball said. ' "Where's your two, then?" I said. "Where are they?" He just shrugged. I can be an irritating little twat, me.'

The next day, England saw vivid proof of Brazil's potential. The defensive flaws Ramsey would remark upon in team talks had to be set against the brilliant attacking surges that brought a 4–1 victory over Czechoslovakia. In midfield, the chain-smoking Gerson looked three times the player he was in 1966, the delicacy of his aerial passing supplemented by a willingness (if provoked) to employ his left foot in less legitimate fashion, and Tosto's confidence had returned with the assurance that an operation to correct a slightly detached retina was a complete success. 'Will Rivelino become a great player?' Pele was asked before the game. 'He already is,' came the reply.

After eleven minutes, Brazil had been a goal down. Petras, in only his second international match, wrongfooted Brito, checked and angled the ball past Felix. In the stands, Phillips nudged Ramsey. 'Yes, doctor, I saw it,' he said. Brazil's equaliser, a stunning free-kick taken by Rivelino, startled the England manager and players as much as it did the Czechs. Approaching the ball at right angles, Rivelino contorted his body to strike a violent left-footed shot straight at Jairzinho, who'd positioned himself on the end of the wall. When Jairzinho dodged out of the way, Viktor could do no better than get a fingertip to the ball on its way into the net. And on the stroke of half-time the crowd watched open-mouthed as Pele's lob from 50 yards out dropped just wide having caught Viktor yards off his line, leaving him to back-pedal like a circus clown teetering towards the end of a plank. Pele's first goal of the tournament came fourteen minutes after the interval when he brought down Gerson's floated pass with his chest for a volleyed finish. Although not totally outplayed, Czechoslovakia could not live with Brazil's virtuosity, which brought them two further goals, both scored by Jairzinho.

A couple of hours after the game, I came across Ramsey at the Hilton. He'd been hugely impressed by Brazil's performance. 'By Christ, these people can play,' he said. And if the thought of coming up against the favourites wasn't enough for England to be going on with, they now found themselves besieged in the Hilton by a coalition of Mexican and Brazilian supporters who kept up a clamour of chanting and drumming throughout the night. Complaints to the police who stood inside the doors of the hotel drew blank stares. Matters came to a head on the Saturday night when a small group of Mexicans managed to penetrate the security and find their way to the twelfth floor, which had been set aside for England's exclusive use. 'It was ridiculous,' Mullery said. 'There we were, about to play one of the most important games of our lives, and people were running around banging on doors in the middle of the night.'

The news that Brazil were not prepared to take a chance with Gerson's troublesome thigh strain brightened bleary eyes. 'Never mind Pele,' Jack Charlton said, 'Gerson's the one who makes them tick. They're going to miss him.' Ramsey, as ever, went over the details. It didn't take much working out that Rivelino would fill

Gerson's role behind the front line with Paulo Cesar coming in on the left. England's only change from the starting line-up against Romania was Wright for Newton, who still hadn't recovered from Mocanu's brutish attentions.

With the mercury climbing towards 100°F, Ramsey spoke of another metal. 'Do you like gold?' he asked the players. (Startled, one or two thought for a moment that Ramsey meant a bonus.) 'Well, think of the ball as gold. Protect it like gold.' This they did for ten minutes, unhurriedly moving the ball around, even creating the glimmer of a chance for Charlton. What happened next has been shown a thousand times. Carlos Alberto fed Jairzinho, who held off Cooper on a stumbling run to the England goal line that looked like taking him out of play; instead, Jairzinho just managed to wrap his right foot around the ball and get it across. Pele's jack-knife jump was perfectly timed, his forehead surely sending the ball in – Mullery heard Pele shout 'Goal!' – only for Banks to make an astonishing save. Was it the best ever? Better than Jim Montgomery's for Sunderland against Leeds in the 1973 FA Cup final? It certainly kept England in a match that thrilled coaches and spectators alike. 'You could take a film of the game and show it, confidently, to every young player in the world,' Bobby Charlton said. 'There is everything in it, all the skills and technique, all the tactical control, the lot. There really was some special stuff played.'

Moore, playing as though his house arrest had been spent on a health farm, was massive. One flawless tackle on Jairzinho in England's penalty area – 'make sure to stay on your feet' – would figure in every coaching video. In training, Moore had come up with an answer to Jairzinho's trick of infiltrating the wall at Rivelino's free-kicks. 'Why don't I just stand behind him?' Moore suggested to Ramsey. When the trick was repeated, Moore cushioned Rivelino's drive, strode forward and clipped a pass upfield to Hurst. Even Zagallo applauded.

When seen on film, the match appears to have a pedestrian tempo, but it didn't seem that way to those who took part. In 1974, I spent a week with Pele in Santos when he was under pressure to appear in a fifth World Cup. 'I have played in many great international matches, but the game against England in 1970 will always stand out,' he said. 'It was never just their defence against our attack. I think they made more chances, and as I said to Bobby

Moore afterwards, England did not deserve to lose. I thought that if we met again in the final it would be a very difficult game for us.'

The only goal came after an hour. Luck was with Tosto when the ball rebounded to him off Moore's shins, wrongfooting Wright. An untidy pass went from Pele wide of Cooper, who had over-covered from the left; Jairzinho strode on to the ball and smashed it past Banks. England, with their vaunted defence, their unbeatable goalkeeper, had fallen behind when on chances they should have been ahead. 'It didn't seem right,' Lee said. 'That game has been on television a few times since [most recently prior to England v. Brazil in the 2002 finals] and I always think what a privilege it was to take part. If you go through the teams, most of the world's best players were on the field that day. The galling thing is that we could have won. I missed a good chance in the first half and we should have equalised late on.'

A big man, good in the air, Astle's inclusion among the substitutes was for just the situation in which England found themselves with less than fifteen minutes to play. 'Get up alongside Geoff and we'll get the ball into you,' Ramsey said as Astle prepared to replace the tiring Lee. Unfortunately for England, the chance came not to Astle's head but his unreliable left foot; the ball scuffed harmlessly past a post. From an equally promising position Ball had the beating of Felix, but he clipped the top of the crossbar.

When Brazil defeated Romania 3–2 three days later, England knew that a draw against Czechoslovakia on 11 June would be enough to see them through. Although assured by Phillips that all those who had turned out against Brazil were fully recovered – Mullery shed nearly a stone – Ramsey decided to make changes, resting Hurst, Ball, Labone and Lee. Lee hadn't got into things, neither had Peters, both at odds with the conditions. England were about to leave the dressing room when Ramsey realised he needed someone to deputise for Hurst as penalty-taker. 'Who fancies it?' he asked. Allan Clarke, who was about to make his international debut, raised a hand. 'I'll have it,' he said. Among the 35,000 spectators who watched Clarke place the ball on the spot three minutes into the second half was his Leeds team-mate Billy Bremner. 'He's millions on,' Bremner remarked. Nerveless, Clarke fired the ball past Viktor. England could now plan for a quarter-final against West Germany in Leon.

The plans were thrown into confusion when, without warning, the Mexican authorities refused England permission to fly into Leon, stating that the runway wasn't long enough to take a large aircraft. Knowing that the Germans had arrived in Leon by air two weeks earlier, Ramsey was furious. 'We suspected that something was going on because the only alternative was to travel by road, a journey of around 170 miles along bumpy roads,' Phillips said. 'There was also the problem of accommodation, which is why Alf decided to send Harold Shepherdson and me ahead of the main party. I told him that I didn't like the idea. My place was with the team. I couldn't be absolutely sure how well the players had come through the game against Brazil and it worried me that Bobby Charlton and Keith Newton had reported sick. It was nothing serious, just a minor stomach upset, but I didn't like the idea of not being with them on that road journey. Gordon Banks shared a room with Bobby and Keith. Gordon said he felt fine. Again, I went to Alf, suggesting that he send one of the FA officials with Harold, but again he insisted on me going. It was one of our few disagreements.'

Phillips and Shepherdson left by car for Leon at four a.m. the next day. Four hours later, Banks went to Ramsey complaining of stomach cramps and nausea. When the main England party arrived in Leon he was put straight to bed. 'I'm pretty sure that if I'd been able to treat him in Guadalajara he would have got over it as quickly as Charlton and Newton did,' Phillips said. 'Now we could only hope that a good sleep would put him right. From the look of him I wasn't all that confident.' Banks improved enough overnight to be put through a light training session by Shepherdson and Cocker, who then reported that the England goalkeeper was fit to take his place in the team. But at a team meeting two hours afterwards, Banks keeled over and was sent back to bed. Still, the idea that Peter Bonetti wasn't alerted until shortly before kick-off against West Germany doesn't meet with Phillips' testimony. 'Peter was told the night before,' Phillips said, 'and it didn't appear to bother him.'

Bonetti was certainly not lacking in confidence. He'd played brilliantly in helping Chelsea win the FA Cup, and had been on the winning side in all his six appearances for England, conceding just one goal. Ramsey retained some doubts – he wasn't aware that

Bonetti had been making clandestine visits to check up on goings-on at the Camino Real hotel in Guadalajara where his wife was staying, along with the wives of Moore, Hurst and Peters – and Cocker's preference was for the third goalkeeper, Alex Stepney. But Bonetti it was.

In the eyes of the England outfield players, Banks was more than just a great goalkeeper. 'He filled us with confidence,' Charlton said. 'I used to watch him in training and think that he was almost unbeatable. The save from Pele was just the sort of thing he could do. Inspirational. It still amazes me to think that Gordon never played for one of our bigger clubs because he must have been worth at least twelve points a season.' In *Bobby Charlton's Most Memorable Matches*, he wrote, 'No disrespect to Peter Bonetti, but we wouldn't have lost to the Germans if Gordon had been fit to play. Banks was Banks. Exceptional.'

For an hour it looked as though Banks would merely be resting up for the semi-finals, England at last looking like world champions, their passing precise, their support play of the highest standard. Having the game of his life, Mullery started and finished the first goal. After playing a one-two with Lee, he passed to the overlapping Newton, ran forward for the return and swept the ball past Sepp Maier. The Germans had been hit from an unexpected quarter. 'In going over the England players we had not considered Mullery as a possible goalscorer,' Helmut Schoen would tell me years later. 'Hurst, Charlton, Lee, Peters yes, but Mullery was the defensive midfielder. In 28 matches for England he'd never scored!' The conditions in Mexico seemed to have seriously reduced Peters' effectiveness. The intelligently applied mobility Ramsey admired was lost in vagueness, but his first notable contribution looked decisive. Newton advanced along the left wing; Peters donned his shroud. Before Maier could move to the cross, Peters appeared from nowhere to flick the ball off the German goalkeeper's toes. England two up.

In each of West Germany's group games Schoen had sent on a fresh right-winger, Jurgen Grabowski, in the second half, mainly to spare Libuda. This time Grabowski's entry was a desperate measure. 'I'd be lying if I said that we'd spotted a weakness in England's defence,' Schoen said. 'It was simply a case of trying something different because we weren't making any headway. Grabowski had done well against tiring defences in the earlier games and maybe

Cooper had spent himself dealing with Libuda. Grabowski was sent out with orders to run at the left side of England's defence.'

Alarmed though he was by the possible effects of Grabowski's directness, Ramsey had already decided to bring off Charlton, saving him for the-semi finals three days ahead. Colin Bell was about to come on for a player making his 106th appearance for England when Beckenbauer left Charlton's side for almost the first time in the match. Sauntering forward, he tried a shot that felled Lee, took the rebound and worked the ball to his right, a move Ramsey had warned against; Bonetti had the shot covered, but he went down late and allowed the ball to pass underneath him. As Charlton reached the touchline, puzzled by his withdrawal, he turned to Ramsey and said, 'We're pissing about.'

Bell's introduction raised England's tempo, and it was his urgent thrust along the German left flank with twelve minutes to go that should have settled the issue beyond doubt. Meeting Bell's centre in front of the near post, his run made to perfection, Hurst glanced the ball across Maier towards an empty net; taking a bounce, it flew inches wide. Lee, who had followed up, held his head in his hands. 'I was so sure the ball was in that I checked my stride,' he said. 'If I'd kept going I could have tapped in. The game would have been over.'

When Gerd Muller threatened for the first time, getting round Newton to test Bonetti from a narrow angle, Ramsey replaced Peters with Norman Hunter. At the sight of Hunter coming on, Jack Charlton made his way out of the stadium. 'Nothing against Norman,' he said, 'but it seemed like an omen. I felt that anybody connected with Leeds United that year was cursed. We'd been the best team in the championship but had finished second. We'd outplayed Chelsea at Wembley in the FA Cup final, then lost the replay. I just knew things would go wrong for England. When I heard a big roar I didn't have to be told that Germany had equalised.' With just eleven minutes left, Labone's untidy clearance had gone to Schnellinger who'd sent the ball back to where Mullery was marking Uwe Seeler; both misjudged the flight, but Seeler got a touch with the back of his head that left Bonetti flailing in no-man's land.

England continued to press forward in extra-time, Hurst getting the ball into the net only for it to be mysteriously disallowed. With eleven minutes left on the clock, Jack Charlton arrived back in his seat in time to see West Germany go in front. Lohr headed across goal, Labone and Moore were out of position, but not Muller. Unchallenged by a transfixed Bonetti, the German leapt, twisted and volleyed into the roof of England's net. All as Jack Charlton had feared.

Two hours after the game I finally tracked Ramsey down in a small chalet at the motel England had occupied since their arrival in Leon. Alone but for Cyril Broderick, a Thomas Cook travel agent who had been seconded to the FA, he sat amid the debris of disappointment: scattered kit, discarded notes, empty champagne bottles. Broderick, slightly drunk and dressed in an England tracksuit, stood beneath a gushing shower. Ramsey looked up. I couldn't think of anything to say, nothing that would have made any sense.

'Do you want a drink?' he asked.

I nodded.

'Pour it yourself,' he replied, handing over a bottle.

'You were so close,' I said. 'You had it won, outplayed them, and . . .'

Ramsey didn't hear a word. He took a sip from a glass and said, 'I still can't believe it. Of all the players to lose, it had to be him.'

Drained by the cumulative effects of altitude, heat and their efforts against England, the Germans fell to Italy in a farcical semi-final that was more Marx Brothers football than the classic it has been ludicrously rated. Classic is a word that should be reserved for Brazil's performance in the final. Winners over Italy by four goals to one, they went into the history books as the best ever. 'What did you learn from Brazil?' Ramsey was asked on his return to London. 'Nothing,' he replied. A mite clumsily, he was stating the truth. How could anyone hope to match such virtuosity?

On the flight home, Ramsey slipped into a seat alongside Bobby Charlton. 'I want to apologise for taking you off,' he said. 'I was thinking about the next match. That was a mistake I shall always regret. Now I'd like to thank you for all that you have done for me and England.'

When England's next team was announced in November, Charlton's name was missing.

'Did Alf call to tell you?' he was asked.

'Didn't have to,' Charlton replied. 'I knew three months ago, on the way home from Mexico.'

8. 1970 TO 1974

Following a meeting of the FA Senior International Committee in October 1970 a statement was minuted expressing confidence in Ramsey and thanking him for his efforts. It was timely, for England would not have a free passage to the next finals for the first time in twelve years. Given the luxury of being in a three-nation group with Poland and Wales – one to qualify – it was a challenge for which Ramsey had two years to prepare.

First there was the European Championship, now growing in importance, and at the very least an opportunity for team building around the survivors from Leon. Of the side that defeated East Germany in a friendly at Wembley in November 1970, Cooper, Mullery, Moore, Hurst and Peters would be past 30 when the 1974 finals came around, a point that wasn't missed by the critics. 'Now, not next year or the year after, is the time to look at fresh faces,' Frank McGhee wrote in the *Sunday Mirror*. But Ramsey wavered. Above all, he had to win games. 'I'm not allowed to experiment,' he complained. 'Every time England play we are expected to win, even against the strongest opposition. I know from experience that it is a big jump from club to international football but I'm always being told to select people who aren't up to standard.'

None of the newcomers promised more than Derby County centre-half Roy McFarland, who had benefited a great deal from playing alongside former Tottenham hero Dave Mackay, later to succeed Brian Clough as the Derby manager. McFarland made his international debut in February 1971 against Malta, a match Moore missed as the result of a suspension imposed by West Ham after he and Greaves were involved in a late-night drinking session on the eve of an FA Cup tie at Blackpool. It was McFarland's absence from the first of two qualifying matches against West Germany in the spring of 1972 that caused Ramsey to accuse Clough of undermining the England team. Having comfortably seen off Malta, Greece and Switzerland, winning five and drawing one of the six matches, England met West Germany at Wembley on Saturday 29 April (the First Division programme was suspended). Three days beforehand Clough had withdrawn McFarland on the grounds of an injury, but

48 hours after England's 3–1 defeat McFarland turned out for Derby in a game vital to the outcome of the League Championship. Clough was unrepentant, stating that McFarland could not possibly have played for England and was only able to play for Derby after intense treatment. 'This man calls himself a patriot, but he has never done anything to help England,' Ramsey snapped. 'All he does is criticise us in newspapers and on television.'

And there was no shortage of criticism. England had not merely been defeated, they'd been taken apart by Gunther Netzer who was at the zenith of his career, albeit only a brief one: he would play only 45 minutes of World Cup football, against East Germany in the 1974 finals. Netzer had first come to Ramsey's attention during England's preparation for a qualifying match against Greece. We were watching a European Cup tie on television together when he stepped forward to take a closer look. 'This is an excellent player,' he said, speaking of Netzer. 'I shall have to find out more about him.'

Still, the Germans had arrived at Wembley with no great confidence. They had not played well since Mexico and had been jeered when held to a goalless draw by Poland. In addition, a bribery scandal in the Bundesliga had left Helmut Schoen without three regular members of his squad. 'We were very nervous in the dressing room,' Beckenbauer recalled. 'Helmut told us not to forget the victory in Leon. But we all knew there was a lot of luck attached to that. England didn't often lose at home and if we no longer had to worry about Bobby Charlton they still had Bobby Moore and Gordon Banks. I felt we were capable of winning but that it would be a hard fight.' Beckenbauer was by now being deployed in the role that would mark him out as one of the game's truly great players. As cover for the team's markers, his duties were not exclusively defensive as his predecessor Schulz's had been. He had licence to break out, using his change of pace and passing skills to link with the midfielders or to open up play. 'After the 1970 World Cup I decided that we needed to take a step forward,' Schoen told me. 'Having a player such as Franz was an enormous advantage. He had outstanding positional sense, could tackle when necessary and always had attacking possibilities in his head.'

To cope with McFarland's absence Ramsey brought in Norman Hunter to play alongside Moore as the central defender – hardly ideal, since it was not a role with which the Leeds man was familiar.

It was loose thinking to suppose that West Germany won the game simply because they were technically superior; England were also second best in the brains department. Operating in an advanced midfield position from where he could quickly link with the German strikers, Netzer caused so much damage that Hunter asked Moore to swap positions. 'Let me have a chance to get at the bastard,' he pleaded. Despite suggestions to the contrary, there was a limit to Moore's authority as captain. Never did he countermand the manager's orders. 'This is the way Alf wants it, and that's how it's got to be,' Moore said.

Netzer's inconsistency in the lead-up to the match is the only possible explanation for his exclusion from Ramsey's team talks; Francis Lee certainly didn't remember his name being mentioned. 'It was easy to make a mistake with him,' Schoen said. 'Netzer was an enigma. All seemed to depend on his mood. He could be brilliant one day, anonymous the next. Against Poland, our last match before we played England, he did very little. It was taking a chance to play him at Wembley, but he tore England apart. Afterwards he did very well. But when it came to a choice between him and Overath, I went with Overath, who was much more reliable.'

Level 1–1 at the interval – Lee had cancelled out a goal by Hoeness – England never looked like winners, although Lee thought the post-match reports misleading. 'The Germans scored three excellent goals,' he said, 'but even when they got their third I didn't think we were completely out of it. The performance wasn't as bad as most of the newspapers made out. But you're always going to get that when things don't go England's way at home. I've seen ordinary teams come here just for a draw in a friendly match, everybody back behind the ball, and if England can't get through they are written off.'

Lee had reached the end of his international career, and he was dropped for the second leg in Berlin a few weeks later. Ramsey, too, was running near the edge. At last finding space for sport on its back page, the *Daily Mirror* demanded an influx of youth – either that or the manager's head. Schoen awaited the announcement of England's team with more than normal interest.

'Do you think Ramsey will be influenced by public opinion?' he asked me.

'No chance,' I replied.

'For us, that is a shame,' he said.

'A shame?'

'Yes, because if he sent out an inexperienced team we would score five or six goals.'

The inclusion of the Arsenal hard man Peter Storey alongside Hunter in England's midfield brought a howl of protest as the move implied that Ramsey's sole objective was to save face. Angered to the point of almost storming out of the press conference on the eve of the game, Ramsey said, tersely, 'I have never selected an England team for any purpose other than to win. To suggest otherwise insults me, the England players and the Football Association.' Neil Phillips had never seen Ramsey in such a mood. 'It was an extremely difficult time for Alf,' he said. 'Most of the old guard, players who had been with him for six years, had gone and I think he realised that English football was on a downturn. The attitude of players throughout the League was changing. A lot of them had picked up on the showbiz thing and were therefore harder to discipline.' In a newspaper interview, Joe Mercer made the point that the longer a manager stays in charge of a club the further he grows away from the players. 'You suddenly realise that you're dealing with players 30 years your junior. How can you hope to understand them? They have different values, an entirely different lifestyle.' This applied as much to Ramsey as any club manager.

If England were going to turn things around in Berlin, they needed luck. With fifteen minutes played, from a corner forced on the right, the ball dropped to McFarland. He shot wide. Unwilling to put their two-goal advantage at risk, the Germans settled into possession football. 'I could understand the way England went about things,' Schoen remarked later. 'If they'd attacked us from the start they might have got a goal, but so would we. All England could do was hang on and hope to get back into the tie. My orders were not to take chances.' The goalless draw increased the pressure on Ramsey, and now it wasn't only the manager who was at odds with the press. The players closed ranks, refusing to speak with reporters at the airport; upset by personal slights, Storey had to be pulled from an angry confrontation with the most caustic of his critics.

West Germany went on to win the 1972 European Championship, beating the Soviet Union 3–0; Ramsey was left to concentrate on qualification for the World Cup finals, a novel experience. It appeared that England had been well treated, given the advantage of a three- rather than a four-nation group. No one imagined that even a troubled England would fail to get past two unseeded teams, Wales and Poland, but problems continued to materialise. In September 1972, the Football League launched an inquiry into newspaper allegations that attempts had been made to bribe Wolverhampton players before the final League game of the previous season, one which Leeds needed to win or draw in order to land the League Championship two days after winning the FA Cup final. Leeds lost the game 2–1. The *Sunday People* named four players, two of whom, David Wagstaffe and Frank Munro, confirmed that they were approached; the others denied it. Wagstaffe said, 'I know from talking to team-mates and from my own experience that offers were made to try and get us to throw the game. In fact, on the day of the match, the manager [Bill McGarry] warned that there might be money flashing about, and to be careful about any approaches made to us. During the match, someone shouted to me to take it easy, indicating that there would be something in it for me if I did. I'm certain it wasn't a joke. It happened a number of times.' Wagstaffe added that he'd discovered approaches had been made to two other Wolves players. 'Frank [Munro] told me he'd been made an offer before and during the game, asking him to throw it for a large sum. He was asked to give away a penalty.' McGarry said that no player had complained to him, and he had heard no talk about bribes. Then why had he warned the players? 'I suppose football managers are sometimes psychic,' he replied.

While the Football League pursued its enquiries into an affair that eventually cost the *Daily Mirror* a large sum in damages, Ramsey received a shattering blow. In October, a month before England played Wales in Cardiff in the first of their qualifying matches, Gordon Banks was involved in a car crash that cost him his sight in one eye. At 34, a third World Cup had been well within Banks's compass, but the accident ended his top-class career. Ramsey could only think of the words he had muttered to himself in Leon: 'Of all the players to lose . . .'

Wales were under the tutelage of Dave Bowen, whose day job was general manager and secretary of Northampton Town, a club struggling for existence in the Fourth Division. Formerly Arsenal's captain, Bowen had led Wales in the 1958 World Cup, their only appearance in the finals. If his resources were slim, his passion was boundless. 'Of course, I shan't say this to our players, but looking at the game coldly I wouldn't back Wales with washers,' he said, 'not unless I can rekindle the spirit of Welsh football. For too long, it seems, I've been looking at England and admiring their qualities. The skill. The composure. The organisation. Well, we haven't many players to call on but some of them – Mike England [Tottenham], John Toshack [Liverpool], Terry Hennessey [Derby], Gary Sprake [Leeds], John Roberts [Arsenal] – are used to the big stuff. Given the emotion of a big game I think we've got an outside chance.'

Ramsey's team talk was uncommonly blunt. 'We'll get nothing here without a fight,' he said. Les Cocker did indeed brandish a fist at Rodney Marsh, the meaning unmistakable. Only Moore, Ball, Bell and Hunter survived from the Mexico contingent, and it was Bell's all-round skills and seemingly inexhaustible energy that gave Ramsey fresh heart. For once, he even found himself in agreement with Malcolm Allison: Bell was a class act, and the expected slog didn't materialise. In keeping with their dismal record of having beaten England only once since the war, Wales were a huge disappointment, most of the game's incidents taking place in their own penalty area. One goal, neatly turned in by Bell, was enough. Kevin Keegan had done little on his international debut; the fastest Tottenham player over 100 yards, Martin Chivers, again made Bill Nicholson wonder whether he'd signed the right man from Southampton.

When the two nations met in the return match ten weeks later, few gave Wales a chance. Crippled by injuries and withdrawals, Bowen's team included three First Division reserves, three players from the Second Division and one from the Third. 'We're on a wing and a prayer,' Bowen remarked. With 23 minutes played the Burnley winger Leighton James sent in a low centre and Toshack answered the prayer. Hunter's equaliser four minutes before the interval spared England a slow handclap, but the relief was temporary. As Ramsey trudged to the dressing room at full time rhythmic derision rang in his ears. In some assessments of England's failure to qualify for the 1974 finals the loss of this home point to Wales is seen as critical, but, as the final table shows, even had England put four unanswered goals past the Welsh they would still have needed an outright victory in the final game against Poland.

That need became apparent on 6 June 1973 when England met Poland in Katowice as part of a four-game summer tour. Following a 2–0 defeat by Wales in Cardiff, the Poles knew they would be eliminated unless they could beat a team that had lost only two of 23 matches played since Mexico, won the British International Championship with a 100 per cent record, and were coming off a 1–1 draw with future European champions Czechoslovakia. Ramsey went for as much experience as he could muster. Martin Peters was recalled to the left side of midfield, Paul Madeley to right-back, and Storey anchored the centre. Deciding that Keegan lacked the maturity for a game of such importance – 'I don't think Alf ever saw me as his type of player,' Keegan would remark – Ramsey brought in Allan Clarke to partner Chivers in attack. England, however, displayed little of the conviction that had marked their visit to the Silesian coalfield shortly before the 1966 finals; instead, it was possible to sense an anxiety that Alan Ball, by then a 64-cap veteran, found difficult to explain. 'It wasn't as though that one match counted for everything,' he said, 'but somehow, I didn't feel the old confidence.'

England could have made a worse start, but not by much. After just seven minutes Gadocha swung in a free-kick that found its way into England's net off Moore and Shilton. Watching the match on television back home, George Cohen threw his arms up in despair. 'It was so untypical of a Ramsey team,' he said. 'Alf was a stickler for dead-ball situations. We used to go over them time and time again. I think the only goal scored against us from a free-kick during my time in the team was in the final. And that was unlucky. England just weren't organised to deal with that one in Poland.' Moore called for calm. 'Settle them down!' he shouted, first to Peters, then to Ball. 'There's plenty of time.' England used it well, mounting a series of attacks that had Poland's defence at full stretch. 'People forget how much we saw of the ball in that game,' Chivers pointed out. 'They only think about the result. In fact we had almost as much of the game as we did in the return at Wembley. Trouble was that we couldn't get through. They had this giant centre-back, Gorgon, and he got to most of the high balls. Still, we should have scored. When a ball came to me in the penalty area, I thought, "This is it!" But the ball skimmed the bar.'

Within two minutes of the restart Moore made an error that would haunt him in the months ahead and remind Ramsey of how much Jack Charlton had contributed to the 1966 triumph. 'One of the reasons I've picked you is that you don't mess about,' Ramsey had told the Leeds centre-half. 'I know that if Bobby Moore dwells on the ball you will step in and cover for him.' Moore and McFarland, however, were out of the same pod, footballing centre-halves. When Moore gathered the ball on the halfway line, McFarland held a position to the right of England's captain. The back line was flat. Immediately, Lubanski, the fastest man on the field, closed Moore down. In trying to sidestep the threat, Moore stumbled. Lubanski whipped the ball away and set off like a startled hare. His low, hard shot went in off the base of Shilton's left-hand post. 'We'd been caught so square that nobody had a chance of getting back at him,' Emlyn Hughes said. 'It was a sickener.'

As England's frustration grew, their tempers shortened. With fifteen minutes left, Peters reacted angrily in a tangle with Cmikiewicz; after eight trouble-free years of international football, Ball foolishly intervened, taking the Pole by the throat and jerking a knee towards his groin. The Austrian referee, Paul Schiller, had no option but to dismiss Ball for violent conduct, thus ensuring that he would miss the return at Wembley.

A few hours afterwards, a group of players were chatting in the room shared by Moore and Ball when Ramsey appeared in the doorway. He accepted a beer from Moore and sat down. 'The first goal was my fault,' he said. 'I should have made sure that somebody filled the space in front of the near post.' Moore and McFarland felt that they should have organised quicker, but as Ramsey rose to leave, he repeated, 'It was still my fault.'

England completed that summer tour with a 2–0 victory in Moscow and a 2–1 loss in Turin – in the circumstances, meaningless results. Ramsey left for a holiday in Cyprus where he would reflect on the fact that England's qualifying group was now wide open, much depending on the outcome of Wales's visit to Katowice in September. If Bowen's team succeeded where Ramsey's had failed, England would be left needing to overwhelm the Poles by four goals to be sure of qualifying.

From within the FA at this time came rumours that Ramsey was unlikely to keep his job if England failed to reach the 1974 finals. Having made enemies from the start, he was now, it seemed, the subject of a conspiracy led by the chairman, Sir Harold Thompson. While the conspirators covertly sharpened their claws – 'I don't think Alf ever realised that people at the FA were out to get him,' Allen

Wade said – on 26 September at Wembley Ramsey was given a lift when England, with Moore on the sidelines, romped to a 7–0 victory over Austria. That same night I watched Wales blow their chances in Katowice, losing 3–0 in a vicious match that saw Trevor Hockey sent off. Wales had hoped to unsettle the Poles with passionate football, as they'd done in Cardiff, but the Poles were a different proposition on their own turf. At the final whistle, Terry Yorath looked up at the scoreboard. 'There it goes, boys,' he said. 'As close to the bloody World Cup finals as I'm ever going to get. All over. Finished. Done with.'

As though itself eager to bring about Ramsey's downfall, the Football League refused to cancel the domestic programme on 13 October, the Saturday prior to the crucial Poland match, a decision accompanied by another crass remark from secretary Alan Hardaker: 'If England do lose the game this country is not going to die. It will be a big thing for six weeks, and then everybody will forget about it.' Ramsey himself focused on travelling to Rotterdam to watch Poland play a warm-up game against the Netherlands. I made arrangements to travel with him from Manchester. He had left behind him at the Lilleshall training centre something of an injury crisis. 'Until the players report back to me on Monday, fit or otherwise, I will have no clear idea of the team,' he said to me. On the short flight to Amsterdam, then during a road journey of about 40 minutes, Ramsey became reflective. He had been in the job for more than ten years, had won a World Cup and, by his own estimate, should have at least reached the final of another. 'I have been through all the emotional hazards that go with this job,' he said. 'I've known success and failure, elation and disappointment. When England wins, everything belongs, quite rightly, to the players. They are the people who have made victory possible. When England loses, it is my responsibility. But football management is a double-edged thing. On the one hand, the manager gets too much credit; on the other, he takes too much of the blame.

'I've never looked for praise,' he continued. 'It makes me uncomfortable. But I know what it is to be depressed. I've never said this before to anyone other than my wife, but when England lost to West Germany in Mexico, I think I lost fifteen years of my life in one afternoon. Physically and mentally, I was shattered, although I couldn't show that to the players. I had to force myself to

JULES RIMET STILL GLEAMING?

congratulate the manager of the German team, Helmut Schoen. Our dressing room was like a morgue. My job was to console the players. I remember Jack Charlton telling me to let myself go. Show some emotion. But it wasn't in me to do that.'

In the tabloids and the broadsheets, on television and radio, Ramsey was seen as an obsessive who seldom let slip the mask of an assumed personality. He had no more consistent a critic than Clough, whose feat of winning the League Championship with Derby while regularly voicing provocative views on television had made him the popular alternative to Ramsey as England manager. As the tension mounted that autumn, Clough argued that no sympathy could be given to Ramsey if he was incapable of producing a consistently successful side from a pool of more than 2,000 players at work in the Football League. It was a typically glib and probably mischievous comment, ignoring among other issues the fact that the League supplied men to the national teams of all four home countries as well as the Republic of Ireland. An hour with the *Rothmans Football Yearbook* would have been enough to expose Clough's assertion as nonsense. Concentrating for obvious reasons on the First Division, once you'd ruled out the Scots, Welsh and Irish players, plus others from outside the British Isles, you had to cull former internationals who had waned, failed candidates and those who were clearly not up to standard – by far the largest group. By my reckoning, in 1973 some 34 genuine contenders survived. 'Three more than I make it,' Ramsey said, caustically.

Of all the appointments in sport, few carry such an overwhelming sense of national responsibility as being manager of England. 'I have never shirked from that responsibility,' Ramsey stated. 'Being the England manager will never make me a rich man, but I can think of no greater honour. Is it wrong of me to expect people to acknowledge that, instead of insulting me with the suggestion that my motives are selfish?' Bobby Charlton, who had won 40 of his 106 caps under Ramsey, could see no justification for that charge. 'I thought he might suppress initiative and flair, but that was never the case,' Charlton said. 'Alf never told anyone how to play for England. It was all about selection. Once he settled on a system he chose people who could make it work simply by playing their normal game. By establishing a mobile bulwark in midfield, Alf more than anyone influenced the way football developed in England, but he cannot be held responsible for the follies of his imitators. I'm sure if he'd been allowed to carry on he would have come up with something different.'

Ramsey gained little from his journey to Rotterdam. Taking no risks with injuries, Poland played out a genteel 1–1 draw. Lato, who had not played in Katowice, showed himself to be a dangerous outside-right, but the Polish defence looked uncomfortable under aerial attack and Jan Tomaszewski's goalkeeping was erratic. 'Some of the Polish players weren't even jumping for the ball,' Ramsey said.

The Wednesday of the following week brought scenes not witnessed at Wembley since the 1966 World Cup final. On entering the stadium, Vic Ziegel of the *New York Post* stood open-mouthed. 'In all my years of covering sport I had never seen or heard anything to compare with that experience,' he would write later. 'It was a statement of nationalism beyond anything I'd known, and few American sports watchers would have understood.' Free of injury worries at last, Ramsey chose the team that had pulverised Austria. Moore remained among the substitutes, having fallen out of favour at West Ham. To England's relief, Lubanski was ruled out by an injury.

On television, Clough proffered the opinion that England had nothing to fear. With very little to go on, he dismissed Tomaszewski as a 'clown'. Every clown has his day, though, and 17 October 1973 was Tomaszewski's. Some of his stops defied description, just flurries of arms and legs. In quick succession, he got to Bell's low drive, Clarke's point-blank header and a shot from Mick Channon that left the Southampton forward's right boot with 'goal' written all over it. 'I would have put the mortgage on any horse he fancied,' Channon quipped. By half-time, England had notched up fifteen goal attempts to Poland's one. 'Just keep playing as you are and the goals will come,' Ramsey said. Better if he'd told his midfielders not to crowd the strikers, the strikers not to snatch at chances.

When Hunter moved to close down Lato on the touchline, near halfway, it was widely assumed that the Polish winger would end up in a seat he hadn't paid for. Ball, or ball and man – either way Hunter was an odds-on favourite. 'To this day I don't know why, but I tried to nick it instead of going through with the tackle,' he said. Watching the match on television, Jack Charlton was astonished. 'I'd seen Norman in that sort of situation dozens of times. I'm looking at it, thinking, "Here we go – bang!" Then Norman's gone in on the wrong side and this little bald Pole is off at our goal.' Drawing McFarland out from the undermanned defence, Lato skimmed a pass to Domarski who was supporting from the right. Domarski's scuffed shot passed through the lunging legs of Hughes and beneath Shilton's dive in an almost mirror image of Bonetti's error in Leon.

Now needing two goals, England renewed the bombardment and drew level within six minutes, Clarke coolly converting a penalty given for a foul on Peters. On the touchline, Moore grew anxious, urging Ramsey to make a substitution. With less than three minutes remaining Kevin Hector scampered from the bench, almost saving the day with a header from England's 23rd corner of the match that was kneed off the line to Clarke, who stabbed the ball wide. To the unconcealed satisfaction of the Scots, who qualified for the first time in sixteen years, England were on their way out of the World Cup.

Inevitably, Ramsey came under heavy fire. The failure to win their group was traced to his 'inflexibility', his rigid adherence to a collective method that 'didn't allow for initiative and flair'. Some of the criticism was valid, but much of it was as clichéd as Ramsey's football was now thought to be. 'I felt really sorry for Alf,' Dave Sexton recalled. 'England were not up against a mug team. Poland were the Olympic champions [and they went on to beat Brazil and gain third place in the finals, won by the hosts West Germany], yet on another day Alf's team might have scored five or six goals. It was just one of those days. How often does a manager come off the field thinking, "How the hell did that happen?" Most everything works, but you can't get the ball into the net. It's happened to all of us.'

Even when alerted to Sir Harold Thompson's next move, the appointment of an FA subcommittee to consider future policy, Ramsey saw no danger. 'Alf was such a proud and honourable man I'm sure it never crossed his mind that the FA would dump him,' George Cohen said. 'Not long after Alf left the England job he was sounded out by Arsenal. His answer was that Arsenal had a manager, Bertie Mee. That's the sort of person he was.' A month after that World Cup exit Ramsey was at the helm as normal for a friendly against Italy at Wembley. He brought back Moore to play as a full-blown sweeper, but the experiment, long overdue, failed and England lost by the only goal.

When the FA subcommittee of Bert Millichip, Brian Mears, Dr Andrew Stephen and Len Shipman met under Thompson's leadership in February 1974 it at last became clear to Ramsey that his days were numbered. In April, ten days after a goalless draw in Portugal, he was summoned to Lancaster Gate to hear the findings of Thompson's men, 'a unanimous recommendation that Sir Alfred Ramsey should be replaced as England team manager'. Ramsey was devastated, and some of the subcommittee members were unable to look him in the face. 'I'd never been deliberately rude to any of them,' he said, 'but they made me feel like a man in the dock waiting to be sentenced. They didn't even have the guts to say why I had been sacked.' It later became clear that the decision had not at first been unanimous. 'I'm ashamed to say that I allowed myself to be forced into it,' Mears revealed. 'I left that room thinking that I'd done a wicked thing. I've never forgiven myself.' Ramsey would be awarded a paltry severance payment of around £8,000 and a meagre pension.

After securing the FA's agreement not to announce the decision until he was out of reach, Ramsey telephoned his wife before going home by the usual route: underground to Liverpool Street station, train to Ipswich. 'People who recognised me were invariably courteous,' he remembered. 'They'd nod, or smile, wish me good luck. I wondered what they'd say if I replied, "Thank you, but I've just been sacked." ' At Liverpool Street Ramsey met up by chance with Ted Phillips, a key figure in his old Ipswich team. 'We hadn't seen each other for a while, and he insisted on buying me a drink,' Phillips recalled. 'Alf came back with large whiskies, which I found odd for someone who normally took a beer or a gin and tonic. I left the train at Colchester. It wasn't until a couple of weeks later that I realised I'd been with Alf on the day he was fired. He never gave a hint of it.'

Two days after the announcement of Ramsey's dismissal, Liverpool and Newcastle met in the FA Cup final. Among those presented to the teams was Ted Croker, a former Charlton player and RAF officer who had succeeded Denis Follows as secretary of the Football Association. When Croker paused to speak with Emlyn Hughes, he heard him say, 'What have you done to Alf?'

9. 1974 TO SPAIN 1982

Engineered by Croker, the impending appointment of Don Revie as Ramsey's successor was the worst kept secret in English football. Despite repeated denials, preliminary negotiations were already under way in the early summer of 1974 when Joe Mercer was made caretaker manager for matches in the British Championship and tour games against East Germany, Bulgaria and Yugoslavia.

The choice of Mercer was a popular one. Easy in his press relations, Mercer's successful career as player and manager spanned almost four decades. 'Joe thought it was the loveliest thing that had ever happened to him in the game,' Mercer's widow, Norah, told me. 'To get that honour just when he was coming up to retirement was wonderful. Even if it was only going to be for a short time, he was at the centre of English football.' Soon, however, Mercer found himself dealing with an incident that would not have developed under Ramsey's firmer control. 'Joe wasn't going to be around long enough to get any benefit from laying down hard rules,' Neil Phillips said. 'But it worried me that the atmosphere was becoming too relaxed. Alf had always insisted on the players being smartly turned out when we travelled; now they were travelling in jeans and T-shirts. We'd kept a careful watch on drinking, but that had also gone by the board. I'd already informed the FA that Alf's dismissal had made it impossible for me to carry on as team doctor, so I was hardly in a position to interfere. Les [Cocker] didn't know where he stood. If Revie didn't get the job, Les would be out.' It had been Ramsey's habit, for instance, to stand over the players while they passed through immigration. When England arrived in Belgrade in early June they straggled through without supervision. The Liverpool trio Kevin Keegan, Emlyn Hughes and Alex Lindsay were first into the baggage hall, where Lindsay leapt on to the carousel. Grabbing the nearest man to him, a guard bustled Keegan into an office where he was held for more than two hours. 'I know we had the business with Astle in Mexico, but that was due to unusual circumstances. What happened to Keegan, who actually hadn't done anything, simply wouldn't have happened under Alf. It proved, and it's been proved many times since, that footballers cannot always be trusted to behave themselves.'

Mercer was able to look back with satisfaction on his brief period in office: he lost only one of seven matches while encouraging a style that was easier on the eye. Privately, however, he feared that English football was about to enter a barren period. When looked at closely, the performances in eastern Europe were not what they seemed. A 1–1 draw against East Germany, a 1–0 win over Bulgaria and a 2–2 draw in Yugoslavia looked fine on England's record, but those results had been achieved against teams unwilling to risk injuries so close to the World Cup finals.

For Leeds United supporters, 'The Revie Years' mean a period of achievement unmatched in the club's history. For England, the phrase came to have a rather different meaning, one of disappointment, uncertainty, even betrayal. Leaving aside the public support for Clough – who lasted only 44 days as Revie's successor at Elland Road, ousted by player power – Revie had no serious rival for the England job in the summer of 1974. Unloved as they were, Leeds had not finished lower than fourth in the First Division since winning promotion in 1964. Champions in 1969 and 1974, they'd finished runners-up five times, and had won the FA Cup, the Football League Cup and a number of European trophies.

Named as England manager in time to make an official appearance at the World Cup final in July, Revie's first move was to summon more than 40 players to a meeting in Manchester; his next, with Croker's enthusiastic support, was to pull together a kit sponsorship deal that gave new meaning to the phrase 'turning out in England's colours'. 'Pulling on an England shirt had always given me a buzz,' Alan Ball said, 'the three lions on the chest. I thought it was the business. But the new strip – well, it were like turning out for a showbiz team.' At that Manchester meeting Revie put forward his intention to press for incentive bonuses. 'He spoke a lot about money,' one of the older hands said, 'which was a big difference from Alf who never got involved in how much we were paid for playing England matches. I think Alf felt that the honour was enough. Anyway, Revie went on about it being wrong that the England players didn't get more in appearance money and were not rewarded for doing well. He said that it was ridiculous that the 1966 World Cup squad got only £22,000 between them. Getting a better share was fine by me, but looking around the room you had to wonder how many of the players were up to playing for England.'

Before two years had passed, Revie came to a similar conclusion. Although England were unbeaten in his first nine games, the results including a 5–1 thrashing of Scotland at Wembley, there was little to suggest that he would successfully make the transition from club to international management. Despite the experience of European football gained at Leeds, Revie struggled to find a winning formula when attempting to qualify England for the 1976 European Championship finals from a group containing Czechoslovakia, Portugal and Cyprus. Ultimately, England's hopes rested on the remote possibility of Cyprus defeating the Czechs in Limassol. Knowing that I had contacts in Cyprus, and of my intention to attend the game, Revie offered to supply detailed information about the Czech team. On the understanding that Revie's name was not be mentioned, I passed on the information to the Cyprus coach Bambos Avramides, who then told me of a suspicion concerning two of his players from a club coached by Josef Masopust, a member of Czechoslovakia's team in the 1962 World Cup final against Brazil. 'They have been told not to try,' he claimed. Only one of them was selected, and the other was substituted after fifteen minutes. But dossiers were of no use to the coach of a team that had given up twelve goals in five matches and didn't have a point on the board. The Czechs sailed through 3–0 and went on to become European champions. Maintaining their dismal record in the competition, England finished in second place.

During a conversation a week or so after England's failure to qualify, I sensed that Revie harboured deep misgivings. 'Leeds were involved in so many things that I completely overlooked the fact that we were using players from five countries,' he said. 'Four of our most influential players – John Giles, Billy Bremner, Peter Lorimer and Eddie Gray, as well as others – weren't English. This applied at other clubs, too: Liverpool, Manchester United, Tottenham. But it wasn't something I'd thought about until I took over England. Then I had to ask myself the question, "How many top-class players have we got?" The answer is not many, certainly not enough.'

In the early summer of 1976, England took part in a tournament hosted by the United States as part of their bicentennial celebrations. They would play Brazil, Italy and Team America, the latter an assembly of mercenaries recruited from the North American Soccer League including Pele, Bobby Moore, Giorgio Chinaglia and Bob

McNab. A competition of no real consequence (the Team America match was rated 'unofficial') saw England lose 1–0 in Los Angeles to a half-paced Brazil and beat Italy 3–2 in New York.

Ahead lay a rather more important encounter with the Italians, for little more than a fortnight later Revie got down to the task of qualifying England for the 1978 World Cup finals. Failure in 1974 meant that England had lost the advantage of being seeded. Finland and Luxembourg came out of the draw as the two lesser nations in Group 2, followed by England and the seeded team, Italy. Revie grimaced. Twice world champions, runners-up in 1970 and European champions in 1968, Italy had only once failed to reach the finals.

Four days before the 1976 Olympics opened in Montreal, an England team containing only four survivors from Ramsey's last squad – Clemence, Keegan, Channon and Madeley – defeated Finland 4–1 in Helsinki. Delighted as he was with the result – 'it showed the benefit of being able to keep the squad together' – Revie was under no illusions. Finland had never lost to England by fewer than three goals, and only two members of their team were full-time professionals. Although all three England strikers, Channon, Keegan (twice) and Stuart Pearson of Manchester United, were on the scoresheet, effort rather than class had crushed the robust Finns.

Croker apart, Revie's relations with officialdom at this time were no less subject to emotional disturbance than Ramsey's had been. Resenting Harold Thompson's habit of addressing staff and players by their surnames, Revie turned on him. 'It's either Don or Mr Revie,' he barked. 'Please yourself.' When Len Shipman, the League President, ordered Les Cocker to take care of his suitcase, Revie snapped, 'He's got enough to do without having to look after you.' But he succeeded where Ramsey had failed, carrying the day when seeking the League's endorsement of his proposal for a suspension of the First Division programme before important international matches. Thus Revie had almost a full week to prepare England for the return match with Finland on 13 October.

Looking for a big win, he made more changes (if not actually the case, it seemed by then that he'd used every one of the 40 players summoned to his inaugural address in Manchester), going to a 4–2–4 formation with Keegan and Denis Tueart of Manchester City occupying the flank positions. After six days of training, bingo sessions, carpet bowls and studying dossiers – Channon remarked that they knew 'everything about the Finns apart from how many times a week they had it off' – England began as though they were out to surpass the record of thirteen goals against Ireland in 1882. Punters betting on the first scorer were spoilt for choice: Keegan, Channon, Royle, Tueart?

It was Tueart, after only six minutes. By the twelfth minute Finland had already defended seven corners and seen their goalkeeper Enckelman make a string of fine saves. 'It seemed only a case of which of us would score next,' Joe Royle recalled. Instead, England fell away and the crowd grew restive as Finland grew in confidence, dealing easily with a stream of unimaginative attacks. Revie yearned for a Giles, a Bremner, a Gray. 'I couldn't believe I was watching a Revie team,' Jack Charlton said. 'He doesn't work that way. I couldn't understand it.' Three minutes into the second half, Finland drew level; four minutes later Royle restored England's lead, but it wasn't nearly enough to satisfy a Wembley crowd of 92,000. As Revie trudged to the dressing room, head down, shoulders hunched, hands thrust deep into the pockets of his overcoat, he heard the dreaded chant: 'What a load of rubbish!' Press criticism was fierce, the reports received by Italy's enlightened coach Enzo Bearzot contemptuous of England's performance. 'A team relying mainly on strength,' he would have read. 'Keegan, as we know, is a dangerously intelligent attacker, but there isn't a great deal else to worry us. Technically, England appear to have gone backwards.'

With two days in which to compose a follow-up column for the *Sunday Mirror*, I telephoned Jack Charlton, suggesting to him that Revie should have remained at Leeds. 'It's easy to think that,' he said, 'but he'd accomplished just about everything on the field, built up the club from nothing. For an ambitious man, the England job was a natural progression. Now it looks as though he's making the mistakes we'd all probably make in similar circumstances. Changing the team from match to match, not sticking to one system. He's terrific on organisation, fantastic eye for detail. Before the start of every season he went back to basics, simple passing practices that bored the hell out of me. It was only after going into management that I fully understood why he did it. Get the basics right, and the rest falls into place.

'I don't know where Revie goes from here because unless he gets a result in Italy next month England will find it extremely difficult to qualify. Revie will carry the can if they don't, but frankly I don't think he's got the players to pull it off.'

One of Revie's big worries was that Italy would outscore England against the weaker teams in the group; indeed, they had begun their campaign with a 4–1 win in Luxembourg. His target, then, was to take at least three points off the Italians. Even with the technical shortcomings evident at Wembley fresh in his mind, Celtic manager Jock Stein, a friend of Revie, felt that England had enough to carry the day. 'I'm sure Don will warn the players against becoming involved in feuds,' he said. 'The Italians try to get you going. A nudge, body checks, trips when the referee's back is turned. If it works, they're at you in a flash. They've got brilliant technique and they think quickly. Italy produces all-round players whereas British football goes for specialists. It's a different game, but I don't see why England shouldn't make it work.'

It was a pipe dream. The need to avoid defeat in Rome in November 1976 prompted Revie to adopt a strategy similar to one he'd employed at Leeds in the away legs of European competitions: he went from his most attack-minded team to his most defensive. Only Clemence, Greenhoff, Brooking, Keegan and Channon remained from the match against Finland a month earlier. Astonishingly, given the circumstances, Revie included the Queens Park Rangers forward Stan Bowles, a precociously brilliant footballer who was about as reliable as a tin watch.

Although Bearzot had pledged to lift the dead hand of negativity from Italian football, on the night Italy played in a familiar manner: they were patient, they took no risks, and they waited for England to make punishable errors. In the 36th minute Antognoni drove in a free-kick that was deflected past Clemence by Keegan. 'Keep playing as you are,' Revie urged his men during the interval. 'It's only one goal. Don't lose your shape. Don't chase the game. We can still get away from here with half a loaf.' England ran and ran, but it would have taken a fog to obscure the difference in class. Thirteen minutes from the end Roberto Bettega headed Italy's second. England's chances of going to Argentina now hung on a slender thread.

In June 1977, England left for matches against Brazil, Argentina and Uruguay. Revie was absent from the first of these games, his failure to attend explained as 'official business'. Having been informed that the FA had lost all faith in him, Revie had taken the pre-emptive step of entering into negotiations with the United Arab

Emirates, and had agreed in principle to become their national coach. While Revie could not be blamed for wanting to safeguard his future after the way in which Ramsey had been dismissed, the announcement of his resignation in a national newspaper in July, reputedly in return for a large sum of money, was shameful.

The FA's decision as a result to approach Ron Greenwood was influenced more by the embarrassment of Revie's defection than by the remote possibility of England's qualification. Greenwood was the most prominent of Winterbottom's disciples, a man of high principle whose work at West Ham had produced three key members of the 1966 World Cup team. On the other hand, Greenwood's achievements in management were negligible. He'd had to live with the criticism that, though West Ham's football was easy on the eye, it was brittle. In charge at Upton Park from 1961 until 1975, Greenwood had won the FA Cup and the European Cup Winners Cup but had finished above halfway in the League only four times. Moreover, the task of steering England through their remaining group games was given to a coach who had not been actively involved in the game for more than a year, his role at West Ham having become purely administrative when John Lyall was made manager. 'We think he's the best man for the job,' Harold Thompson insisted. After Revie, respectability seemed to be the preferred option. Thompson had told Greenwood, 'No promises, but the image of the game is all wrong and we need a firm, stable hand immediately. Everyone is being roasted, myself and the rest of the International Committee. We don't like it. See what you can do.'

In the short time available it was impossible for Greenwood to create a team. Sensibly, he called on as many players as possible from Liverpool, the European champions, plus Keegan, who had recently upset the Kop by completing a move to Hamburg. 'At least they'll know each other,' Danny Blanchflower quipped in the *Sunday Express*. Even after a drab goalless draw in a warm-up match in September against Switzerland at Wembley, it was widely supposed that England would run up a big score away to Luxembourg on 12 October. Instead, they struggled through by two goals, a performance poor enough for critics to suggest that the game had passed Greenwood by, that his appointment was a folly.

When Italy travelled to meet England at Wembley the following month, it was with the comforting knowledge that they would qualify if they avoided defeat. With a home match against Luxembourg to come, they could even afford to lose by one or two goals. Claudio Coutinho, a former army officer and volleyball international who had surprisingly been made manager of Brazil, gave England little chance. 'People are again asking what has gone wrong with English football,' he said when we spoke a few days before the match. 'It is important that they do well, even though their task looks impossible. For the good of football England must show that they haven't forgotten how to play the game they invented.' It was Helmut Schoen's view that England had stood still in the seven years since Mexico. 'That was a fine England team and we were fortunate to win,' he said. 'But where are their playmakers now? There is no Bobby Charlton, no Bobby Moore. We changed. Italy changed, became less defensive. But nothing seems to change in England. England needs a new manager less than they need a different policy. I thought Ron Greenwood was a good appointment because he has always been an advanced thinker. He thinks European. Unlike a lot of people in English football he can see beyond Dover.'

It was not enough, but the manner of England's two-goal victory over the Italians left their supporters reflecting on what might have been. At last there was a semblance of class as Greenwood's philosophy took hold. Keegan scored in the eleventh minute, Brooking nine minutes from time. In between England played football described by Bearzot as the best he'd seen from them in some time. Greenwood had restored England's pride, and his elevation from caretaker to full-time manager brought no complaints.

Despite the good impression he'd created, Ron Greenwood's appointment was not automatic. Along with Brian Clough, Lawrie McMenemy, Bobby Robson and Allen Wade he was one of five applicants interviewed by the International Committee. Predictably, Clough was the public's choice, heavily outscoring his rivals in a poll conducted by the *Sun* newspaper. For Greenwood, now well into his fifties, it was the England job or retirement. He had no intention of going back to West Ham. 'That chapter of my life was closed,' he said. The next chapter opened with a mandate until the 1980 European Championship when, if England reached the finals, his position would be reviewed.

Brooking apart, the England players hadn't known what to expect. 'With Alf, everything was practical,' Emlyn Hughes said. 'Revie filled our heads with information, terrific in its way, but not what I'd grown used to at Liverpool where everything was kept simple. West Ham were looked on as a soft touch away from home and the impression got around that Ron was a blackboard man. As it turned out he was nothing of the sort. In his own way, Ron was as enthusiastic as Bill Shankly and Bob Paisley, and their ideas were basically similar. Pass and move, always support the man on the ball. Ron was as sharp as a tack. Saw everything.'

In his 1984 autobiography, Greenwood wrote: 'The wide range of playing methods used by our clubs gives the Football League its strong, highly individual flavour. Some teams play it short and some long. Some play through the middle and some look for corner flags. Some employ wingers and some fill centre-circles. Some play football from the back and some don't play football at all. From Liverpool through to Watford, by way of Manchester United, West Ham, Nottingham Forest and Arsenal, there is such a variety of styles and priorities that every game is different. But while this is fine for the spectators it is not so good for England's manager, who is expected to make up a complicated jigsaw puzzle with pieces from a lot of different boxes. Variety may be the spice of life, but it does not produce players who can step quickly and easily into international football.'

It was with this handicap – no other international manager had had to deal with such a diversity of style – that Greenwood set out to restore England's prestige. Where Ramsey and Revie had kept the circle of assistance small, Greenwood went for expansion, recruiting a number of club coaches to work with him on a part-time basis; where Ramsey and Revie preferred to keep their own counsel, Greenwood actively sought the views of League managers. His choice of Clough and Peter Taylor to work with the youth team raised eyebrows, even more so when they pulled out following complaints made by Frank O'Gorman, the doctor, and Ken Burton, the coach. Burton resigned, saying, 'I can't put up with it.'

Helpfully, during this period, with his 58th birthday fast approaching, Greenwood was spared the pressure that haunted the faces of a number of leading managers in the 1978 World Cup finals in Argentina. 'Compared with this World Cup the others I have been in were garden parties,' Helmut Schoen remarked. 'Football is the most followed game in the world and therefore attracts extreme reactions. If I'd known it was going to be like this I would have retired earlier.' At least Schoen had the comfort of knowing that he would shortly hand over to Jupp Derwall. Greenwood's friend, the chain-smoking Enzo Bearzot, soldiered on – a wise decision since he went on to lift the 1982 World Cup.

Over a year after Greenwood was given the post an article appeared in the *Observer* describing his appointment as 'inspired'. After starting in February 1978 with a 2–1 defeat at the hands of West Germany in Munich he'd won ten and drawn three of England's next thirteen matches. The most recent, a 3–0 win over Bulgaria in Sofia on Derby Day 1979, strengthened England's grip on a European Championship qualifying group that included Denmark and the two Irelands. It also drew the admiration of Bulgaria's coach Izvetan Ilchev. 'This is a new England,' he said. 'They are still physically strong but they no longer concentrate on power. They have ideas, sophistication, a team who play modern football.'

Keegan, a better all-round player after two seasons with Hamburg, had become the key figure in England's development, as enthusiastic as ever but more mature. By his own admission, Keegan was not a naturally gifted footballer; he hadn't fallen out of bed with a body swerve, dribbling skills and a cannonball shot. Ron Ashman was manager of Scunthorpe when Keegan took his first steps in the League. 'Practically everything Kevin achieved as a player came from exceptional determination,' he confirmed. 'It never came easy for him. But he worked and worked to make himself a great player. Although I knew he'd get there, none of the clubs who showed an interest, including Liverpool, could make up their minds. I must have had half a dozen conversations with Bill Shankly before he finally agreed to pay £35,000. "And that's me taking a chance," Bill said.'

Having played in an era of English football illuminated by such notables as Matthews, Finney, Mannion and Mortensen, and having seen many fine young players come through the youth and under-23 teams, Greenwood had never subscribed to the view that a dearth of talent could be explained by social changes. If it existed, the fault lay with years of stagnation brought on by the 1966 success, and Greenwood relished the challenge. It was, he said, the most invigorating period of his professional life, 'a huge bonus'. 'At this stage of my career I could not ask for more than to be working with talented players and coaches. I think people abroad are again looking towards British football. Progress is being made, exciting progress. Liverpool and Nottingham Forest have proved this in the European Cup. There is a lot of good work being done.'

When on 13 May 1980 England defeated world champions Argentina 3–1 at Wembley, expectations soared out of all proportion to progress. What price now the rest of Europe? Four days later, England, risking five changes, were walloped 4–1 at Wrexham by a Wales team playing to impress a new manager, Mike England. 'England to be champions of Europe?' Welsh half-back Peter Nicholas said. 'You can bet them with me. Now.'

Even so, by June, when England arrived in Italy for the European Championship finals, Greenwood had lost only three of 29 games since taking over. The eight nations were split into two groups of four, with the winners to meet in Rome. England were drawn with Italy, Belgium and Spain. Greenwood's relations with the press had generally remained cordial, but all was about to change.

A 1–1 draw with Belgium in Turin on 12 June raised fresh questions about the team – incidental in the context of a riot by English supporters who fought running battles with police at the Stadio Communale and on the streets outside. England feared expulsion from the championship, but they got away with an £8,000 fine. It seemed to many that English football had begun to export hooliganism on a grand scale. I wrote: 'Riots in Paris, Rotterdam, and now Turin; thuggish behaviour in Luxembourg three years ago when England were striving to reach the 1978 World Cup finals. The record is truly appalling.' Michel Daphinoff, a senior UEFA official who'd been dispatched from Rome, said, 'There is a recurring pattern of violent behaviour by English football supporters. It cannot go on. We are alarmed because the rest of society cannot be expected to tolerate it.' Turin's mayor, Diego Novelli, immediately ordered a clampdown. When England met Italy three days later riot squads stood by in the stadium and patrolled the streets outside. Fearing reprisals, hundreds of England fans had already left the city. Greenwood and his players felt let down. They lost the match 1–0, and a 2–1 victory over Spain in Naples on 18 June counted for nothing. West Germany defeated Belgium in the final, claiming their third major championship in eight years.

A little less than twelve months later, Greenwood decided that his time was up. England's attempt to qualify for the 1982 World Cup finals had begun to fall apart, threatening to bring about a repeat of the disappointment in 1978. From the first five of eight qualifying matches England had managed only five points. Of the three ties that remained, two were against Hungary and one was away to Norway. Even with two to go through from the group England's prospects looked bleak.

Greenwood arrived at his decision within a few minutes of England's 2–1 loss to Switzerland in Basle on 30 May 1981, intending to have it announced by the FA after the forthcoming match against Hungary in Budapest on 6 June. In typical tabloid fashion, Greenwood was berated for England's failure to overcome 'a bunch of cuckoo clock makers and waiters' when in fact all but two of the Swiss players were full-time professionals. The *Sun*'s headline writer knew his history, putting up FOR GOD'S SAKE, GO, but Greenwood had already got the message. To make matters worse, English hooligans attacked Swiss supporters during the interval and afterwards ran riot in the streets. 'If they are not seen here again for 50 years, it will be too soon,' the local chief of police said. But just when all seemed lost, England pulled back from the brink, beating Hungary in Budapest for the first time since 1909, inspired by a Brooking goal struck with such force that the ball had to be prised from a stanchion.

When they finally heard of Greenwood's decision to retire, the players successfully pleaded with him to reconsider. One thing led to another, crazily. Don Howe, by then a key member of Greenwood's staff, recalled, 'I think we all went through that summer thinking that only a calamity could keep us out of the finals. We'd got out of a mess and were back on track. September has never been a good month for the England team, wrong time of the season. It was reaching the point where no international team could be taken lightly. However, I felt we'd be too good for Norway.' But they weren't, and a calamity it was. England, after taking the lead through Bryan Robson, lost 2–1 in Oslo and were as good as out of the World Cup. Immediately, Greenwood came under a bombardment of 'told you so' criticism: he was 'too old', he had 'too many fancy ideas'.

Then, in early November, ten days before England were due to meet Hungary at Wembley for their final qualifying tie, came the news that Romania had lost at home to Switzerland. When they dropped another point in Berne the door was open for Greenwood's team. All England needed was a draw. Already assured of first place in the group, Hungary offered little more than token resistance, leaving England to rejoice over a 1–0 victory. 'I wore my Swiss tie for two weeks,' Greenwood joked.

Had there been a prize for 'most complicated journey to a World Cup', I would have won easily that summer of 1982. The morning after Larry Holmes stopped Gerry Cooney in their World Heavyweight Championship clash I flew from Las Vegas to London via San Francisco. From London I drove to Paris, put the car on an overnight train to Biarritz, and then drove to Bilbao. I arrived in northern Spain to discover that England's approach to the tournament had undergone a distinctive change. The old informality, the easy communication with management and players, had given way to a strict routine of press conferences and prearranged interviews. England's hotel, some ten miles from the city, was off limits to the media. Contact was restricted to an annexe, and was by appointment only.

Still, enough information was available to establish that Brooking and Keegan, both now past 30, were behind schedule in the treatment room. With an average age of 28, the squad was strong on experience but it creaked in some positions. Significantly, Greenwood had left his conventional wingers at home, reverting to Ramsey's preference for wide midfielders; Peter Shilton had finally edged past Ray Clemence as the first-choice goalkeeper; Hoddle, the most naturally gifted English footballer of his generation – it was often said of him that 'Brazil would have him in a flash' – still had plenty to prove at international level. The big plus was Bryan Robson. Fully recovered from having broken his leg no fewer than three times, and now with Manchester United, he met Bill Shankly's description of the perfect half-back: 'someone who can pass, tackle, run all day and score goals with the heart of a lion'. Comparison with the Tottenham hero Dave Mackay was valid. Kenny Sansom, his 23 caps exactly matching his age, took the field against France on 16 June as the team's youngest player, by only a few months from Terry Butcher. He was thrilled to be playing in the finals. 'Every footballer who gets to a World Cup for the first time says that it's the stuff of dreams, but you have to be there to know just how exciting it is,' he said. 'It gives you such a buzz. All the best players are there, men you didn't often come up against in those days, posing different problems from the League. It's like nothing else a player ever comes across.'

England got off to a flier, Robson scoring inside 30 seconds, 'from a throw-in I was supposed to take,' Sansom pointed out. 'Instead, Steve Coppell picked up the ball and when Terry Butcher flicked the throw on with his head there was Robbo – bingo, a goal. Afterwards we learnt what we'd already guessed, that it was the quickest ever goal in the World Cup finals [it won Robson a gold watch]. When you start like that it really gives the team a lift, but I remembered Don [Howe] saying not to get carried away if we went in front. To keep our shape, not just go galloping forward. France had some outstanding players – Platini, Giresse – but even though they equalised before half-time I felt we were good enough to beat them. And when Robbo scored again we were on our way.' Paul Mariner completed the 3–1 victory, and Robson was named man of the match.

'How are things with Kevin and Trevor?' Greenwood was asked after the match. He had nothing positive to report. Keegan and Brooking were sharing a room – 'misery loves company' – and their worries. Brooking had a groin injury that 'was taking a lot longer to clear up than I'd expected, but there again I was at an age [33] when you don't heal as quickly'. In an attempt to accelerate his recovery a specialist was flown in from London to give him an injection. Keegan's case was even more worrying. Perky on arrival in Spain, his back had gone into spasm during a training session, basically as a result of wear and tear. For years he'd been unsparing in his efforts for Liverpool and Hamburg, and he'd looked sprightly enough in Southampton's colours, but Keegan's body was telling him different.

Secretly, Keegan spent 24 hours in a nursing home near Bilbao so that X-rays could be taken of his back. When these and other tests failed to identify the problem he became depressed, even suggesting to Greenwood that it might be better for everyone if he dropped out of the squad. 'I feel bloody useless,' he said. The extraordinary outcome was that Keegan borrowed a car and drove through the night to Madrid; from there he flew to visit a specialist in Hamburg, returning four days later. Greenwood wrote: 'I would not have let anyone else make the journey, but Kevin was such a man of the world that I knew he would be all right.' Not a word of this leaked out until Keegan was back with the squad, and even then Greenwood withheld the details of his captain's moonlight flit. Keegan's ghost-writer Vince Wilson wasn't told the full story until England were out of the World Cup. 'All Kevin told me was that he'd been to Hamburg,' he confirmed.

Although Keegan and Brooking were in light training, neither was fit enough even to be considered as a substitute for the next match against Czechoslovakia, so Greenwood sent out an unchanged team. The Czechs hadn't looked up to much when Greenwood and Howe watched them draw 1–1 with Kuwait in Valladolid, and they did nothing in Bilbao to suggest that the England coaches had missed something. England's two goals were gifts: the Czech goalkeeper Seman dropped a corner at Trevor Francis's feet in the 63rd minute, and three minutes later Barmos turned the ball into his own net. Played two, won two, and England were through to the next round.

Sir Stanley Rous's contention that sixteen finalists was the ideal format for the World Cup had carried no weight with Brazil's João Havelange, who had ousted Rous from the presidency of FIFA in 1974. Havelange's big vote-catcher was expansion to 24 finalists from a broader qualifying base. Thus, in 1982 the finals commenced with six groups of four, the top two from each going forward into four groups of three, these four group winners contesting the semi-finals. Some 52 matches were played over 29 days. Of the lesser nations at the finals, Kuwait were the most interesting. They had a Brazilian coach, Carlos Alberto Parreira, a former goalkeeper who would guide his country to success in the 1994 finals, and so much money that one player was reputed to have spent £20,000 on presents. Sparing no expense in trying to become a power in the game, they had reached the quarter-finals of the 1980 Olympics and won the Asian Championship the same year. When England lined up against them on 25 June, a draw between France and Czechoslovakia had already confirmed England as group winners with France in second place, so there was no pressure whatsoever on Greenwood's team. Hoddle came in for the injured Robson and England should have scored five, but they settled instead for Francis's strike in the 27th minute. As when going out of the 1980 Olympics, the Kuwaitis demanded immediate transportation home. 'In their eyes it was all very simple,' Parreira told me. 'If there isn't a flight then go out and buy a plane.'

On the day England defeated Kuwait I watched West Germany beat Austria 1–0 in Gijon, an outcome described by the world's press as 'the biggest scandal in World Cup history'. After West Germany went ahead in the eleventh minute neither team showed any interest in taking things further. Hugh McIlvanney wrote, 'if this non-contest had been a horse race the stewards would have held an instant inquiry'. It was certainly tough on the Algerians, for the result denied them a place in the next round. It was not, however, the 'fix' they imagined; actually there was no evidence to support the widespread suspicion of an officially prearranged result. By changing the format, FIFA had created a situation in which West Germany needed a victory while Austria could suffer a narrow defeat and still survive, and the players had figured that out for themselves on the pitch. 'I was afraid something like this would happen,' Franz Beckenbauer said when we spoke after the game. 'I am ashamed of our team, but I understand. The World Cup has become so important it is no longer enough just to play. The teams must look ahead and consider every possibility. I have sympathy for Algeria. However, if they had not allowed Chile to steal two goals this game would have been an honest one. I don't think there was a plan between the coaches. It was the players themselves who made this happen. There are strong personalities in our team and you could see from the way things were after we scored that they arranged a pact with the Austrians.'

On the subject of West Germany's football, Beckenbauer was equally scathing. He had seen nothing to convince him that they would overcome England at the Bernabeu Stadium in Madrid in the opening game of the second phase's Group B. He complained particularly about the failure to establish lines of communication. 'It is as if each man is playing on his own,' he remarked. Pele joined in the criticism of Jupp Derwall's team. 'He is sending out Rummenigge and ten robots,' he said. As it turned out, Rummenigge almost won the game in the final minutes, hitting the crossbar with a long shot. Otherwise it was a game dominated by the fear of losing – drab, negative and almost completely lacking in incident until Rummenigge's single act of aggression. 'I thought we did a tremendous job containing their attacking full-backs,' Greenwood reflected the next day. But England's attackers had again been impotent and uninspired, unable to free themselves from West Germany's disciplined marking.

Still, Greenwood's 40 years in football had narrowed to a week that contained the prospect of leading England into a World Cup final. If England could beat hosts Spain (losers by two goals to one against the Germans) by two goals they would meet either France or Northern Ireland, the tournament's surprise package, in the semi-finals. The margin was crucial because in the event of a group tie England and West Germany would draw lots from a bag containing six balls, four of them unmarked. 'We believed that our better results in the first phase would put us through,' FA secretary Ted Croker said, 'and that the wording of the rule was unclear.' FIFA would have none of it.

England now found themselves quartered at Navacerrada, a wooded area in the shadow of hills about an hour's drive from Madrid. There, speculation centred on how Spain would approach a match that held nothing for them but pride, and on whether Greenwood would start with Brooking and Keegan, both greatly improved but seriously short of match fitness. Along with Geoff Hurst, Greenwood had watched the match between West Germany and Spain. They felt Spain were a moderate team although not lacking in spirit. 'It is impossible to tell how they will respond against us,' Greenwood said. 'In similar circumstances we would give everything, but I simply don't know enough about the Spanish character.' Spain's coach, José Santamaria, the Uruguayan-born pillar of Real Madrid's defence in the fifties, announced that the task of restoring national pride would be entrusted to the men who had failed the host country. 'There will be no experiments,' he said. 'For some it will be the end, but they have a responsibility to Spain.'

Off the field, England had never been better served in the brains department. Apart from Howe, his chief assistant, Greenwood could call on the observations of Dave Sexton, Bobby Robson, Terry Venables and Geoff Hurst. All agreed with Greenwood's opinion that it would be foolish to try to force the pace. In his conversations with the players Greenwood advised caution. 'You must be patient, keep your heads,' he urged. The manager's selection of Tony Woodock for the injured Coppell meant that he was sending out three strikers: Woodcock, Mariner and Francis. And, at last, Brooking and Keegan put in an appearance: both were named among the substitutes. 'We weren't fully fit,' Brooking admitted, 'but Ron told us that we'd go on if things weren't going well. He said that he'd try to get the moment just right so that we'd give Spain fresh problems.'

Brought off the bench in the 63rd minute (Keegan for Woodcock, Brooking for Rix) with the score at 0–0, they proceeded to squander

England's best chances. Brooking shot straight at Luis Arconada, and Keegan headed a Robson cross wide. ('A sickener' he later called it. 'I'd scored from 50 worse positions.') England's best players for so long, the sum total of their World Cup experience was 27 minutes, and neither was capped again. England went out of the tournament without losing a match, but privately Greenwood conceded that their football had lacked imagination and decisive pace. Those faults, and others, could be traced back to an absurdly congested domestic fixture list, blinkered coaching and too much faith in spirited scufflers. Northern Ireland's remarkable feat of getting within one game of the semi-finals had in fact been achieved with mostly second-rate players, good organisation and shrewd management. And it was mostly sound organisation that got West Germany through to the final against Italy, who had broken millions of hearts by eliminating Brazil. Playing more defensively than some historians suggest, Italy won 3–1 and put their name on the trophy for a third time.

Elsewhere, Bobby Robson was in something of a quandary: should he stay with Ipswich or take up an offer to manage his country?

10. 1982 TO ITALY 1990

The circumstances in which Bobby Robson became manager of England were remarkably similar to those surrounding Alf Ramsey's appointment twenty years earlier. Both had to weigh up the many advantages they enjoyed at Ipswich against the prestige of running the national team. As late as the last week of his service with Greenwood at the 1982 finals, Robson was still undecided, telling Terry Venables, 'On the one hand I've got this terrific opportunity, an honour; on the other a club where I'm happy and appreciated. I just don't know.' Venables looked hard at him and told him to go with his instincts.

Although the popular press was yet again touting Brian Clough – 'Why not the best manager in England?' the *Sun* asked – Robson's arrival at Lancaster Gate caused no adverse reaction. After all, his CV was impressive. As a player he'd made twenty appearances for England, including five in the 1958 World Cup finals; as a manager he'd got over disappointments in Vancouver and at Fulham to make his mark at Ipswich. After a slow start he'd won the FA Cup and the UEFA Cup and engineered a string of top-six finishes; with five more points Ipswich would have won the championship in 1981, and again in 1982. So, for the second time in two decades Ipswich said farewell to 'an irreplaceable manager'. 'I just hope I'm doing the right thing,' Robson said.

It had all been seen and heard before. The 'honeymoon' was brief, lasting barely six weeks from Robson's appointment. During that period England gave up a European Championship qualifying point to Denmark in Copenhagen and lost 2–1 to West Germany at Wembley. Meanwhile, Robson was roasted in some sections of the press for leaving Keegan to figure out for himself that his international career was over.

On the face of it, to be drawn in a qualifying group with Denmark, Greece, Hungary and Luxembourg was no big deal. Hungary had been among the qualifiers in Spain but had failed to get beyond the first phase, thrashed 4–1 by Argentina. The result in Denmark was, however, sobering. 'They'd come on a bundle,' Sansom said. 'It was no freak result. You could see how much some of their players had improved from going abroad.' Denmark's 1–0 victory at Wembley in September 1983 – 'the worst experience of my international career,' Robson called it – more or less put paid to England's chance of qualifying for the finals, the issue settled when the Danes won in Greece. The typically arrogant conclusion was that England had lost to a team that had no right to be on the same field. It was the 'cuckoo clock maker' syndrome all over again, a pathetic media-fed assumption of superiority that had no basis in fact.

Undeservedly seeded, England were given every chance of qualifying for the 1986 World Cup finals in Mexico when they were drawn in a group with Northern Ireland, Romania, Finland and Turkey, with two to qualify. Whether Robson would be with England all the way was another matter, however. In May 1984, a couple of months after being systematically taken apart by France in Paris, where technical shortcomings were again evident, England lost 1–0 away to Wales and then gave such a poor performance against the Soviet Union at Wembley that Robson's reputation was left in tatters. His ill-advised experiment with 4–2–4 (a tactical relic) that June day proved disastrous. The Soviets couldn't believe their luck. They took one look at the formation, broke into smiles, and ran England ragged. Only Shilton's goalkeeping kept the score at 2–0. A storm of abuse broke over Robson as he made for the dressing room. The depression he'd felt when England had lost at home to Denmark was nothing to this. To make matters worse, his father was at the game. 'I thought of him sitting there listening to it all, people shouting for me to be sacked. It must have been awful for him.'

When England, depleted by withdrawals from the squad, left for a three-game tour of South America it was generally felt that Robson's future was in the balance. After two years in office he was no further forward in team development than Revie had been at a similar stage. 'We are all right in some positions,' he said on arrival in Rio de Janeiro, 'but when it comes to real class we are thin on the ground.' Forty-eight hours later, Robson was off the hook. Quite unexpectedly, England defeated Brazil 2–0 at Maracana, a match remembered for a virtuoso goal that worked wonders both for John Barnes and his boss. The result, however, was not quite what it seemed. 'Have you ever seen such a poor Brazil team?' Don Howe whispered to me in the dressing room. It wasn't simply the absence of such stars as Socrates, Falcão, Zico, Cerezo and Oscar; crippled economically,

Brazilian football was in disarray. 'With a real centre-forward we would have won the World Cup in Spain, now nobody wants to play,' Saldanha told me before the game. 'Brazil must be Brazil, but there are people here who advocate the European style. There is only argument.' Argument so decisive that nobody of note wanted to manage the team. Nevertheless, England were the first foreign team to win in Brazil for more than ten years. 'The effect was tremendous,' Ray Wilkins said. 'It improved our spirit no end and we all felt that the gaffer had turned a corner.' After the joy of Rio, a 2–0 loss to Uruguay in Montevideo was acceptable even to Robson's most waspish critics.

As England boarded a flight to Santiago for the final match of the tour against Chile, they were horrified to discover that fellow travellers included a group of about twenty England supporters who had been seen making a nuisance of themselves at the airport. Throughout the journey they hurled racist abuse at Barnes and Mark Chamberlain –'Blacks out, send them back!' – chanted anti-Semitic slogans and insulted Ted Croker. On arrival in Santiago they unfurled a National Front banner and gave fascist salutes. Most dispiriting of all was the realisation that England's hooligan element had the financial capability to form long-range groups.

Concluding the tour with a goalless draw, England could now concentrate on the World Cup qualifying campaign scheduled to start in October against Finland at Wembley. Heeding the lessons of history, Robson had carefully avoided September when negotiating fixtures in Group 3, using the slot for a friendly against East Germany which England won 1–0. By the time they came to London, the Finns had already taken two points off Northern Ireland, who in turn had beaten Romania 3–2 in Belfast.

Welcome as the victory in Rio had been, the South American tour had done little to alter Robson's view that an injection of class was vital. 'I think we are better for the experience,' he said, 'but too much of our football is untidy. Players who are now beginning to make their way in the team, John Barnes for example, must learn to broaden their game and establish a level of consistency.' Still, England flew out of the blocks. It was hardly a class performance, but at least England had on their shooting boots: two up at half-time, they ran out 5–0 winners.

Turkey were next, managed by Jupp Derwall, who'd been dumped by West Germany following their defeat in the 1982 World Cup final. Derwall's consolation was a contract worth £150,000 a year – five times Robson's salary – to work jointly with Istanbul club Galatasaray and the Turkish national team. Deaf to Derwall's counsel, Turkey proved to be no match for a rampant England. Scoring from England's first corner, Robson rattled in a hat-trick; Viv Anderson's first international goal brought the final tally to eight. 'I lost count,' Peter Shilton said. 'I thought we'd scored nine and I was shouting for double figures.' Derwall was hugely impressed. 'It was lucky for Turkey to lose only eight goals,' he said when we spoke at his home the following day. 'This is a very young and inexperienced Turkish team, and last night they were in awe of England's reputation. But even when I allow for many mistakes by Turkey I think England have real possibilities with a number of their players. Football is speeding up, and I think maybe England will benefit from the trend. The team isn't perfect by any means and it will be interesting to see how well it can defend against better opposition. But Shilton is still very good and I like the blend in midfield. Robson is everywhere. He makes tackles, he supports and he is always trying to make goals for himself. Wilkins is a good organiser who can control the play in areas where one pass can open up a defence. In conditions that suit them England would be too powerful for most teams, and at Wembley they will beat anyone.'

But it was almost a year until England's next competitive fixture at Wembley, and three and a half months had elapsed before the squad reassembled at the end of February 1985 to prepare for a difficult match against Northern Ireland in Belfast. Though England had not lost in Belfast since 1927, their victory at Windsor Park there the previous year stood as the only home loss suffered by Billy Bingham since taking charge in 1980. Taking no chances, prepared to settle for a draw, Robson decided to meet fire with fire, opting for a method direct enough to suggest that his players should have taken the field wearing a pilot's insignia on their shirts rather than the three lions badge. The ball was hardly out of the air, the most likely injury a stiff neck. Fourteen minutes from time Mark Hateley fastened on to an aimless punt forward and slid the ball past Pat Jennings, who was making his 108th senior international appearance, equalling the British record set by Bobby Moore.

The word most commonly used to describe England's performance that day was 'rubbish'. Coming under fire again, Robson reacted angrily to the implication of being influenced by the director of coaching, Charles Hughes. Hughes's long-ball philosophy had become a contentious issue. Used successfully by Graham Taylor at Watford and Dave Bassett at Wimbledon, and rapidly catching on, in the mid-eighties it was threatening to take English football back years. 'Belfast was a one-off,' Robson insisted.

With three wins out of three, England held pole position, and after a fortunate goalless draw on 1 May against Romania in Bucharest, where Gheorghe Hagi emerged as a rising talent, they could look forward to playing three of their remaining four games at Wembley. But though they were the bookmakers' favourites to qualify from Group 3, England still hadn't convinced the press or the public that they possessed genuine World Cup potential. The next two games, a 1–1 draw against Finland in Helsinki and a 1–0 loss to Scotland at Hampden Park, brought fresh outbursts of criticism, aimed mainly at Robson. England's commitment that June to an acclimatising tournament hosted by Mexico came as something of a relief.

The disaster at Bradford eighteen days earlier and a vicious outburst of hooliganism by Millwall supporters at Luton in March had not prepared anyone for the criminal tragedy at the Heysel stadium in Brussels on 29 May when Liverpool and Juventus met in the European Cup final. Together with a number of the England players, I was sitting by a swimming pool when Peter Shilton emerged from a doorway with a shocked look on his face. 'It seems that something terrible has happened at the European Cup final,' he said. 'Lots of people dead.' The tragedy, which had begun with Liverpool fans charging Juventus fans before the match had even started, held serious implications for English football. Suddenly, it seemed not only possible that English clubs would be thrown out of European competitions – an indefinite ban was eventually imposed – but that the national team would not be welcome at the 1986 World Cup.

It was in this incriminating atmosphere that England lost to Italy (2–1) and Mexico (1–0) in Mexico City. A 3–0 victory over West Germany on 12 June meant little to anyone other than the ITV commentators, who naively played it up as a triumph; playing at altitude just four days after the end of their league season, the Germans, now managed by Franz Beckenbauer, lasted barely twenty minutes. 'If the question had come up before I was appointed, we would not be here,' Beckenbauer said. 'Coming so soon after the last matches in the Bundesliga with no time to acclimatise was foolishness. With so little time for preparation it was impossible for our players to last the whole game. I'm told Bobby Robson is under pressure. If so, we have done him a favour.'

Thoughts about the pressures of the game were on many minds on 10 September 1985 when, on the final whistle of a World Cup eliminator between Scotland and Wales in Cardiff, Jock Stein collapsed and died. Matt Busby's remark, 'Football has lost a colossus,' was no exaggeration. A manager of infinite wisdom, and unswervingly a man of the people, Stein had set towering standards of play and principle. But the pressure was largely off Robson when England marched out alongside Turkey at Wembley a month later because they were already sure of reaching Mexico. Northern Ireland's victory in Bucharest earlier that day had left Romania needing to score ten in their final match against Turkey if they were to overtake England. England removed all doubt with a 5–0 victory that included a Gary Lineker hat-trick. By drawing 0–0 at Wembley in mid-November Northern Ireland joined England on the trip to Mexico. (The Romanians, 3–1 winners in Istanbul the same night, cried 'Fix!')

That the World Cup was being played in Mexico at all was a miracle or a disgrace, depending on how you looked at FIFA's decision to go ahead despite the earthquake that devastated large sections of Mexico City in September 1985, claiming many thousands of lives. While the Mexican government pleaded for foreign aid, the World Cup Organising Committee gave its full support to rebuilding communication facilities, particularly the studios of Televisa, a television company owned by Emilio Azcarraga who was said to be the fourth richest man in Mexico. One of FIFA's vice presidents, Guillermo Canedo, was a senior Televisa executive. Following his return from a reconnaissance, Alec Weeks of the BBC's sports department told of having seen untagged bodies thrown into trucks as the ground was cleared for reconstruction. 'In view of what has happened there is no moral justification for holding the World Cup in Mexico,' he said. The job of restoring Mexico's television links was completed within four months. West Germany, the alternative venue, was told to stand down.

Though hundreds who had survived the earthquake, many of them crippled for life, were living from hand to mouth, all the competing nations flew to Central America in the summer of 1986, England with none of the advantages they'd enjoyed in 1970 as the defending champions. As an unseeded nation, it hadn't been until the draw was made that any plans could be put in place, though England had come out of it pretty well, thrown into the weakest group along with Poland, Portugal and Morocco. Banished for security reasons (though this was denied by FIFA) to Monterrey, less than a hundred miles from the United States border, the squad arrived to discover that there had been another administrative cock-up (shades of Leon in 1970). The hotel into which they'd been booked was on a busy highway, making sound sleep impossible. After a number of telephone calls they found alternative quarters in Saltillo, some 5,000 feet above sea level and far enough away – around 40 miles – to discourage unwelcome visitors. 'It was bloody hot,' Peter Reid recalled. 'You could have fried an egg on the pavements. It was that hot I trained wearing a blue floppy hat, even in practice matches. By comparison, Majorca was at the North Pole. Fortunately, all three of England's games would kick off at four p.m.; unfortunately, Robson and Howe had miscalculated the heat's effect, choosing a strategy entirely unsuitable to the conditions. They'd gone for a pressing game that called for a lot of energy – impossible in that heat.'

Then there was the worry over Bryan Robson. More than two months before the end of the 1985–86 League season it was made clear to Manchester United that Robson's troublesome shoulder required an operation. Desperate to have his captain fit for the finals, Bobby Robson wanted it done there and then, but the Manchester United manager Ron Atkinson refused, insisting that Robson first complete the season. The pain Robson felt when taking a tumble during World Cup preparation in Colorado indicated that his shoulder could go again at any moment. Bobby Robson decided to take a chance.

It was Bryan Robson who led England out against Portugal in the Tecnologica Stadium, Monterrey, on 3 June 1986, and Bobby Robson who led the players on a miserable trek back to Saltillo later that day. Just as Reid and other members of the squad had feared, the tactics were all wrong. Periods of comfortable possession concealed the fact that passes aimed over England's full-backs drew the centre-backs, Terry Butcher and Terry Fenwick, out of position. The truth finally dawned when Portugal took the lead fifteen minutes from time. With

England's defence all over the place, Carlos Manuel closed in on the far post to sweep the ball past Shilton. Portuguese supporters set off on noisy circuits of Monterrey, the England contingent stood around in morose groups, and the inquest in Saltillo was inconclusive. 'A few us had a moan but Bobby didn't want to change the way we were playing,' Terry Fenwick said. Because of a change in format – sixteen teams were to go forward – defeat in the opening game wasn't the handicap it might have been in previous World Cups, but the effect on morale was a different matter. Where there had been confidence, now there was doubt.

Three days later England returned to the Tecnologica Stadium with an unchanged team to face one they had never previously met. In a television studio back home, Alf Ramsey referred to England's next opponents as 'the Moroccians'. Making only their second appearance in the finals, Morocco had already held Poland to a goalless draw, and would go on to top the group. England approached them warily but were expected to win; the phrase was not new, but in the circumstances it was appropriate. England began badly and fell away. Whatever Bobby Robson had planned to say at the interval was rendered useless in the 38th minute when his captain's weakened shoulder failed to withstand the impact of a cartwheel tumble in Morocco's penalty area. Clearly unable to continue, Robson had barely reached the bench when Wilkins was yellow-carded. Less than a minute later he was given offside when he thought he'd been fouled. In frustration, he threw the ball towards the Paraguayan referee Gabriel Gonzalez and was dismissed for a second bookable offence. Until then the holder of an unblemished record at every level of the game, Wilkins had now become the first England player ever to be sent off in the World Cup finals.

Harsh words were exchanged in England's dressing room. 'We're always being told to think for ourselves, now somebody had better start thinking for us,' one of the players said. Down to ten men (Steve Hodge had replaced Robson), England were led back out by Peter Shilton, their third captain on the day. 'In that heat it had been hard enough with eleven men, so our instructions were to try and keep the ball,' Fenwick told me. 'Fortunately Morocco didn't come at us. Maybe they didn't want to risk losing. But with one thing or another, being a man short, the temperature, the system, we were there for the taking.'

Robson was back under fire. England fans filled the notebooks of news reporters with bitter complaints about the manager and his employers. Claiming to speak for the nation, the *Sun* demanded England's recall: BRING THEM HOME. Its chief sportswriter branded Robson 'the fool on the hill'.

A few hours after the game Robson called a squad meeting at which Fenwick challenged the choice of system. 'I was so annoyed that I just stood up and spoke my mind,' he told me. 'I told the manager that unless we got back to a system we were used to he might as well book us on a flight home. Thinking about it now, I was probably out of order, but somebody had to say something. The room went very quiet. Players don't want to rock the boat, but when I looked behind me Peter Reid and Alvin Martin were on their feet agreeing with me.' Martin was in Mexico as cover for Butcher and Fenwick. 'Fen made sense,' he said. 'I could see that if I got called into the team I'd be stuck with the problem.' After seeking Butcher's thoughts, Robson reverted to 4–4–2. Abandoning the idea of a winger (Chris Waddle) and a tall target man (Hateley), he brought in Hodge and Trevor Steven as wide midfielders and Peter Beardsley to provide close support for Lineker. Reid was also brought in, supposedly to stiffen the midfield, but his inclusion also had the effect of transforming Glenn Hoddle.

The most naturally gifted English footballer of his generation, Hoddle had iconic status with everyone who blamed England's comparatively poor World Cup record on a preference for industry over craftsmanship. That he had not been an automatic choice since making his international debut under Ron Greenwood in 1980 (he arrived in Mexico with 33 caps) was not, however, down to idleness or suspect stamina but a flawed positional instinct. The space in play most easily available is that between two players of the same team as long as they can see each other. Hoddle didn't have an eye for it. He didn't hide from the ball, but getting it to him was consistently a problem. Tottenham dealt with this on a collective basis. Steve Perryman, who was captain when Hoddle began to make his mark in the team, said, 'Glenn had terrific skill and imagination, but because he wasn't easy to find we weren't getting the best out of him. As a team, we decided to give him the ball as much as possible. I was playing right-back at the time, and I told Glenn to come square to me whenever I got possession from our goalkeeper. It didn't matter if somebody closed down on Glenn or my pass was hurried because he had the skill to control the ball however it came to him.' This, more than any other factor, explains why Hoddle's international career didn't fully meet expectations. Nobody in football admired technical fluency more than Bobby Robson's predecessor, Ron Greenwood, but he, too, had reservations about Hoddle, using him only twice (once as substitute) in the 1982 World Cup finals. Although Hoddle was a fixture come the 1986 finals, England did not get the full benefit from his deft touch and exceptional vision until Reid was brought in against Poland following Wilkins' expulsion in the previous match. This is not meant as a slight to Wilkins, but if Hoddle wasn't immediately in view he fell into the old habit of playing safe passes which had made England's movements predictable. A canny pro, Reid simply altered his own position to where he could see Hoddle and force the ball at him.

England, other results going in their favour, would have been safe with a draw against Poland; instead they woke up and swaggered into the next round. Much more comfortable with 4–4–2, they played with a precision unimaginable after the first two matches. All three goals came from England's left, all from Lineker whose hat-trick was England's first in the World Cup since Geoff Hurst's. Along with his pace and predatory instinct, Lineker's firm ankles looked priceless assets. 'I guess I achieved something with my outburst, but at a price,' Fenwick remarked. 'I couldn't see myself playing again for England after that World Cup.' He didn't. 'It was different again,' Fenwick continued. 'There was much better understanding, a lot more purpose. We looked a real team.'

England's poor form in the first two games actually worked in their favour: as winners of Group F they would have remained in Monterrey to play West Germany; as the second-placed team they went forward to meet Paraguay, a less daunting prospect, at the Azteca Stadium in Mexico City. Dave Sexton was a busy man in Mexico: by day he scouted other finalists, writing up reports for Robson; by night, at the age of 55, he studied for an Open University degree in philosophy. 'I try not to get the two mixed up,' he joked. Sexton's view of Paraguay was that they were skilful, could be spiteful, but had a porous defence.

Sexton's report was spot on. Paraguay dazzled for 30 minutes, gave up a goal to Lineker, and then turned nasty (Reid, no pussy cat himself, had limped away from a whack in the first minute). Lineker was off the field receiving treatment for an elbow in the throat when Beardsley put England two up in the 57th minute. 'After that it was "Who can get an Englishman?"' Reid said. 'Elbows, trips, sly kicks, the lot.' Reid limped off to be replaced by Gary Stevens of Tottenham. Lineker returned to score his fifth goal of the tournament. England were through to the last eight, the end of the line in all but one of their World Cup ventures.

On 18 June, four days before England met Argentina at the Azteca, I received a telephone call from the *Sunday Mirror* suggesting that my preview should focus on the Falklands conflict four years before. Links between the two countries, diplomatic and sporting, were still severed, England hadn't played Argentina at anything since 1982, and people hadn't forgotten. It was the Falklands all over again, this time on a football field.

I listened to all this with a heavy heart. I thought about all those who had died, unnecessarily in my view, and told the *Sunday Mirror* what they could do with their request. A month after the World Cup I ended a 24-year association with Mirror Group newspapers to join the *Independent* in time for its launch the following October. What I did write for the *Mirror* was that the match would probably come down to a duel between the world's greatest outfield player and the goalkeeper who was reckoned to be the best then at work in the game: Diego Maradona versus Peter Shilton.

Sad, bloated figure that he became, Maradona's reputation in 1986 was that of a genius capable even of surpassing Pele. As a nineteen-year-old in Argentina's colours at Wembley he'd caught everybody's eye. 'Phenomenal,' Ron Greenwood said. At 25, Maradona was approaching his peak. Freakishly built, standing only 5ft 4in and weighing several pounds more than eleven stone, he had none of Pele's muscular symmetry; instead he possessed a squat upper body, powerful shoulders and formidable thighs. 'To see him wrench that body into improbable twists and turns makes you think that he must have a cast-iron pelvis,' Sexton said. Like Puskas before him, Maradona's used his right foot merely to remain upright. His left foot was a marvel. 'When I got to Barcelona, the players there told me that Maradona's left foot was like a hand,' Lineker told me.

England's hopes of keeping Maradona at bay were inseparable from their goalkeeper's record in the World Cup finals. In 1982

Shilton was beaten only once in five matches, and so far only once in Mexico. 'Having the big man in goal is a big bonus,' said Greenwood, who had interrupted his retirement to follow the finals as an analyst for BBC Radio. 'And now he is skipper he is even more determined that he won't let anything go past him.' How to deal with Maradona became the main point of discussion. 'Of course we spoke a lot about him,' Fenwick confirmed. 'The coaches didn't think that man-marking him would work [West Germany gave the job to Lothar Matthaus in the final] because nobody in the squad was used to doing that sort of job and he was so powerfully elusive with all that strength in his legs he'd be gone in a flash. It was decided to share the responsibility around, making sure that somebody was close whenever he got the ball.'

The closest player to Hodge when he sliced a clearance back over his head towards the penalty spot was Shilton. Seeing Maradona closing in, Shilton elected to punch. It was no contest in the air, but Shilton had been slow to make up his mind and had taken his eye off the ball. Maradona got a fist to it. 'We couldn't believe the referee when he gave a goal,' Fenwick said. 'The linesman must have seen what happened, but he bottled it. I went after the referee, so did Shilts, but the others seemed too shocked to do anything. I was angry with them because we should have caused more fuss [an echo here of Winterbottom's remark when England were sucked into Brazil's free-kick routine in 1962].' England were still fuming when Maradona scored one of the great World Cup goals just four minutes after the 'Hand of God' incident. Collecting the ball just inside his own half – 'some of our players were still so upset that they'd lost concentration,' Fenwick maintained – Maradona wrongfooted Beardsley and Reid and set off on a bewildering staccato dribble that took him past Butcher and Fenwick as though they were traffic cones set out for a training session. In marquee terms, it was Shilton versus Maradona: The Legitimate Confrontation. Maradona dropped down a gear, dummied, and drove the ball home.

Robson went for broke. Taking off Reid and Steven, he sent on his wingers, Barnes and Waddle. Argentina had made no plans to deal with unorthodox brilliance. With ten minutes left Barnes got away on the left to provide Lineker with a goal. Urged on by Robson and everyone else on the bench, England almost snatched an equaliser, too. This time, however, it was Lineker who ended up in the net, not the ball from Barnes. 'Say you'd punched it in,' it was suggested to Lineker. He shrugged.

Looking back, Fenwick is glad that a marvellous goal stood between the two teams. 'Over the 90 minutes Argentina had too much for us,' he said. 'But it would be rotten to think that the little bastard cheated us out of it.' That their conquerors also went on to defeat West Germany in the final was some consolation for England, particularly after the early tribulations in Monterrey. Eighth place in the FIFA rankings was about right for the side; ever mindful of public opinion, the popular press unanimously agreed that Robson should stay in office. The FA's endorsement was a formality.

Between the end of the World Cup and the opening fixture of the 1988 European Championship, England lost just two matches, one of them away to the World Cup finalists and soon-to-be world champions in Düsseldorf. Drawn in a group with Turkey, Northern Ireland and Yugoslavia, they reached the finals in West Germany in cruise control, dropped just the one point, scored nineteen goals and conceded only one. Not since 1966 had they gone into the latter stages of a major tournament in such confident mood.

England's opening game on 12 June was against the Republic of Ireland who had surprised everyone bar Jack Charlton by qualifying for their first major tournament. In fact, surprise had been the general reaction when Charlton became the first non-Irish national manager in February 1986. A story popular in Dublin was that Charlton's appointment had resulted from an error in voting. If so, it was the luckiest mistake Irish football ever made. Charlton wasn't interested in prolonging a tradition of moral victories. His instructions were easily understood: 'Don't take risks in your own half, don't piss about in the middle of the field, get the ball forward.' If not as crude as some reports suggested, it certainly wasn't pretty. And it was hard to play against. 'I went to watch the World Cup finals in 1986 and hardly took a note,' he said. 'I saw nothing new. I saw teams playing more or less as they did when I was turning out for England. Tactically, international football had got into a rut, and for most of the time I was bored stupid. Apart from what I saw in Mexico, I thought about the sort of attacks that most bothered me as a defender. Not so much the close-quarter stuff, one-twos, players running at you, but angled balls coming over my shoulders, making me turn. I was a good defender, so if those attacks bothered me they would bother others.'

In qualifying the Republic for the finals, Charlton was already a hero. When they defeated England 1–0 in Stuttgart he was on his way to sainthood. England were still in shock three days later when they lost 3–1 to the Netherlands in Düsseldorf, and then by the same score to the Soviet Union. The morning after England's exit, Robson admitted that he did not regret the absence of any player apart from Terry Butcher, who was injured. Back home, there was outrage. Never before had an England team finished bottom and pointless in the finals of a major tournament. The *Sun* called it a 'disgrace to the nation'. In the *Independent*, I spoke against celebration of mediocrity, the failure to compensate for the disappearance of street football and arrogant assumption. Nervously, the FA, who hadn't given Charlton even the courtesy of a reply when they'd invited applications for team manager following Revie's defection, kept Robson in place. But how long would he last?

England's attempt to qualify for the 1990 finals in Italy began in October 1988 against Sweden at Wembley. The European club ban was already beginning to have an effect. Apart from Lineker at Barcelona, only two of the selected eleven, Butcher and Stevens, with Glasgow Rangers, were getting experience against foreign opposition. Held to a goalless draw, England ran up another dismal first: never before had they failed to win their opening game in a World Cup qualifying competition. Robson and his players left the field with abuse ringing in their ears.

On a visit to Albania with the England under-23 team, Les Cocker had described its capital Tirana as 'Accrington without lights'. England's football against the group's no-hopers in March 1989 could hardly have been described as illuminating, but a 2–0 win was welcome enough. Sweden had already picked up two points in Albania and had England to come in Stockholm. Lineker was again missing from the score sheet that day. Recovering from hepatitis, and out of favour with Barcelona's coach Johann Cruyff, he had now gone eight games without an international goal, but he recovered his touch the very next month with three of England's five goals against Albania at Wembley, and then netted the first of the three Robson's team scored against Poland in June.

In 1966, Ramsey's England had used Poland as a stepping-stone to the finals; it was a friendly that had established their potential. Robson's England went to Katowice in rather different circumstances.

With two to go forward from Group 2, a draw would eliminate the Poles and ensure England's qualification. It was touch and go, Poland a revelation to their supporters. Supposedly a rag-tag team, they ran England ragged. Robson's players had more than 450 caps between them but they were made to look like novice internationals by Polish flair and industry. It took a series of outstanding saves by Shilton to keep England in the game. Nails were being bitten on England's bench when the tired Poles threw in one final assault. In the last minute a 30-yard shot from Tarasciewicz smacked against England's crossbar, Shilton palpably beaten. England were through. 'It's a long time since we had to survive such pressure,' Robson said. It was only when Poland were swept aside by Sweden, who thereby topped the group, that England fully realised how close they'd been to elimination. Had Tarasciewicz's shot dipped a couple of inches lower, the second place to Sweden would have been taken by Denmark.

Whatever awaited England in the 1990 finals, it was clear Robson's days were numbered. Embarrassed by sleazy tabloid revelations about his private life, the FA were already casting around for a replacement. Alex Montgomery was one of four journalists present when this fact was let slip by Bert Millichip the FA chairman. 'He didn't come right out with it, but he gave a pretty clear indication that Bobby was on his way out,' Montgomery said. Robson would in due course be officially informed of the decision; for now, having reached the finals, he felt that he had survived the worst the tabloids could hurl at him. 'The personal abuse has been hard to take,' he said, 'but now I've got used to it, it no longer hurts. I know I'm doing the job to the best of my ability and that the players are giving me their utmost.'

But another storm was brewing. For security reasons, England were sent to play their group games on the island of Sardinia, drawn, as fate would have it, with the Netherlands and the Republic of Ireland, two of their conquerors in the 1988 European Championship. The fourth team was Egypt. Within a week of arrival the England squad had cut off all contact with the press. This breaking point was reached when tabloid news reporters (the 'Rotters') joyfully revealed that Isabella Ciaravolo, a Sardinian liaison officer, had been relieved of her duties after unsubstantiated reports of clandestine meetings with several of the England players. 'Things changed a lot during my time with England,' Butcher said. 'I'd always got on pretty well with the press, feeling that the majority could be trusted. But by then there were people around who had been sent just to dig up scandal, watching our every move, prepared to make something out of nothing.'

Veteran World Cup observers, those who came to report on the football alone and in whose ranks stood one or two with a full attendance record since the Second World War, agreed that Italia 90 was the worst ever, with no outstanding team, style at a premium, and hardly an individual performance worth speaking about. 'The game has lost its soul,' Saldanha said shortly before his death in Rome two days after West Germany defeated Argentina in an instantly forgettable final. Thinking modern developments a curse, especially the rapid spread of commercialism, the great football philosopher went sadly. 'The last of the romantics,' someone said of him, and certainly there were precious few at work that summer.

The reign of Robson covered a period when technical standards in English football declined. Inventiveness was sacrificed to speed, power and collective efficiency. But in what always looked like being a lacklustre World Cup, it seemed as though those prosaic qualities, augmented by Paul Gascoigne's flair, might work for England. Until Kevin Sheedy removed all reason for optimism. Given the lead by Lineker in the ninth minute, England were grimly playing out time when Sheedy pounced on Steve McMahon's error to gain a point for the Republic of Ireland. A narrow victory would not have spared England the bombardment of criticism they took for being sucked into copying Charlton's long-ball tactics. How could it? The ball was in play for only 50 minutes. 'It must have been an awful game to watch,' Butcher said, 'but no matter what people said about Jack's policy, the Irish could make life difficult. They never held the ball long enough for you to get at them. Jack was right when he said that nobody enjoyed playing against them. Watford and Wimbledon made a similar style work for them in the First Division. Nobody enjoyed playing against them either.'

It was once said of Bobby Robson that his indecision was final. Unfair, perhaps, but as in Mexico four years earlier he was now talked into changing formation. Mark Wright was brought in as the covering player in a back line of three; effectively it was a five-man defence. Paul Parker's pace got him the nod over Gary Stevens as the right wing-back. Nobody, least of all their own supporters, knew what to expect from the Dutch on 16 June; the players had wanted Johann Cruyff as coach but had got Leo Beenhakker. 'It depends on which team turns up,' Johann Derkson, a Dutch journalist, said. 'Will it be the team that can take your breath away? Or the team that sulks?'

Apart from the nervousness welling inside him over the tactical switch, Robson also had the worry of Bryan Robson's injured toe and Gascoigne's unpredictability. A painkilling injection would suffice for England's captain, but Dr Freud himself would probably have given up on Gascoigne. At 22 (going on ten) he was the youngest player in the squad, and as far as many of its members were concerned he was a pest. That was off the field. On it he could hit a level of performance to justify Bobby Robson defining his fellow Geordie as 'one of the finest players to emerge in British football for many years'. Gascoigne's principle assets were balance, a deft touch, exceptional dribbling ability and limitless imagination. If no speedster, he was deceptively strong, difficult to shake off the ball. On the downside there was his lack of discipline and a volatile temperament. Gascoigne could lift a manager to the heights or plunge him into despair, though Terry Venables never once regretted paying Newcastle £2 million to get him for Tottenham.

It was mainly through Gascoigne's efforts as an all-purpose inside-forward, and Des Walker's flawless policing of Marco Van Basten, that England more than held their own against the Dutch who were indeed in one of their soporific moods. 'They had some terrific players – Van Basten, Rijkaard, Gullit, Koeman – but they didn't seem half the team that won the European Championship two years before,' Butcher said. 'Not that we thrilled any hearts.' A goalless draw left the group wide open.

When it became clear to Bryan Robson that his injury wasn't responding to treatment, he arranged for a faith healer to be flown out. It didn't work. Robson was out of the game against Egypt and out of the tournament. In Mexico he'd upset Manchester United by remaining with the squad instead of returning for an operation on his damaged shoulder. This time the club were firmer, and Robson was ordered home. The England manager proved firmer too: going against the tactical preference of senior players, he reverted to a four-man defence with Wright and Walker as the centre-backs. 'It was the first time Bobby left me out, either for Ipswich or England,' Butcher said. 'He wanted to play an extra attacker because the Egyptians had shown they were difficult to break down. There wasn't going to be much midfield cover so he wanted his quickest defenders out there just in case Egypt tried to catch us napping.'

Egypt's intentions didn't take much working out: if they could take another point, they would finish the group stage unbeaten; if results elsewhere went in their favour, they would then have a chance of going through. As it turned out, Shilton's ninth clean sheet in World Cup finals, a new record, was his easiest. Egypt seldom ventured from their own half, defending so deep that a price was offered against England being offside more than five times. With almost an hour played it might have been possible to get a price against England scoring, for they hadn't created one clear-cut chance. Then Wright got on to Gascoigne's inswinging free-kick to register his only England goal, enough for them to end up top of Group F, with the Republic in second place and Holland third. The prize for third place was a match with West Germany; the Irish got the Romanians and England would face Belgium in Bologna. In keeping with the tournament's overall sterility, Group F produced only seven goals. If drearily achieved, England's victory over the Egyptians stood alone.

Dave Sexton had been tracking Belgium. 'Belgium's coach [Guy Thys] wasn't a chopper and changer,' he told me. 'He had a nucleus of experienced players, although some were getting on a bit. They had excellent teamwork. I'd seen [Enzo] Scifo before and really liked him. I warned Bobby that Belgium would give us a hard game.' It was an understatement. 'In truth, they deserved to beat us,' Butcher said. 'I got back in the team when Bobby decided to use the sweeper system, which worked well enough. One of our problems was that we couldn't keep Scifo quiet. He was sharp and alive, all over the place.' Although Barnes had a goal wrongly disallowed for offside, Belgium were generally more threatening, striking the base of Shilton's right-hand post twice, Ceuleman in the first half, Scifo in the second. Scifo's effort led to the withdrawal of McMahon, who had succumbed to the effort of marking him. On came David Platt.

As the game went on through extra-time the dreaded prospect of a penalty shoot-out loomed. But with barely a minute left, Gascoigne had enough strength left to carry the ball deep into Belgian territory, only to be impeded by the veteran full-back Gerets. Looking around as though unsure what to do with the free-kick, Gascoigne then saw that Robson and Howe were on their feet urging him to put the ball into Belgium's penalty area. 'Bobby and Don were waving, pointing at Belgium's goalmouth, shouting "Put the bloody ball in there!"' Butcher said. Gascoigne's chip looked too long, but as it dropped over Platt's right shoulder he spun through almost 360 degrees and volleyed England into the quarter-finals. Butcher wasn't alone in thinking them fortunate.

More good fortune was on the way. 'I have to admit it,' Butcher said, 'Cameroon tore us to pieces [without four first-choice players, missing through suspension]. We knew they had some extremely talented players but we weren't prepared for their teamwork and effort.' When Platt gave England the lead with a header in the 25th minute it was glibly supposed that Cameroon would either collapse or turn nasty (they had already picked up two red cards and eight yellows). Instead, they startled England with attacks of such precision and swiftness that Robson's defenders felt as though they were chasing shadows. 'They seemed to come at us from everywhere,' Butcher recalled. 'Running, shooting. It's wrong to say that we took them for granted. We didn't. But apparently some of the press had done exactly that, writing up the game as though it was a lucky dip for England, a bye into the semi-finals. Some bye!'

England began the second half with Beardsley on for Barnes; Cameroon called on the talismanic Roger Milla, a player of infinite skill and indeterminate age. Officially, Milla was 38, but who really knew? Persuaded out of semi-retirement, he'd been used exclusively as a substitute, yet he already had four goals to his name. In the 62nd minute he lured Gascoigne into giving away a penalty from which Kunde equalised. 'Then they really came at us,' Butcher said. 'It was difficult to know who to mark. They didn't seem to have any positions.' Sexton was watching the game on television in Milan. 'If it hadn't been against England I would have been on my feet applauding Cameroon,' he said. 'For an hour they were astonishing, knew no fear.' Four minutes after drawing level, Cameroon took the lead when Ekeke fastened on to a pass from Milla that ripped open England's defence. Switching to an orthodox formation, Robson replaced Butcher with Trevor Steven. 'Sitting on the touchline, growing more anxious by the minute, I couldn't see us scoring until Gary Lineker panicked them into giving away a penalty.' The legitimacy of that award has never been in doubt, but the penalty from which Lineker put England through in extra-time was as dubious as Geoff Hurst's second goal in the 1966 World Cup final.

Still, England had made it to the World Cup semi-finals for the first time on foreign soil. But if West Germany could beat them in Turin it would provide Franz Beckenbauer with an opportunity to emulate Mario Zagallo's feat of winning the World Cup both as a player and manager. And Beckenbauer, like Robson, was due to hand over control of his national team. A few days before the game I spoke with Beckenbauer at Erba near Lake Como. 'It is remarkable how many times the paths of West Germany and England have crossed in football,' he said. 'Some of my great personal memories are of matches between us. Now I must try to defeat England again. As a small boy, one of my first football heroes was an Englishman. Stanley Matthews. I have warm feelings about Bobby Charlton and Bobby Moore, great players and, yes, friends. One thing I know about the match is that England will be difficult. They never give up.'

What England knew, and tried to forget, was that the Germans had made a habit of reaching World Cup semi-finals. This would be their eighth since 1954. German football seldom set pulses racing, but their consistency was second to none: twice winners, they'd appeared in five World Cup finals; all of Beckenbauer's three predecessors as manager, Sepp Herberger, Helmut Schoen and Jupp Derwall, had won major championships. A German journalist and friend, Hartmut Scherzer, said, 'For the German people, reaching the last four of the World Cup is no big thing. It may sound arrogant, but it is the truth. I have read that even if England fails to reach the final they will be heroes at home. Before the World Cup final of 1982 it was already known that Derwall was not staying on. Had that not been the case Derwall would have been hounded by the press for losing and not playing well. The English tabloid press is not uniquely brutal. Things can be equally tough for the national team manager in Germany, tougher even, because whoever has the job is judged by many past achievements. Qualifying for the World Cup and doing fairly well is not enough. Nobody knows this better than Beckenbauer. He is protected by a huge reputation, but that wouldn't save him from criticism if Germany does not win this World Cup.'

In reaching the semi-finals the Germans had scored ten goals in their group, thirteen overall; England had scored six, two from penalties against Cameroon. However, they'd kept only one clean sheet to England's three. Sexton had been tracking the Germans in Milan. 'Athletic, strong, well coached, plenty of experience' were the general points in his report to Robson. Jurgen Klinsmann, magnificent against Holland when both teams were down to ten men, was a real danger. 'But the Germans are not as strong defensively as I expected,' Sexton added. Robson worried that Germany's man-markers would try to wind up Gascoigne – 'I like him, a real talent,' Beckenbauer had said. For England it was the sweeper system again. Surely at least one game in the dreariest of World Cups would rise above the numbing mediocrity.

Ever since Herberger's team defeated 'unstoppable' Hungary in the 1954 final after giving up eight goals to them in a group game, one of West Germany's strengths had been the confidence to work steadily through a tournament. Surely they would now step up a gear? Instead, it was England who came on to a game. By contrast, the Germans fell back in form, their defence as hesitant as Sexton had suspected, their build-up lacking its usual efficiency. Before the game, on a darkened side of the Estadio Delle Alpi in Turin, shuffling, silent columns of English supporters had made their way to the game under heavy escort, moving like a chain gang. As half-time approached they were in full voice, thrilled by England's improvement. To then see England fall behind to a fluked goal was a palpable shock. With 60 minutes played Thon touched a free-kick to Brehme, whose shooting had been mentioned in England's team talk. Parker remembered. The first Englishman to move, he flung himself in the path of Brehme's drive but succeeded only in getting a touch that sent the ball looping over Shilton. Robson repeated the substitution he'd made against Cameroon, replacing Butcher with Trevor Steven. Again the switch in formation worked. With ten minutes left, Lineker burrowed between two defenders to equalise.

For the third consecutive match England would have to endure a further 30 minutes' play. Ramsey's instructions in 1966, 'You've won it once, now win it again', became Robson's. 'Now you can win it,' he said. Butcher sat through the additional half an hour feeling helpless. 'I'd been out there, now I couldn't do anything but wait.' And watch. Watch Waddle hit a post. Watch Buchwald do the same. Watch Gascoigne in tears when shown the yellow card that would keep him out of the final if England got through.

It all ended with penalties, and more English tears. 'The only genius Germany showed us was from the penalty spot,' Butcher recalled. 'The pressure on the kickers was enormous. Walking up to the ball, knowing that billions are watching. You can practise every day, put the ball exactly where you want it time after time, and still make a mess of the responsibility. Nothing much disturbed Stuart Pearce, yet he couldn't score. Chris Waddle shot over. And the Germans were so clinical. Perfect technique, ice cool.' Outside the stadium after the match West Germany's bus drew alongside England's. 'We could see the German players jumping about, hear them singing and shouting,' Butcher recalled. 'I'll always remember that.'

Brehme's penalty against Argentina in the final was enough to secure West Germany's third World Cup success, bringing them abreast of Brazil and Italy. At least Argentina had not profited from the policy of cynical containment that had marked their progress to Rome. They'd entered the final without four of their best men, all through suspension, and had a further two sent off. Unquestionably, the worst World Cup ever.

11. 1990 TO FRANCE 1998

The irony of Bobby Robson's departure from office was that it came at a time when public support for him was stronger than it had ever been. Since the FA's decision, taken well before England got through to the semi-finals in Italy, also meant losing the vast experience accumulated by Robson's chief assistants Don Howe and Dave Sexton, it made very little sense.

On the morning after West Germany put England out, I was sitting together with Howe and two colleagues when Sexton walked towards us. 'There is the man who should now manage England,' Howe said. At 59, Sexton had the bearing of a much younger man. His knowledge of the game could not have been bettered anywhere, and his enthusiasm for it was undiminished. He'd been at every World Cup since 1958. In that year, the modest bonus Sexton and a friend had picked up for helping Brighton gain promotion from the Third Division went on the second-hand car they drove to Sweden for the finals. Living in a tent, they went from training ground to training ground, picking up match tickets where they could. As Chelsea's manager, Sexton had won the FA Cup and the European Cup Winners Cup in successive seasons; he was Manchester United's manager when they lost to Arsenal in the 1979 FA Cup final; he'd coached Arsenal, too, during Bertie Mee's reign at Highbury, and Fulham; under his guidance, Queens Park Rangers finished runners-up for the League Championship in 1976, just one point behind Liverpool; when the FA established a School of Excellence at Lilleshall, the 'headmaster' was Sexton; and under Robson, he'd successfully managed the England under-23 team.

Howe's contention that the FA could not have turned to a better candidate was, however, flawed. A dignified, self-contained man, Sexton had inherited toughness from his father Archie, a contender in the 1930s for the British and Empire middleweight championship. But it was impossible to imagine that he could handle the growth of media attention that had put years on Robson. Later on, I asked Sexton whether at any time he would have taken on the task of England manager. 'I was never asked,' he replied enigmatically.

Not since Walter Winterbottom had there been an England manager without top-class playing experience; only Greenwood, a 'B' international, had been unable to answer the challenge 'Show us your caps.' Graham Taylor, a moderate full-back, had spent his playing days in the lower leagues with Lincoln and Grimsby; undeterred by technical limitations on the field he had, however, made considerable progress in management. Taylor's ascent to the most important (and exposed) office in English football began in the 1975–76 League season when, at 31, he guided Lincoln City to the Fourth Division title with a record haul of 74 points and 111 goals. An alliance with Elton John at Watford then sent Taylor's stock soaring. In successive seasons, he took Watford up two divisions. By 1982 they were competing at the highest level of English football; the following year they finished runners-up to Liverpool in the championship; and in 1984 they reached the FA Cup final. Taylor's only concession to artistic merit in that time was the inclusion of John Barnes at outside-left; other than that it was mostly long ball supported by hard-running midfielders. Wolves had done it in the 1950s with better players.

Nobody gained more pleasure from Taylor's success than the FA's director of coaching. Charles Hughes could point to Watford and Wimbledon as proof that direct football worked. Many in the game were appalled, even more so when Taylor made his system work for Aston Villa. Promoted in his first season, they finished runners-up to Liverpool two years later, just as the FA were deciding that Robson's time was up. Had Taylor remained at Watford the FA would probably have looked elsewhere, but then his work at Watford was the clincher. Where Robson had dithered, Taylor leapt at an opportunity he could not have imagined in his first year of management. From Sincil Bank to Lancaster Gate in fifteen years was some progress.

Two big questions existed. Was Taylor prepared to run the risk of employing his preferred style of play at international level, and the wrath of the press that would inevitably result from its failure? And, could he handle big-time players? One thing was for sure: Taylor could have talked for England. Media friendly, his press conferences often took the form of lengthy tutorials. Open and amiable, he astonished football writers by handing out his home telephone number.

Taylor chose as his assistant a big man with a big personality. Lawrie McMenemy hadn't been much of a player either, but he knew his way around the game. Recovering from a grim spell at

Sunderland, he'd managed Southampton with confidence and no little style, guiding them to victory in the 1976 FA Cup final. According to the grapevine, he'd come within one vote of securing the managerial berth at Manchester United. Importantly, McMenemy wasn't intimidated by the prospect of dealing with star players; his Southampton teams had included Kevin Keegan and Alan Ball, snapped up, along with others, at the back end of their careers.

Though a year passed before Taylor's first defeat, the 1–1 draw against the Republic of Ireland in a European Championship qualifier at Wembley in March 1991 set off the first tremors of doubt. Whereas Taylor had compromised over use of the long ball, the Republic were still devotees of the system, if with refinements England hadn't expected. Playing with formidable enthusiasm and vigour, and drawing level through Niall Quinn after unluckily falling behind, Jack Charlton's team played Taylor's off the park; for long periods England's overmanned defence was under bombardment, their uncertainty manifest in seizures of anxiety. England hardly mounted a coherent attack, and Bryan Robson, now approaching the end of his international career, was second best to Ray Houghton in midfield. 'If there was any justice, we'd have won easily,' Charlton said. 'England aren't one thing or another. You've got to settle on a style and stick with it.'

Two months later Taylor lost the player around whom his predecessor had intended to build a new team. While playing for Tottenham Hotspur against Nottingham Forest in the FA Cup final, Paul Gascoigne went so viciously at Gary Charles that he wrecked his own right knee. Diagnosed as a rupture of the cruciate ligament, it put in doubt Gascoigne's agreed deal with Lazio and raised the fear that his career might be over. Gascoigne would fight back, but he would never again be the same player. In warming to his tears during the 1990 World Cup semi-finals, tears that increased his popularity, people had ignored the emotional excesses of his nature. Over-indulged, an over-hyped product of his sporting time, unarguably an artist in an age of house painters, Gascoigne always seemed to be heading for a traumatic experience from which he might find it difficult to recover. Unlike many great footballers from the past, he did not appear to possess an uncomplicated appreciation of the good things that had happened to him, no capacity for honest, unquestioning gratitude. 'Sadly, a thing about Paul is that he doesn't really understand what it takes to be a star,' it was once said of him.

In September 1991, Taylor tasted his first defeat as England manager, a 1–0 loss to Germany, now one nation, at Wembley. But a far more important fixture was imminent. Ramsey, Revie, Greenwood, Robson – all had found trouble in the European Championship, and now it was Taylor's turn. If England failed to take a point from Poland in Poznan on 13 November, they would not be going to Sweden. It was close, too, Lineker's equaliser not coming until late in the game.

Robson's second tilt at the European Championship, in 1988, had brought the humiliation of three straight defeats and searching reappraisal. Taylor's effort in the summer of 1992 was only marginally better: goalless draws with Denmark and France followed by a 2–1 defeat by the hosts in Stockholm that left England propping up the group. For the first time as England manager, Taylor came under attack. Slammed for his choice of tactics, he'd made matters worse for himself by substituting Gary Lineker when the Tottenham centre-forward was just one goal short of Bobby Charlton's national record of 49. Lineker, in the last of his 80 games for England, was furious, hinting that he'd never hit it off with Taylor. The *Sun* excelled themselves. Superimposing Taylor's face on a turnip, they ran the headline SWEDES 2 TURNIPS 1. Taylor changed his telephone number in anticipation of a tricky schedule for qualification for the 1994 World Cup finals.

In 1966, Norway had provided England with shooting practice for the World Cup. Four years later, an old friend of mine, George Curtis, who had served as Alan Brown's assistant at Sunderland before managing Brighton, was in Norway coaching Rosenberg. 'If Norway could get players out into the world, the game here might take a great leap forward,' he'd told me. 'They are very athletic, have good skills, and they're quick learners. All they need is experience of top-class football.' Norway had certainly made enough progress by 1992 to be a threatening factor in England's attempt to qualify for the World Cup, to be held in the United States. The other teams in England's group were Holland, Poland (again), Turkey and San Marino. England and Holland were clear favourites; Norway and Poland were potential troublemakers. Gascoigne had recovered sufficiently to be back in contention, but there was little else to suggest that England were heading for football's last frontier. England had gone four games without a victory, and had won none of their last nine. Alan Shearer was a big hope at centre-forward, but he was still adjusting to international football.

At the 1992 Olympics in Barcelona I had the company of the former Arsenal captain Frank McLintock when watching a game between Italy and the USA. Central to our interest was a major law change, the first for many years, that had been introduced by FIFA to combat the sterility of Italia 90. Launched at the Olympics, it prevented goalkeepers from fielding back-passes other than those delivered with the head. I shared McLintock's reservations, agreeing that this might lead to a further downgrading of build-up play. The wider feeling was that it would eventually work to the satisfaction of most people. For sure, goalkeepers would be spending a lot more time in kicking practice.

Norway arrived at Wembley in October 1992 under full sail. Their eccentric coach Egil Olsen already had six points in the bag. 'People said it was nothing to put ten goals past San Marino, but have England ever scored ten in a World Cup tie?' Olsen asked. No, never. At home two weeks later, Norway had lowered Holland's colours in Oslo, and then completed a double over San Marino. 'Wembley holds no fears for my players,' Olsen said, a statement Norway justified by holding England to a 1–1 draw. If by now a mite wary of the press, Taylor didn't flinch from repeating in public what he'd said in the England dressing room. 'We were much the better team, we deserved to win,' he stated. Indeed, he considered it the best attacking performance England had given under his management.

On 17 February 1993, desperately ill with cancer, Bobby Moore summoned up enough strength to broadcast on the match between England and San Marino at Wembley. It was his way of justifying one last visit to the scene of his greatest triumph. He died fewer than two weeks later. As Hugh McIlvanney put it, 'the impact of his death, and the remarkably widespread ache of deprivation left by it, cannot possibly be explained in terms of accumulated nostalgia. Even the length and sustained distinction of his professional career [his total of 108 international caps remains a record for an English outfield player] do not take us halfway to an explanation. The encouraging truth may be that Moore's place in the hearts of such a large percentage of the population confirms the survival among us of the capacity to recognise and applaud heroic style.'

Little of the style Moore so consistently represented could be found in European football as between November 1992 and March

1993, against Turkey (twice) and San Marino, England added six points and twelve goals to their World Cup tally. Taylor's team was essentially functional, compact, combative, energetic. Even on his one good leg – it was noticeable that he no longer had a full range of movement in the other – Gascoigne could turn a game, but after nearly 70 appearances for the national team John Barnes remained an enigma. Gifted, intelligent and strong, he still hadn't grasped the basic geometry of the game.

Dutch football wasn't in much better shape. Barry Hughes certainly painted a bleak picture of it: lowered standards, declining interest, hooligan supporters. In his mid-twenties Hughes, a Welsh under-23 international, had been transferred from West Bromwich Albion to Blau Whit of Amsterdam. He'd lived in Holland for more than 30 years; as coach of Haarlem he'd been responsible for the development of Ruud Gullit. 'The game here is not what it was,' he said. 'So many players have gone abroad it doesn't come as a surprise to hear people say they've lost interest.' Dennis Bergkamp was next in line. Internazionale had agreed to pay £8 million for the tall, blond, moody 23-year-old who could be one thing or another, brilliant or peripheral. Internazionale gave up on Bergkamp after just two seasons, finding him ill fitted for the role of conventional striker. Bergkamp would find the Premiership more to his liking.

With Bergkamp, Gullit and Marc Overmars in their team, the Dutch, however, were expected to have plenty of attacking ideas when they came to Wembley at the end of April, though defensively they were suspect. Taylor decided to go for them, and England went in front after only two minutes. Barnes, Platt and Gascoigne hovered around a free-kick; Barnes eventually took it, curling the ball over the wall and out of Ed de Goey's reach. Normally restrained, Taylor leapt up from his seat, applauding. Twenty-two minutes later Les Ferdinand's shot rebounded from the far post to Platt. The hero of Bologna didn't miss chances like that, and England were two up.

Although unable to break away from Carlton Palmer and Paul Ince in midfield, the Dutchmen were too wise in the head for panic. Surely England could not maintain this pace for another hour. Suddenly, out of nowhere, Bergkamp looked a snip at eight million. Tony Adams thought he'd got him until Bergkamp pulled Wouter's forward pass out of the air; the Dutchman's second touch was a shot on the turn that flew into England's net. In an attempt to get more of the ball, Holland's coach Dick Advocaat then pushed Frank Rijkaard into midfield. 'It was a tough night,' Rijkaard recalled. 'England didn't give us an inch and their energy was remarkable. We were hardly ever able to put more than two passes together.' But with fifteen minutes left it was noticeable that Ince and Palmer were not covering as much ground, almost burnt out. Getting no change on the left, Overmars switched wings. Taylor checked his watch and raised four fingers. The signal was barely received when Des Walker blundered in on Overmars. Quick as he was, Walker couldn't give a yard start to the swiftest player on the field; panic-stricken, he tugged Overmars down just inside England's penalty area, and van Vossen levelled the scores. Taylor said he'd felt like crying.

The following month Terry Venables was voted out as chief executive of Tottenham Hotspur. A shaky alliance with the club's chairman and principal shareholder Alan Sugar finally broke up three days before the 1993 FA Cup Final. The bitter legal wrangle that followed would become entwined in the affairs of the England team, but in the early summer of 1993 all that was in the future. For the present, thoughts turned to whether England could cancel out the loss of home points that would have established them as favourites to qualify.

By the time England travelled to Detroit for a four-team tournament that was staged to drum up US enthusiasm for the finals, tabloid knives were sparking on the grindstone. It was bad enough that England had only just got away with a point in Poland on 29 May, the equaliser coming just six minutes from time when Ian Wright's shot squeezed through Bako's hands. The manner of England's 2–0 defeat at the hands of Norway in Oslo four days later was something else, though, all too much for Taylor's dedicated critics. It didn't take the brightest of minds to realise that Taylor had confused the team with a system unlike any he'd used before, one that had succeeded only in producing the worst performance of his reign. Given just one day to take their manager's latest theory on board, the England players had stumbled around as though playing blindfold, which in one sense they were. Rumours of unrest were made credible by England's lack of fight. Lee Sharpe, who had replaced Barnes on the left side of England's midfield, said, 'I didn't really understand what I was supposed to be doing out there. A lot of the time I found myself playing left-back.' It was to Taylor's credit that he didn't try to defend his mystifying tactics. 'I got it wrong,' he said. 'It's unbelievable to me that the players showed no passion, but I have to bear the responsibility. I'm the manager. I'm the one here to be shot at.' Scenting blood, the tabloids took Taylor at his word, trying to outdo one another in the pun stakes (NORSE MANURE; OSLO-RANS). Leaving late for Detroit, I had McMenemy for company. He, too, seemed unsure about where he now stood with Taylor. 'I don't know what's going on,' he admitted. On 9 June things went from bad to worse when England, outdoing their 1950 counterparts, lost 2–0 to the USA.

The Republic of Ireland team knew that if they defeated Lithuania in Dublin on 3 September they would need only one point from matches against Spain at home and Northern Ireland away to reach the World Cup finals for the second successive time. England, on the other hand, would probably be eliminated if they lost at home to Poland. Jack Charlton hadn't moved far from a direct method; by contrast, Taylor was no closer to a settled pattern of play than he'd been at the end of his first year as England manager. Unquestionably, this was related to the pressure imposed on him by the media-fed assumption that England remained a great footballing power. However, there was little on the credit side of Taylor's technical account. If admittedly more of a hostage to tradition, with all that that implied, he had not shown any of Charlton's dogged rejection of compromise. While the expectations of Irish football were not as high as those of England, the impression was that Taylor had been so sensitive to public perception and specious historical comparison that the quest for an acceptable and winning system had taken him up blind alleys.

There was nothing for it but to gamble. Taylor changed his goalkeeper, bringing in David Seaman for Woods; Stuart Pearce was recalled after missing the last eight internationals through injury, and made captain; and costly errors explained Walker's absence from the team after five years as a regular, Taylor preferring the centre-back partnership of Tony Adams and Gary Pallister. Ahead through Ferdinand after six minutes, England chased away the bleak memory of Poland's killing draw at Wembley twenty years before, scoring two more in the second half. Afterwards, Taylor restated his belief that England were at least good enough to qualify and reach the last eight in America the following summer.

None of the permutations that existed when England met Holland in Rotterdam five weeks later involved Norway, who'd qualified by defeating Poland at home. With Poland more or less out of it, Norway could sit back and watch Holland and England fight it out for the remaining place. To the astonishment of media-linked former players present at a press conference on the eve of the game, Taylor was drawn into a heated debate over changes in tactics and personnel. Under any circumstances it would have been foolish; on the eve of such an important game it made no sense at all.

Taylor already had reasons to suspect that the football gods were not with him. Now came another. When Ronald Koeman was panicked into hauling down Platt, it seemed for a moment as though England had themselves a penalty, that the big Dutchman would be sent off for a professional foul. Instead, to Taylor's fury, England had to settle for a free-kick on the edge of the area while Koeman got away with a yellow. The German referee Assenmacher was right on the first count, wrong on the other. Within three minutes England had further cause to curse Assenmacher's leniency when Koeman gave Holland the lead with a retaken free-kick. The sight of Bergkamp surging through to put Holland two in front with twenty minutes left to play was all too much for Taylor. He leapt from the bench, brushing aside a FIFA official, raging that the referee had got him the sack.

For a month, England lived in hope. 'If Holland lose in Poland and we win by seven against San Marino . . .' It was to end in farce. Arriving at Windsor Park, Belfast in mid-November for the game between Northern Ireland and the Republic, I heard loud laughter coming from a clubroom. No wonder: San Marino had gone in front against England after only eight seconds – the quickest international goal ever! Now needing eight, England replied with seven, none if it mattering when the news came through that Holland had beaten Poland 3–1. Meanwhile, a 1–1 draw earned the Republic a place in the finals on goal difference. For the first time since 1950 none of the four British nations had qualified.

In the midst of Irish celebrations, Jack Charlton expressed sympathy for Taylor and Terry Yorath, whose hopes of taking Wales to the finals had been dashed that night by Romania's victory in Cardiff. 'Football can be a cruel game,' he said. 'I feel for them. Luck is so important. I sent on Alan McLoughlin who hadn't scored for us in fourteen games, and he puts us level with almost his first kick. But for a poor decision by the referee England might have won in Rotterdam. Things went one way for me, another way for Graham. Funny thing, but Graham once told me that he was a lucky manager.'

Much to the FA's relief, Taylor resigned.

In late January 1994, ending weeks of speculation, Terry Venables was appointed as the new England manager. Humour ran strong in Venables. There was a hint of melancholy, too, a Celtic legacy, but humour was the important thing. Without it, he thought, the last nine months of legal wrangling with Alan Sugar and media probing might have been unbearable, might even have driven him over the edge. Sport tells anyone who watches intelligently about managed news and the disfiguring effect stress can have on even the most confident of men. In the job that had undermined Taylor's reputation, Venables knew that he would be at the mercy of forces over which he had no control; critics who, if not openly hostile, might not be qualified or objective; a public whose sympathies could change as quickly as the weather. And when it came to the England team, patience was not a national virtue. Cautiously, for Venables was still heavily involved in legal proceedings, the FA offered him a contract spanning two and a half years and covering the 1996 European Championship finals in England, after which the situation would be reviewed.

In the minds of his detractors, Venables was east London man, arch, glib, quick-witted, a flash opportunist, but Malcolm Allison thought him to have one of the most advanced minds in world football. The *Sun* 'exclusively' revealed that Venables wanted England to play like Brazil when in fact he'd merely said that it was important to adopt Brazil's policy of establishing a system and sticking to it. One of the first things Venables did was to add Dave Sexton to his back-up team of Don Howe, Bryan Robson, Ray Wilkins and Ted Buxton. When an FA official complained about Sexton being 63, Venables replied, 'I don't want him to play.'

His and England's only opportunity for competitive football before hosting the European Championship was a summer tournament in 1995 for which they brought over Brazil, Sweden and Japan. Even allowing for the absence of nine regulars from the squad, things did not go well. England played poorly when defeating Japan 2–1, scrambled to a 3–3 draw against Sweden and lost 3–1 to Brazil.

Before the draw for the European Championship finals was made that December, Venables realised that he did not have the full support of the Senior International Committee. 'By then it was fairly common knowledge that I wasn't happy with the situation,' he told me. 'I didn't know exactly about the court cases coming up after Euro 96, but I wanted to know where I stood with the FA. Whether I was going or staying. I got on well with the FA secretary Graham Kelly and told him there were a couple of things I needed to sort out. Money didn't come into it. I simply wanted to know what they had in mind for the future, and we agreed to talk in Birmingham at the draw for the championships.'

Venables met with Kelly, the FA chairman Bert Millichip and the chairman of the Senior International Committee, Noel White. Immediately, Venables challenged White over remarks attributed to him in a national newspaper. 'A lot had been going on, the court case and "world exclusives" about me in one of the tabloids – tat no other newspaper found important enough to follow up – but Noel White at least could have taken the trouble to speak to me before making statements which, from my point of view, were entirely negative.' White's claim that he had been caught off guard didn't wash with Venables. 'I stressed that the job was hard enough to do, trying to build a team, dealing with the media, without fighting your own. I said the next thing, the players would be at it.' When Venables asked White to explain publicly what he had meant by supporting him only until after Euro 96, he got no satisfaction. 'He went on about me not having had any competitive games. Competitive games! I'd had competitive games all my life. It was fairly obvious that they wanted to see how England shaped up in Euro 96 before coming to a decision, so I said, "I don't do auditions," and left them to it. Some people seemed to have the idea that I was calling their bluff, but that was bollocks. They could have appointed Glenn Hoddle three months before they did because they knew I wouldn't change my mind. It was nothing to do with money. I'd taken the same salary as Graham Taylor. I didn't care about the money.'

When it came, Euro 96 generated great excitement. The song 'Three Lions', composed by the comedy duo Frank Skinner and David Baddiel, was barely up to the meagre standards of the Eurovision Song Contest, but it was catchy and it took off. Unfortunately, England didn't. Stupidly, overlooking the fact that

Venables would hand over to Hoddle once England's fate was settled, one critic called for his dismissal after a poor performance in the opening game against Switzerland on 8 June. Then England moved up a gear. Gascoigne scored a brilliant goal to help his team beat Scotland, then they collectively thumped Holland 4–1. Members of the Senior International Committee wore worried frowns; what if the manager they'd let go proved to be a winner? The frowns were still in place after England luckily scraped past Spain in a penalty shoot-out to reach another semi-final with the Germans, which again went to penalties. As in Turin six years earlier, the Germans put theirs away with nerveless precision. Gareth Southgate missed his, and England were out. Germany defeated Czechoslovakia in the final and smugly pointed out that Bertie Vogts had emulated his predecessors. Every German national coach was a winner.

At 38, Hoddle was England's youngest ever manager. Like Venables, he'd played in Tottenham's midfield, but with more distinction, winning 53 caps for his country. Some Spurs supporters considered him to be the club's best ever player, which was pushing it a bit when the other candidates included such notables as Ron Burgess, Dave Mackay, Danny Blanchflower and Jimmy Greaves. Hoddle had developed a taste for coaching when playing under Arsène Wenger at Monaco. He'd gone on to become player-manager of Swindon, then Chelsea. It was said that Chelsea's irascible chairman Ken Bates wasn't sorry to see him go, for, contrary to an assumption based on images of him as a player, Hoddle was not an adventurous coach. His preferred system of play was a version of Venables' five-man midfield. Venables had used wingers, Darren Anderton and Steve McManaman, who could double as midfielders; Hoddle was more likely to use midfielders in the wide positions.

At this time, Alan Shearer was clearly one of England's pluses. Given a close-season choice between Manchester United and New-castle, the England centre-forward had found the pull of his own folk irresistible. Shearer's strength, powerful shooting and headwork reminded people of the former Bolton and England hero Nat Lofthouse. After a slow period in his international career, Shearer had scored ten times in 29 matches. Another came in the first match under Hoddle, a 3–0 victory away to Moldova on the first day of September – 'Where is it?' one of the players had asked – that got England off to a flying start in the 1998 World Cup campaign. The other teams in Group 2 were Italy, Poland and Georgia. Only one was sure of automatic qualification.

When Poland stepped out at Wembley on 9 October, it was within a few days of 23 years since they'd driven England to despair. 'It still haunts me,' Alf Ramsey told the *Daily Mirror*. The *Independent* spoke to Norman Hunter about the uncharacteristic tackling error that had helped to bring about England's absence from the 1974 World Cup finals, and to end Ramsey's reign. 'Strange, but until a couple of days ago I'd never been asked for an explanation,' he said. 'I was on my way in when the bastard [Lato] checked. It caused me to go in with my right peg, which was never a good idea, and I missed him.' Hoddle told his men to forget about history, but after only seven minutes it hit them square between the eyes. Poland, who had not scored on their three most recent visits to Wembley, attacked down the right and scored. For the next seventeen minutes, England were hardly in it. Then, with the crowd growing restive, David Beckham put Shearer in to equalise. Gaining only his second cap that day, Beckham had given the first hint that he could make the big step up. Beaten by Shearer's second goal of the night, the Poles reckoned they were unlucky losers. The press agreed.

Bobby Charlton once said that he'd spent around twenty years travelling the world as a footballer, and seen little but hotels and football grounds. The England players who visited Tbilisi, Georgia, in November were ordered not to try to broaden their cultural experience. Amid civil unrest and UN patrols, Hoddle's order of the day was to take no chances, on or off the field. Francis Lee, who had become chairman of Manchester City, warned that Georgi Kinkladze could dribble England dizzy. Small, compact and inventive, Kinkladze earned his living with City in the Premier League, and was presently Lee's favourite player. Lee's admiration for the Georgian was not, however, unanimously supported in City's dressing room ('He only lends you the ball'). Kinkladze did indeed lead Georgia in a demonstration of ball skills, but England were well equipped to deal with exhibition football. Teddy Sheringham scored after fifteen minutes, Les Ferdinand got a second before the interval. England completed their one hundredth World Cup match at a stroll and had two more points in the bag.

In the mid-nineties, Matthew Le Tissier was frequently in contention for goal of the month. Left foot, right foot, volleys, half-volleys, the tall Channel Islander had a repertoire that lifted him higher in the affection of Southampton's supporters than anyone who had ever played for them. Consistency, however, was not one of his strong points. As one Premier League manager put it, 'He's the sort of player who can get you the sack. Supporters love him for what he can do, and he really can do astounding things, but they don't see how much time he spends on the edge of the game.' Scouting reports on Le Tissier often read 'brilliant but unreliable'. Naturally drawn to Le Tissier's artistry, in February 1997 Hoddle took a chance on him, selecting him for the toughest qualifier so far: Italy at Wembley. Until then, five of Le Tissier's seven caps had come as a substitute. LE TISSIER'S BIG CHANCE, the *Daily Express* exclaimed; standing room only on trains from Southampton.

Italy's coach Cesare Maldini, father of their left-back Paolo, announced a squad that included three Premier League players: Gianfranco Zola and Roberto Di Matteo of Chelsea, and Fabrizio Ravanelli of Middlesbrough. Zola was nearly 31 and past his best, Italian critics said when Parma sold him to Chelsea for £4.5 million in 1996. So much for those critics. An instant hit at Stamford Bridge, the little Italian would shortly be voted Footballer of the Year by the football writers of his adopted country, and none of the previous 49 recipients had better represented the award's citation: By Precept And Example.

Early on, Le Tissier missed a chance to shape the game and the rest of his career. Zola scored in the 18th minute. On the hour, Hoddle replaced Le Tissier with Ferdinand. Le Tissier's 'big chance' had gone; he was never seen again in England's colours. Italy had three wins out of three, England three out of four.

It should have been pretty obvious to anyone who regularly watched football in the Premier League that there was room for technical improvement. This, more or less, is what the Leeds manager George Graham implied on Sky TV in the first week of April following his team's goalless draw with Blackburn Rovers, a match so inept it had an effect similar to that induced by mistaking Valium for coffee sweetener. Frustrated in his search for attackers, Graham gave it as his view that there was too much money chasing too little homegrown quality. 'The problem drives you abroad, and I have been all over Europe,' he said. Money, on a ridiculous scale, had brought many foreign players to the Premier League. That money, pouring in from Sky and sponsorship, had created an inflated market, transfer fees often out of all proportion to ability and unforeseen difficulties in player development.

A couple of weeks after Graham's remarks were broadcast, England defeated Georgia 2–0 at Wembley, Sheringham and Shearer the scorers. England's supporters were happy with the result, but they were still grumbling about the quality of the football. Sheringham and Shearer were on the mark again at the end of May when England won 2–0 in Katowice, a result that put Poland out of the reckoning. It was all narrowing down to the match against Italy in Rome in October.

England's performance in Le Tournoi, a summer tournament hosted by France, nourished the view that they were more than capable of achieving automatic qualification. When England followed up a good 2–0 victory over Italy with a 1–0 win against France, the trophy was theirs. The 1–0 loss to Brazil was lightly taken. While Hoddle was understandably encouraged, close analysis of England's efforts suggested that too much had been read into them. It was traditional for the England team to play flat out whatever the circumstances, their commitment as complete in friendly matches as in World Cup ties. The impression held in some quarters was that England had taken Le Tournoi rather more seriously than their opponents. In their dogged resistance to this unpopular point of view, some pundits were as perilously placed as horse-players blind to evidence of deliberate idleness in running.

To continue the betting analogy, England had never been hotter favourites than they were on 10 September against Moldova at Wembley in their last home qualifying match: ten to one on. Not since Busby's days had Manchester United supplied so many players to England. Beckham, Scholes and the Neville brothers were selected, and Nicky Butt would come off the bench. Moldova were pointless and, in cockney slang, potless. 'The wages of one England player would cover our whole league,' Moldova's coach, Ion Caras, said. 'If we lose five to nothing it will be a triumph.' They kept England down to four, the first coming from Scholes whose play bore the mark of an old-fashioned inside-forward. As a fifteen-year-old he'd been rated higher than Beckham by the coaching staff at Old Trafford.

Suddenly, as the result of a goalless draw in Tbilisi that brought Cesare Maldini under heavy fire, Italy, three times winners and beaten finalists in 1994, were confronting a World Cup crisis. A draw in Rome would send England through and cast Italy into a play-off, which would be England's fate if they lost.

To make the level at all, international footballers must survive tests of their skill and temperament. As they rise, pressure rises with them, but given the imprecision of human behaviour, one can never anticipate how they will react. Bobby Moore performed at his best when most was at issue, his attention often diffusing over a long club season, refocusing only when important games came along. Manchester United's defeat of Juventus in the Champions League two weeks before England set off for Rome was achieved in the main through the sustained intensity of their teamwork. Much less was required to overcome Crystal Palace easily in a League game a few days later. 'You couldn't help feeling that they were bored,' it was said. Hoddle had grown to know international football as a world apart, with its own set of imponderables. No matter how closely the England coach studied his players, he could not be sure that all those called on for Rome would be at their best mentally.

Sportswriters and broadcasters were not slow to point out that England had not won on Italian soil since May 1961, when a goal from Jimmy Greaves helped them gain a 3–2 victory in Rome. Greaves told *Sun* readers that England would probably need as much luck as they'd enjoyed 36 years before. 'Italy outplayed us for most of the game, but we got away with it,' he recalled. Hoddle spoke about playing positively, but a pretty safe bet was that England, with the advantage of two options, would seek to establish a balanced pattern of play. Shearer would have been ideal in the circumstances, any circumstances, but a serious ligament injury sustained at the start of the season would keep him out for another five months. The inclusion of three strikers in Maldini's team suggested that England would be on the back foot for most of the game.

In his excitement after 90 minutes with no goals, Sky's lead commentator Martin Tyler forgot the diversity of audience culture. 'Be proud to be English!' he yelled as television cameras covered England's leaping celebrations. England were through, but only just. In injury time, Italy – down to ten men from the 75th minute when Di Livio got his second yellow card of the night – had launched one last attack; Del Piero's cross from the right was perfectly delivered, but somehow Vieri managed to head a simple chance narrowly wide.

Italy eventually qualified by defeating Russia in a play-off; Scotland, under the scholarly Craig Brown, had gone through before the kick-off in Rome.

Ten World Cups was enough for a man in semi-retirement. France 98 would be my last as a working journalist. Given a roving assignment by the *Independent*, I set off by road, heading first for Bordeaux where Chile and Italy were due to open Group B. Gascoigne's surprise omission from England's 22 would have been a big enough story without the extraordinary details of his reaction to the news. Shocked when given the news in Hoddle's room, Gascoigne had launched into an emotional outburst whose every word and gesture, it seemed, had quickly reached the press corps. On a calmer note, much satisfaction was expressed over the inclusion of eighteen-year-old Michael Owen of Liverpool, who'd emerged as a goalscoring sensation. Owen had disappointed in a couple of England friendly matches, showing poor positional sense, but he had the priceless asset of speed. The scoring of a classic goal in a warm-up game against Morocco in Casablanca had made up Hoddle's mind. Opposing the argument that Owen was being rushed ahead of his time was the ancient tenet: if they're good enough, they're old enough. David Beckham was five years ahead of Owen in age, and by ten caps in experience. The view held in some quarters was that Manchester United's right midfielder would serve England better in a more central position. Beckham's great assets were a marvellous right foot and prodigious energy. On the downside, there was his lack of genuine pace and dribbling ability. The most likely candidate for the creative role was Paul Scholes.

News from England's base camp at La Baule in western Brittany suggested that things were not as I used to know them. A friendly in Caen had been played behind closed doors. 'With other teams allowing much freer access to press and public, it was another example of the way England seem to be paranoid,' wrote my colleague Glenn Moore. 'Whether the secrecy, which is even extended to banning other hotel guests from using the swimming pool, bonds the team or makes them withdrawn and fearful is yet to be seen.' Flying from Toulouse, I arrived in Marseille on the morning of England's opening game in Group G against Tunisia, after which they would meet Romania and Colombia. So many high hopes and low fears were stirred before England's debut in France 98 that an extravagant response to the 2–0 victory gained at the Stade Vélodrome was perhaps understandable.

Those of us who had been down the World Cup road more often than it was comfortable to remember knew the risks involved in reaching conclusions at an early stage, especially since the expansion from sixteen qualifiers. It was not that any of the outsiders were likely to cause more than passing, if lively, interest, but that unorthodox individual brilliance made better teams nervous. 'Because not very much is expected of the small teams, they play adventure football,' Argentina's coach Daniel Passarella said. 'Maybe they feel some pressure, but they have nothing to fear.' Watching Graeme Le Saux rush into an embrace with Hoddle's assistant John Gorman after sending in the free-kick that enabled Shearer to head England in front against Tunisia made you realise just how much tension the England players had been under. Personally, I had not seen this from an England player before. It made me wonder how far the celebrations would be taken if England made significant progress in the days ahead.

The one thing that stood out when Romania limbered up at the Municipal Stadium in Toulouse a few days before returning there to play England was how relaxed they appeared to be in preparation. Grateful for the cool breeze that coincided with their arrival on the banks of the river, the Romanians proved more agreeable than expected, raising no objection to scrutiny and interrogation. The work being done was of no more value in terms of assessment than a fighter's in the gymnasium or a golfer's on the practice ground. However, Romania's coach Anghel Iordanescu appeared pretty confident that his players would give a good account of themselves, pointing out that Romania's colours had not been lowered by England since a 1–0 defeat in the 1970 World Cup finals. 'Partly from what I've seen myself, partly from speaking with [Chelsea wing-back] Dan Petrescu, I'm aware of technical developments in English football,' he said. 'But if they no longer concentrate so much on direct play, they still send in lots of centres and are very strong physically.' Certainly, Iordanescu was determined that his defenders should not fall for Shearer's trick of winning free-kicks by holding up the ball to invite tackles from behind; where Shearer had won eight free-kicks in dangerous positions against Tunisia, he got only one in Toulouse.

It was a bad day all round for England. They lost Ince with an ankle injury, and his replacement, Beckham, did little to persuade Hoddle that he was 'properly focused'. England were chasing the game from the 47th minute, when Moldovan scored the first competitive goal Seaman had conceded for twenty months. With a quarter of an hour left there was only one thing for it: Hoddle sent on Owen, who equalised seven minutes from time. The cheers of England's supporters had barely died down when Petrescu held off his Chelsea club-mate Le Saux to regain the lead for Romania with a shot that passed through Seaman's legs. In the seconds that remained, Owen hit the foot of a post. 'I just told Michael to go out and enjoy himself,' Hoddle said. 'He did very well.' 'I warned our players that if Owen came on it would be like trying to catch a wind,' Petrescu said. 'He is so quick.' Iordanescu smiled when it was put to him that some of England's football prior to Owen's introduction was prehistoric. 'I think we played a more thoughtful game, particularly in the second half when they came back strongly at us,' he said.

Statistically, England's loss to Romania changed nothing. They still had to take a point from Colombia, the same as if they had won or drawn in Toulouse. The big question for Hoddle was whether it made any sense to persist with his preferred system of play: three defenders and a five-man midfield with wing-backs. Romania had found no great difficulty in dealing with the predictably wide angles of England's attacks, or in keeping the ball, and the ease with which they were able to infiltrate the space between England's midfield and the defensive line cast fresh doubts on Hoddle's thinking. Owen's selection, however, was no longer an issue. He simply had to play. In the event, Colombia were all tricks and no penetration, brilliant individually but never a collective threat. England should have scored six, never mind one each for Anderton and Beckham. Beckham's was a curling free-kick that launched a phrase – 'Beckham Territory'.

Shortly before the game, England had learnt that they would face Argentina in the next round. Among the many traps into which a football coach can fall is that of winding up the opposition. 'Why did he say those things?' a Danish sportswriter asked about remarks attributed to Hoddle. 'Why does he have to bring up the past?' The past, of course, was Diego Maradona's 'Hand of God' goal in 1986, Hoddle's mistake to elaborate on how he'd felt when it happened. 'Maybe Hoddle's words were twisted by reporters, but that's not how it will seem to the Argentinian players who have done nothing here to suggest they are cheats,' the Danish reporter added.

Fuel for a fresh outbreak of xenophobia, Hoddle's indiscreet digression threatened to work against him in St Etienne, where only 2,000 places had been allocated to English supporters. As night turned to light, a man in middle age and of no small football experience put forward the thought that England would not win the World Cup again in his working lifetime. Just one victory from ten appearances in the finals, and that gained on home soil, England had figured only twice in the last four competitions. For expectation had again turned to despair, David Batty's miss in a penalty shoot-out against Argentina putting England out of France 98 in the second round.

The game had begun as dramatically as it would continue. In the sixth minute Diego Simeone was sent flying by Seaman – 'I should have stayed on my feet,' he reflected – when trying to reach Batistuta's headed pass. Seaman guessed right, but he couldn't get a strong enough hand on Batistuta's spot kick. Owen, meanwhile, was learning fast. Barely touched, if at all, by Roberto Ayala, he tumbled in Argentina's penalty area; Shearer's kick was struck with such force it was a wonder the net stayed in place. Ten minutes played, one goal each.

Argentina had been fully informed about Owen's pace, his lines of running, his stronger and weaker sides. But how could they have known about his precociousness? A more experienced player might have looked for support when getting the ball at halfway; instead, Owen did what came naturally: he went for goal, leaving Jose Chamot for dead. 'Don't dive in on him,' Argentina's coach had warned his defenders. Ayala would admit that he'd been panicked by the suddenness of Owen's surge. 'In those situations you try to give yourself time to adjust. Owen had run well ahead of any other England player so it was in my mind to push him wide, to my left. He did that anyway, but so quickly that I couldn't get at him.' Owen's next move turned him into a superstar. Darting right, he unleashed a tremendous cross-shot that was in Carlos Roa's net before the burly Argentinian goalkeeper could blink. Owen leapt into the arms of his team-mates, the England bench leapt about in excitement, and English journalists ignored the golden rule of not cheering in the press box.

Twice England spurned chances that if taken might have put the game beyond Argentina's reach; three times England managed to prevent Ariel Ortega from engineering an equaliser. The tall Danish referee Kim Nielsen had just checked the amount of remaining first-half time when Ortega worried Sol Campbell into conceding a free-kick just outside the front of England's penalty area. Sexton's report had singled out Juan Sebastian Verón as Argentina's most influential player – 'extremely skilful, intelligent, energetic, organises all the free-kicks'. In the split second before Verón made contact with the ball, Javier Zanetti peeled away behind England's wall; controlling Verón's pass with his right foot, he put the ball past Seaman with his left. Zanetti came tearing out of England's penalty area, excitedly pointing out that he'd scored with his weaker foot, his 'swinger'.

'We've seen just about everything now,' somebody commented during the interval, but not by a long way. No sooner had the second half begun than Simeone sent Beckham to the floor with a tackle from behind. Then, Beckham's petulance surfaced in a way that would make the next year of his life miserable. It was no more than a flick of the right foot that caught Simeone behind the knee, but he made the most of it. Had FIFA not recently ordered referees to be less lenient Beckham might have got away with a yellow card, which was Simeone's punishment for the tackle. But Beckham got the full treatment. As he walked off the pitch, Hoddle seemed to be looking straight through him.

The England coach switched to a four-man defensive line and withdrew Owen to midfield, leaving Shearer as the lone attacker. 'Against most teams I would have been confident of winning,' Passarella said, 'but England never allowed us to take full advantage of the extra man. They defended very well, and I always feared they would break away and score.' England thought they had when Campbell headed in from a corner, only for a free-kick to be given against Shearer.

Almost certainly, Beckham and Scholes would have been among England's first five penalty-takers, but following the shortsighted substitution of the latter during extra-time Hoddle was left without either. His amended list included Paul Ince, who had ducked the responsibility in Euro 96, and Batty, who had never taken a penalty since turning professional. Both missed.

The TV audience, some 28 million in the UK alone, included Jack Charlton. 'It was heartbreaking to see England go out on penalties again,' he said. 'People were quick to blame David Batty, but what about Paul Ince? If he'd scored then perhaps we could have won before Batty stepped up. When the Republic of Ireland had a penalty shoot-out with Romania at Italia 90 I told the players to sort it out for themselves. The only other thing I told them was to make up their minds where they were going to place the ball and to stick with it. We scored five out of five and won.'

As in Italia 90, the England players watched dejectedly as the victors drove off in triumph. First Germany, now Argentina. Hoddle ignored Beckham. Ridiculously, Owen was compared with Pele at a similar age; a BBC executive reckoned that he was a shoe-in for Sports Personality of the Year, which he duly won. Argentina were eliminated by Holland in the next round, last-minute losers when Dennis Bergkamp's breathtaking effort overtook Owen's as goal of the tournament, and France, at last, won the World Cup, easily defeating Brazil 3–0 in a final played amid a mystery surrounding Ronaldo's health.

But if England did not live up to expectations in France, there seemed plenty to build on over the next four years. Owen, Beckham, Scholes and Campbell clearly had big international futures ahead of them. Doubts about Hoddle's man-management skills still existed, but he was generally considered to be tactically sound and was still in charge of the squad come September when England began their tilt at the 2000 European Championship.

12. 1998 TO JAPAN AND SOUTH KOREA 2002

In mid-December 1998, Graham Kelly resigned as chief executive of the FA, and a unanimous vote of no confidence in its chairman Keith Wiseman was passed following an internal investigation into the misuse of funds. Nick Harris of the *Independent* reported: 'The FA investigation was centred on Mr Wiseman, who allegedly agreed to deliver grants totalling £3.2m over eight years to the Welsh FA in return for votes to support his bid to secure a place on the executive committee of FIFA, the game's governing body. It is understood that Mr Kelly's signature was on a letter concerning the payments to the Welsh FA, and it is thought his resignation was primarily through shame by association rather than any involvement in wrongdoing.'

The FA's director of public affairs, David Davies, was made up to chief executive. Shortly before that, Davies himself had become involved in controversy as the co-author with Hoddle of a secret World Cup diary that somehow escaped the FA's normal vetting procedure. Published under Hoddle's name, it divulged private matters between him and the players, who might have been inclined to feel that all future communication with the coach should be confined to name, rank and number. In his new role, Davies said that Hoddle's position would not be affected by the upheaval at Lancaster Gate. Hoddle, however, would not survive publication of an interview he gave to *The Times* in which he aired his unorthodox spiritual beliefs, including views on reincarnation which suggested that afflicted people were being punished for their sins in a previous life. Widespread indignation left the FA with only one course of action. In February 1999, Hoddle was fired.

In 1992, after eight years out of the game, Kevin Keegan had made a hero's return as manager to Newcastle United. Nearly five years of thrilling championship challenges ensued, then he sensationally quit midway through the 1996–97 season. Casting around for a manager with the drive and personality to help fulfil his ambition of turning Fulham into a major club, Mohammed Al Fayed saw just the man in Keegan. Fulham were carrying all before them in the Second Division when Keegan was given the opportunity of becoming Hoddle's successor. Cautiously, as unsure of the FA as they, in truth, were of him, Keegan agreed to try the job on for size. In the summer of 1999 he took it full-time.

In the meantime, the former Leeds manager Howard Wilkinson had been made the FA's technical director with responsibility for all levels of player development below senior level. John Cartwright was among the longer-serving professional coaches who felt that the coaching system had taken the wrong direction. 'Far too little time, if any time at all, was being spent on skill,' he said. A former West Ham player, Cartwright was at his best working with young players: he'd run the under-21 team for Ron Greenwood, followed Sexton at Lilleshall, and produced an outstanding youth team at Crystal Palace, from which nine players graduated to League football, three becoming internationals. 'I'd coached for almost twenty years, but all that experience obviously didn't mean anything under the new regime,' he added. 'Of course, it didn't help my cause when I spoke out against what was happening in English football, how little we were doing to improve individual ability. And it made me angry to discover that some former players were being fast-tracked into the system, virtually getting a badge by post.' In November 1997, Cartwright had received a letter from the FA's solicitors warning of legal action should he persist in publicly implying that a chosen few were being brought in without going through proper qualifying procedures. 'In effect, I was being warned off. The FA saw me as a troublemaker. Three times I applied for posts they advertised, but the best I got in reply was a formal rejection. In the end I gave up.' In 2002, Cartwright helped launch a company with the objective of recreating the long-lost experience of street football. 'I wasn't going to change things at the FA, that's for sure,' he said.

By his own admission, Keegan was no tactical coach. He abided by fundamental principles of play, and his biggest asset was enthusiasm. He inherited a team that had made a poor start to qualifying for the finals of Euro 2000, losing away to Sweden and drawing against Bulgaria at Wembley. 'We can only give it a go,' Keegan commented, perkily. 'I think we've got the players and the spirit.' Where Hoddle had been aloof, Keegan was lively. England's supporters took to him in the way they had taken to Venables, but whether Keegan could make his attacking instincts work at international level was another thing.

England's first competitive fixture under Keegan was against Sweden at Wembley in June 1999. The Swedes, who were galloping away with the group, were happy with a goalless draw. England's last qualifying match, in September against Poland, was also goalless, a result that left England having to play Scotland in a two-leg play-off. Still, gone were the days of the great Scottish stars such as Law, Baxter, Mackay, Bremner and Dalglish. In their place stood journeymen. 'Sometimes you have to think that it's all over for us,' the former Manchester United and Scotland wing-half Pat Crerand said. 'Time was when players came through naturally; now they look as though they've all come out of one pod. I don't see things changing.' Working with meagre resources, Craig Brown had organised Scotland well and made them difficult to beat, but goals were hard to come by. 'If we can beat England at Hampden, it will give us a chance,' Brown said. Scotland lost by two goals to nil at home, then won 1–0 at Wembley. England scraped through to the Euro 2000 finals on goal difference.

According to some newspaper reports and comments passed across the airwaves, Michael Owen had taken a tumble. From boy wonder to little boy lost was how one scribe cynically put it. No sooner had he returned from the 1998 World Cup and set off on another Premiership season than newspaper reporters and television commentators were making him man of the match just for warming up in Liverpool's colours. 'So much in only two years,' is roughly what one commentator said. And since Owen's terrific strike against Argentina in France there had certainly been plenty of proof that his pace was exceptional; unfortunately, the media overlooked important aspects of his development, seeing him as the finished article when he still had much to learn. A persistent thigh strain didn't help him, but during the qualifying campaign Owen had looked so out of touch that Keegan publicly suggested he might benefit from a run in the under-21 team.

Shortly after England secured their place in the finals to be held in Belgium and Holland, there were more changes within the FA. It was announced after an extraordinary general meeting that the new chief executive Adam Crozier would have the power to hire and fire the national coach. In addition, as part of the FA's restructuring process an operating board had been formed to improve relations between the FA, the Premier League and the Football League.

Thus Keegan must have felt a tad insecure when England proceeded to make a mess of the finals. Two goals up after eighteen minutes against Portugal on 12 June, they squandered the lead and lost 3–2. Keegan's tactics were perceived as naive and he was roasted in some sections of the press for replacing Owen at the interval. Apart from the struggle England now faced in qualifying for the quarter-finals, they ran into more trouble when it was revealed that Beckham had been caught on camera making a one-fingered gesture to fans as he left the field. It turned out that he'd been answering abuse that had been hurled at him and other England players at the entrance to the players' tunnel, at half-time and full-time. Keegan said, 'I heard the abuse and I was ashamed to think it was coming from English people. It was disgusting. If it had been directed at me in the way it was directed at David Beckham I don't think I could have kept my temper.' All hope of progressing in the competition disappeared a week later when an 89th-minute penalty conceded by Gary Neville sent England to another 3–2 defeat, this time against Romania.

A hard-fought 1–0 win over the Germans was the only crumb of comfort for England, and they drew Germany again in their 2002 World Cup qualifying group. Of the other three countries England had to face, only Albania fell into the no-hope category: Greece had reached the 1994 World Cup finals, and Finland had grown stronger from the experience key players were getting abroad.

Wembley Stadium had stood for almost seven decades and been the home of the national team for more than half that time, but in the autumn of 2000 it was about to close. Wembley's fate would hang in the balance for more than two years, but the stadium as it stood had only one event left to stage. Appropriately, England's last match at football's most famous arena, the scene of the 1966 triumph, was against Germany.

The public's faith in Keegan had already diminished, and Keegan himself had begun to doubt whether he was up to dealing with the complexities of international competition. Now without Alan Shearer, who had announced his retirement from international football, England struggled from start to finish against Germany, unable to get back into the game after going behind after just a quarter of an hour when Hamann took full advantage of poor defensive organisation to score from a free-kick that skidded off the damp turf to Seaman's left and into the corner of the net. England's

1–0 defeat was met with howls of derision, much of it directed at Keegan as he made for the dressing room. Somewhere along that wretched route he reached a decision that would explode on to our television screens shortly afterwards. Keegan is a romantic, and like all romantics he acts on impulse. That night, 7 October 2000, he quit. Despite the pleadings of players and officials, Keegan remained adamant that he'd had enough. 'The fans, more than anyone, put me in this job,' he later explained to the press. 'Walking off, the fans who were still around told me that maybe it was time to go.'

Left rudderless for the qualifier against Finland in Helsinki four days later, the FA turned to its technical director Howard Wilkinson. England were without Beckham, Steven Gerrard and Gary Neville, all of them injured, and they were extremely fortunate to escape with a goalless draw, Wilkinson incurring the wrath of the press for leaving Owen on the bench for the entire game while persisting with Andy Cole, whose tenth appearance for England again failed to produce a goal.

Although stories linking Sven-Goran Eriksson with the England job were at first dismissed as products of creative-school journalism, it soon became clear that the Swedish coach of Lazio was the man Crozier wanted. The very idea of appointing a foreigner to coach the national team was anathema to many in English football. The Charlton brothers spoke out against it; so did John Barnwell of the League Managers Association and Gordon Taylor of the Professional Footballers Association. 'If we can't find one of our own then there must be something terribly wrong in English football,' Bobby Charlton said. He and Taylor later came round to Crozier's way of thinking. In any case, where was the English manager with the sort of standing, experience and record of accomplishment Crozier had in mind?

Thirty-eight years after Alf Ramsey accepted the job for a salary of around £7,000, Eriksson's contract exceeded £2 million when he took over in January 2001. He brought no fancy ideas with him; it was going to be 4–4–2. 'We may have to change the formation from time to time, but I want to keep things simple,' he told the players at his first squad meeting. They were impressed.

With Wembley decommissioned, England went on the road, taking their games around the country, first to Villa Park at the end of February where under Beckham's captaincy they defeated Spain

3–0. The next stop was Anfield for the home qualifier against Finland. Having already given up three points, and with the away fixture against Germany to come, England could not afford another slip. Defeat by Finland would all but ruin hopes of qualifying for the World Cup finals in Japan and South Korea, the first to be held in Asia and the first to be hosted by two nations. Fielding two Liverpool players, Jari Litmanen and Sami Hyypia, the Finns were again a problem, taking the lead with a Gary Neville own-goal in the 26th minute and almost equalising at the death after goals from Owen and Beckham had put England in front.

If not always true, at the dawn of the new millennium there was substance to the argument that easy pickings no longer existed at international level. During qualification for the 1990 finals England had put seven goals past Albania, but since the collapse of communism a number of their players had been able to fashion for themselves careers abroad, which meant they were unlikely to be the pushovers of old. And so it proved. Well organised, and defending stubbornly, Albania made England work hard for a 3–1 victory, all the goals coming in the last eighteen minutes. Owen and Scholes got the first two, and Cole the third, at last breaking his duck at international level.

If England's football under Eriksson had so far been more methodical than exciting, three successive victories silenced criticism of his appointment. At first dubious, the *Sun* became positively ecstatic, recruiting Gary Lineker to support their new-found conviction that Eriksson was the man for the job. 'You can already see this guy knows his stuff,' Lineker wrote. 'OK, he didn't know all our players when he took over, but it was a great time to come in, with three games in which he could afford to experiment a little and still get the right results. That was the perfect scenario, but you have to be impressed with the start Eriksson has made. He is clearly very intelligent, articulate, and tactically he is very sound. In an ideal world, of course you would want an Englishman in charge, but so long as he keeps on winning that is not going to be an issue, and I've thought that from the moment he was appointed. If he takes us to the World Cup, I'm convinced we will do very well.'

England's 2–0 defeat of Greece in Athens in June gave Eriksson five wins out of five, three of them in World Cup qualifiers, narrowing the gap with Germany and taking Eriksson closer to his first target of finishing second to earn a play-off. But none of the colleagues I spoke to about the Swede could provide illuminating answers to my questions. Their contact with him was confined to formal press conferences at which he gave very little away. Unlike his predecessors, he took no active part in training sessions, leaving the practical work to his assistants, Steve McClaren and Peter Taylor.

Eriksson's first setback came in August with a friendly against Holland at White Hart Lane, during which his favoured method of forceful football was made to look archaic by a team superior in technique and cohesion. The 2–0 defeat did not augur well for the upcoming qualifier against Germany, but Eriksson was quietly confident that England would win in Munich. It startled him to discover that Germany were unbeaten at home in World Cup qualifiers, for the report on them he'd received from Dave Sexton was encouraging. Sexton, at the head of a team of scouts, had come back from watching Germany with the news that their defensive play was flawed.

Before England could attempt to exploit the details of Sexton's report, they were a goal down, their own defence seriously at fault when allowing the cumbersome Carsten Jancker time in which to make a laboured turn and poke the ball past Seaman. But within seven minutes it was all-square. In a misguided attempt to catch England offside, Germany were caught flat-footed when Barmby's header found Owen, who was on to the ball in a flash, hooking it into the net. Almost forgotten in the euphoria of England's subsequent victory was the fact that the outcome might have been very different but for the simple chance wasted by Deisler and Seaman's alert save from Bohme before Gerrard's blistering low drive in first-half stoppage time gave England the lead. Shocked by the suddenness of it, Germany fell apart, conceding another three goals to Owen (twice) and Heskey.

Putting five goals past Germany in their own backyard was quite a feat, extending way beyond the belief that England were equipped to exploit serious defensive shortcomings, but as Eriksson sensibly stated, it was too early for talk of a renaissance. So how good were England that early September night, and how poor were Germany? All England's goals carried the stamp of Liverpool, yet only a week before Owen, Heskey and Gerrard had been kept at bay by a Bolton defence that boasted no international defenders. England's defence needed further education, but Germany's didn't exist. Somewhere between these conclusions was the key to the future.

England could not have found a better venue than St James's Park, Newcastle for the qualifier against Albania four days later. Some 52,000 turned out in expectation of a crushing victory over the weakest team in the group. Eriksson was staggered by the reception. 'We still hadn't qualified, but it was as though we'd won the World Cup,' he said. Although Albania would complete their fixtures without a win and only three points, they had conceded on average fewer than two goals a game when they turned out against the Munich heroes. England made hard work of overcoming Albania's stubborn resistance. Owen followed up his hat-trick against the Germans with a neat volleyed goal two minutes before the interval, but the outcome was in doubt until the 88th minute when Robbie Fowler, on as a substitute for Heskey, got past two defenders to score with the coolest of chips. Now level with Germany on points and games played, England topped the group on goal difference.

Expecting Germany to defeat Finland in their final game, Eriksson called for a maximum effort against Greece at Old Trafford on 6 October. To be sure of automatic qualification England needed all three points – surely not a problem against opponents whose dismal away record included a 2–0 defeat in Albania. Making light of Owen's absence, the *Sun* concluded that Eriksson could pick Lineker and Hurst and still beat Greece. But, as Eriksson had privately feared, Greece made nonsense of form. Clearly the better side in the first half, they deservedly led 1–0 at the interval. Eriksson brought on Andy Cole for Barmby and switched Heskey to the left side of midfield, but still England struggled to establish a cohesive pattern. Eriksson's second substitution, however, proved more successful. Replacing Fowler midway through the second half, Teddy Sheringham scored with his first touch, a near-post header from Beckham's free-kick. With Germany still goalless in Gelsenkirchen, the odds had swung back in England's favour, but not for long. It took Greece barely more than a minute to regain the lead. Ferdinand failed to deal with a centre from the right, and Nicolaidis swept the ball past Seaman.

Only Beckham responded fully to the crisis. Forsaking his station on the right wing, England's captain was everywhere, chasing, tackling, passing, filling the game with his presence. But even such a remarkable effort of will seemed to be in vain as the contest passed into injury time. Then, taking a leaf out of Shearer's book, Sheringham conned the Dutch referee Dick Jol into awarding England a free-kick 30 yards out. Since Beckham had failed with six previous dead-ball opportunities, Sheringham wanted to try his luck with this one, but the captain pulled rank, set his eyes on the target, drew a deep breath and sent the ball curving over the wall into the top right corner of the Greek goal. There was just time to restart the game, then Jol's whistle sounded its conclusion. The roar that followed was as much one of relief as triumph. Over in Gelsenkirchen, the German players slumped in despair. Although held to a goalless draw by Finland, they had clung to the hope that Greece would hang on to their lead. It was the first time Germany had failed to qualify automatically for a major tournament, though home and away play-offs against Ukraine eventually saw them through to the finals on a 5–2 aggregate.

Eriksson's fingers were crossed when he attended the draw for the finals. As a result of the failure to qualify in 1994 and to reach the quarter-finals in 1998, England were placed in the second tier; the top six seeds comprised France, Brazil, Argentina, Italy, Germany and Spain. Of those, Argentina, France and Italy were the teams Eriksson wanted to avoid. Contrary to the belief that they had a lucky coach, England drew Argentina, Sweden and Nigeria in what was immediately dubbed the Group of Death. 'I hope we have more luck in June than we had tonight,' Eriksson told a gathering of English sportswriters. 'We've got the best team in South America [Brazil had only just qualified for the finals], maybe the best from Africa and a very good European team, so we will have to be in good shape right from the start. There is no place to hide. When there was just one team left to complete the group, I thought to myself, we only need Nigeria now for the set, and out they came. We will have to play extremely well, but we can do that.'

Beset by revelations about his private life, Eriksson ran into further trouble in the months leading up to the World Cup when an injury sustained by David Beckham in a European Champions League game against Deportivo La Coruña was diagnosed as a broken metatarsal. Sir Alex Ferguson's first reaction was that Beckham had very little chance of recovering in time to play in England's first game against Sweden on 2 June, but Eriksson refused to give up hope. As it turned out, Beckham had been left with just enough time to recover his mobility, if not his match fitness, but more problems followed. Two weeks later a similar injury ruled Gary Neville out of the tournament. Lucky coach? No sooner had Eriksson absorbed those blows than he was informed by Liverpool that Steven Gerrard would have to miss the finals because of a groin injury, and that Michael Owen was nursing a thigh strain. The question of how many fully fit players Eriksson would have available in Japan was further complicated when the Newcastle midfielder Kieron Dyer was carried off at Southampton with what was at first thought to be an injury serious enough to prevent him starting the next League season, never mind travelling with England to the World Cup.

The death of Sir Walter Winterbottom in February 2002 prompted reflections on how much things had changed since he'd led England on their first World Cup adventure 52 years earlier. England had travelled to the 1950 World Cup in Brazil without a doctor, arriving just three days before the tournament commenced. Winterbottom had the assistance of just one trainer who had the added responsibility of treating injuries. In contrast, Eriksson had his chief assistant Tord Grip, a battery of coaches, a fitness expert, scouts, medical back-up and a press officer.

This large group plus the squad arrived at Awaji Island in central Japan on 25 May, after the players and their families had spent a week in Dubai. Dyer had made it as the result of a call to Eriksson by Newcastle's manager Bobby Robson, who felt that Dyer had recovered sufficiently from his injury to take part. The next day, in their final warm-up match, England drew 2–2 with Cameroon. Even before France were seen to be a busted flush and England wrecked Argentina's confidence, my personal impression was that the World Cup had never been more likely to fall into the hands of a half-decent team playing to its maximum potential, and because England seemed to have a chance of figuring in that category and Eriksson could indeed be a lucky general, I took the 14–1 on offer shortly before the tournament got under way. But England's inability to keep the ball in their opening game against Sweden – Ron Atkinson was the only TV pundit to pronounce the truth: 'Poor in the first half, awful in the second' – suggested that they might find it difficult to reach the latter stages of the competition.

Troubled by the failure of his midfield during that 1–1 draw, Eriksson introduced Nicky Butt for the game on 7 June against

Argentina in Hokkaido, where the enclosed, air-conditioned Sapporo Dome would favour England's energetic method. There have been countless crucial incidents in World Cup history that owed nothing to tactical decisions, only to strokes of good fortune. One such happened for Eriksson after nineteen minutes' play against Argentina when Owen Hargreaves, who had started badly, collided with Owen and limped off for treatment. The only other fully fit midfielder on England's bench was sent on to play wide left, allowing Scholes to take up his preferred central role. If the result of this switch wasn't startling, it gave England a better shape and improved the service to Owen. A minute before the interval, shortly after shooting against the base of an upright, Owen wrongfooted Pochettino and won a penalty. Beckham, whose lack of match fitness had been patently obvious, now made a decisive contribution, smashing the spot-kick past Cavallero. Under siege for most of the second half, the defending as desperate as it was often fortunate, England hung on for a victory that caused nationwide celebrations.

Before a ball had been kicked in Japan and South Korea, a popular assumption was that there are no longer any easy international matches – then Germany, who were not considered serious contenders, put eight goals past Saudi Arabia. However, when Nigeria took their only point from a goalless draw with England, Rio Ferdinand took up the old theme. 'We knew it wouldn't be easy,' he said, 'because there aren't any easy games.' Coaches preach this point of view to concentrate the thoughts of their players. 'You must fight for the right to prove your superiority' is another way of putting it.

England had reached the last sixteen without scoring a goal from open play. Criticised for selecting only seven midfielders, and with three of them – Beckham, Dyer and Joe Cole – not fully fit, Eriksson's luck was holding. Holding on to the ball was a different matter, though. England were not so much disputing possession as conceding it, unable to boss the tempo of their games. As in the previous three, so with the fourth, a 3–0 drubbing of Denmark who were out of it by half-time as a result of suicidal defending. Two days later, England learnt they would be facing Brazil in the quarter-finals.

Until the latter stages of the South American qualifying competition it seemed likely that Brazil would fail for the first time to qualify. They ultimately scraped home in third place behind Argentina and Ecuador after being 90 minutes away from finishing fifth, which would have meant a play-off against Australia. As a result, no coach of Brazil had come under more criticism than Luiz Felipo 'Big Phil' Scolari. As his team struggled through the qualifiers, one abject performance following another, Scolari warned that the 'beautiful game' was dead. Even though Brazil's group record was three wins out of three with eleven goals, they'd struggled to get past Belgium to reach the last eight and the defence had looked vulnerable. Clearly way short of full fitness, Ronaldo was being nursed through the tournament. On the eve of the game, Pele said, 'England are the most difficult opponents left. Their defence is the best in the World Cup, yet those defenders are young enough and fit enough to support the attack. It is important that Ronaldo and Rivaldo have a big game because I fear for our defence. Brazil have played England three times in the finals before, have never lost, and each time we have gone on to win the World Cup. If we beat England again, we can win a fifth title, no matter who else we have to play.'

England took a risk with Owen, who had been able to do only light training, and hoped that Beckham would at last produce a performance worthy of his reputation. In the 23rd minute a hopeful forward pass from Heskey carried no threat until Lucio inexplicably allowed the ball to bounce off his right leg into Owen's path. Owen easily rounded Marcos to give England the lead. Brazil's equaliser came out of nowhere. In the time allowed for David Seaman to recover from a heavy fall, Beckham vaulted out of a concerted challenge by Roberto Carlos and Roque Junior. The ball was switched infield where Ronaldinho nudged the ball away from Scholes to arrow at England's defence. Passing his right foot over the ball, Ronaldinho flew past Cole and laid the ball on perfectly for Rivaldo to sweep it past Seaman.

If blameless in that instance, Seaman had taken such a heavy knock that a case could have been made for replacing him with Nigel Martyn for the second half. But the Arsenal goalkeeper assured Eriksson that he was fine. Five minutes after the interval, he found himself looking at Ronaldinho shaping up to take a free-kick from fully 40 yards out. Seaman positioned himself to deal with the expected cross, but the ball swung and dipped over his head into the top far corner. Fluke or not, England were behind.

Encouragement came when Ronaldinho was red-carded for an innocuous-looking tackle on Mills, but England simply didn't know how to take advantage of their numerical superiority, their play so lacking in imagination that Brazil's goal was never seriously threatened. Hardly anything came from Beckham; Owen was so ineffective that Eriksson replaced him with Vassell. As Pele had predicted, after overcoming England, Brazil went on to lift their fifth World Cup.

It was certainly a disappointing end, though admirably in line with England's record of success in over half a century's worth of World Cups: the national team has refused at the quarter-final fence on five occasions (1954, 1962, 1970, 1986 and 2002), going on only twice, in 1966 and 1990. Ahead of them in the league table of success in the world's premier football competition are the multiple winners: Brazil, (West) Germany, Italy, Argentina and Uruguay. France's record of one win and three semi-final appearances also comfortably beats them. Bearing comparison are the achievements of countries such as Holland, Czechoslovakia and Hungary (all runners-up on two occasions), Sweden (one runners-up spot, two semi-finals and a 'final pool' place in 1950), and Yugoslavia (two semi-finals and three quarter-finals). At best, England are in seventh place; if reaching the final twice is a more noteworthy achievement than to win it once, they're in tenth place. Prior to 2002, England hadn't been able to progress beyond the second round for sixteen years, and qualification, as 1994 proved, is never assured. The road ahead, in an international footballing world more complex and radically different to that into which Walter Winterbottom strode as England's first ever manager some 57 years ago, shows no signs of being any less difficult to negotiate.

APPENDIX:
ENGLAND WORLD CUP SQUADS
1950–2002

1950 SQUAD
Bert Williams; Ted Ditchburn; Jack Aston; Alf Ramsey; Laurie Scott; Bill Eckersley; Billy Wright [c]; Laurie Hughes; Jimmy Dickinson; Bill Nicholson; Willie Watson; Jackie Milburn; Stan Mortensen; Roy Bentley; Wilf Mannion; Tom Finney; Eddie Baily; Jimmy Mullen; Stanley Matthews; Henry Cockburn; Jim Taylor.

1954 SQUAD
Gil Merrick; Ted Burgin; Ron Staniforth; Roger Byrne; Ken Green; Billy Wright [c]; Syd Owen; Jimmy Dickinson; Bill McGarry; Stanley Matthews; Ivor Broadis; Nat Lofthouse; Tommy Taylor; Tom Finney; Albert Quixhall; Dennis Wilshaw; Jimmy Mullen.

1958 SQUAD
Colin McDonald; Eddie Hopkinson; Don Howe; Tommy Banks; Peter Sillett; Billy Wright [c]; Maurice Norman; Ronnie Clayton; Eddie Clamp; Bill Slater; Tom Finney; Bryan Douglas; Peter Brabrook; Alan A'Court; Derek Kevan; Bobby Smith; Johnny Haynes; Bobby Robson; Peter Broadbent; Bobby Charlton.

1962 SQUAD
Ron Springett; Alan Hodgkinson; Jimmy Armfield; Ray Wilson; Ron Howe; Peter Swan; Ron Flowers; Maurice Norman; Bobby Robson; Stan Anderson; Bobby Moore; Johnny Haynes [c]; George Eastham; Bryan Douglas; Jimmy Greaves; Gerry Hitchens; Bobby Charlton; John Connelly; Roger Hunt; Alan Peacock.

1966 SQUAD
Gordon Banks; George Cohen; Ray Wilson; Norbert Stiles; Jack Charlton; Bobby Moore [c]; Alan Ball; Jimmy Greaves; Bobby Charlton; Geoff Hurst; John Connelly; Ron Springett; Peter Bonetti; Jimmy Armfield; Gerry Byrne; Martin Peters; Ron Flowers; Norman Hunter; Terry Paine; Ian Callaghan; Roger Hunt; George Eastham.

1970 SQUAD

Gordon Banks; Keith Newton; Terry Cooper; Alan Mullery; Brian Labone; Bobby Moore [c]; Francis Lee; Alan Ball; Bobby Charlton; Geoff Hurst; Martin Peters; Peter Bonetti; Alex Stepney; Tommy Wright; Norbert Stiles; Emlyn Hughes; Jack Charlton; Norman Hunter; Colin Bell; Peter Osgood; Allan Clarke; Jeff Astle.

1982 SQUAD

Ray Clemence; Viv Anderson; Trevor Brooking; Terry Butcher; Steve Coppell; Steve Foster; Kevin Keegan [c]; Trevor Francis; Glenn Hoddle; Terry McDermott; Paul Mariner; Mick Mills; Joe Corrigan; Phil Neal; Graham Rix; Bryan Robson; Kenny Sansom; Phil Thompson; Ray Wilkins; Peter Withe; Tony Woodcock; Peter Shilton.

1986 SQUAD

Peter Shilton; Gary Stevens; Kenny Sansom; Glenn Hoddle; Alvin Martin; Terry Butcher; Bryan Robson [c]; Ray Wilkins; Mark Hateley; Gary Lineker; Chris Waddle; Viv Anderson; Chris Woods; Terry Fenwick; Gary Stevens; Peter Reid; Trevor Steven; Steve Hodge; John Barnes; Peter Beardsley; Kerry Dixon; Gary Bailey.

1990 SQUAD

Peter Shilton; Gary Stevens; Stuart Pearce; Neil Webb; Des Walker; Terry Butcher; Bryan Robson [c]; Chris Waddle; Peter Beardsley; Gary Lineker; John Barnes; Paul Parker; Chris Woods; Mark Wright; Tony Dorigo; Steve McMahon; David Platt; Steve Hodge; Paul Gascoigne; Trevor Steven; Steve Bull; David Seaman.

1998 SQUAD

David Seaman; Sol Campbell; Graeme Le Saux; Paul Ince; Tony Adams [c]; Gareth Southgate; David Beckham; David Batty; Alan Shearer; Teddy Sheringham; Steve McManaman; Gary Neville; Nigel Martyn; Darren Anderton; Paul Merson; Paul Scholes; Robert Lee; Martin Keown; Les Ferdinand; Michael Owen; Rio Ferdinand; Tim Flowers.

2002 SQUAD

David Seaman; Danny Mills; Ashley Cole; Trevor Sinclair; Rio Ferdinand; Sol Campbell; David Beckham [c]; Paul Scholes; Robbie Fowler; Michael Owen; Emile Heskey; Wes Brown; Nigel Martyn; Wayne Bridge; Martin Keown; Gareth Southgate; Teddy Sheringham; Owen Hargreaves; Joe Cole; Darius Vassell; Nicky Butt; David James; Kieron Dyer.

INDEX